PEOPLE LIKE US

PEOPLE LIKE US

The Report Of The Review Of The Safeguards for Children Living Away From Home

Sir William Utting

Catherine Baines
Marian Stuart
John Rowlands
Roz Vialva

London: The Stationery Office

Applications for reproduction should be made in writing to The Copyright Unit, Her Majesty's Stationery Office, St. Clements House, 2–16 Colegate, Norwich NR3 1BQ.

ISBN 011 322101 0

Printed in the United Kingdom for The Stationery Office
J70802 C10 1/99 9385 9797

CHILDREN'S SAFEGUARDS REVIEW

Rooms 634-636 Wellington House, 133-155 Waterloo Road, LONDON SE1 8UG
Telephone 0171 972 4272/4527/4338 Fax 0171 972 4421

Secretary of State for Health

Secretary of State for Wales   30 July 1997

Dear Secretary of State

The Prime Minister announced this review to the House of Commons on 13 June 1996 and the Secretary of State sent me a commissioning letter with terms of reference on 17 June. The attached report discharges that commission. I feel greatly privileged to have been invited to undertake it.

I have been splendidly supported in this work. Catherine Baines and Roz Vialva worked full-time on the review, John Rowlands and Marian Stuart part-time. Each has made a distinctive and invaluable personal contribution. We worked as a Team; overall responsibility is mine.

I am greatly indebted to officials in Departments of State and to the many organisations, individuals and young people who contributed so substantially to this report.

Yours sincerely

W. B. Utting

SIR WILLIAM UTTING

Review Team: Sir William Utting, Miss Catherine Baines, Mrs Roz Vialva and Ms Marian Stuart

TERMS OF REFERENCE

– to review the safeguards introduced for England and Wales by the Children Act 1989 at its implementation in 1991 and the further measures since taken to protect children living away from home, with particular reference to children's residential homes, foster care and boarding schools;

– to assess whether these safeguards are the most effective that can realistically be designed to protect such children from abuse and other harm and whether they are being satisfactorily enforced;

– to make recommendations accordingly to the Secretary of State for Health and the Secretary of State for Wales.

FOREWORD

The report begins with a free-standing summary.

Principal recommendations are listed and cross-referenced to relevant chapters. They are selected on grounds of being important in their own right and affecting large numbers of children.

After a general introduction, each chapter of the report is preceded by a synopsis which refers to all its recommendations. Many of these are important in themselves and for particular groups of children.

The chapters on specific setting are followed by chapters on cross-cutting issues which affect all children living away from home. Readers whose interests are confined to a particular setting should consult these chapters – or at least their synopses – too.

CONTENTS

PEOPLE LIKE US

The Review of the Safeguards for Children living away from Home

SUMMARY REPORT

People like us:

- lived away from home as children,

- are parents of children living away from home,

- care for and protect children living away from home,

- abuse, harm and fail children living away from home.

CONCLUSIONS

The Government established this Review as a result of continuing revelations of widespread sexual, physical and emotional abuse of children in children's homes over the preceding 20 years.

Repetition of abuse on that scale in children's homes is unlikely. Far fewer children live there: 8,000 in 1995 compared with 40,000 in 1975. Homes are much smaller, with an average capacity of 10 children. The exposure of abuse has attracted public attention and led to improvements in the recruitment and management of staff.

There are no grounds for complacency about either children's homes or the other settings in which children live away from home. Abuse is documented in them all. People who wish to exploit children seek occupations or voluntary work where they have access to children. They will find the weak points in our defences. Institutions may be corrupted by evil people, or decay internally through neglecting their primary purpose of serving the interests of children.

A protective strategy includes

- a threshold of entry to paid and voluntary work with children which is high enough to deter committed abusers;

- management which pursues overall excellence and is vigilant in protecting children and exposing abuse;

- disciplinary and criminal procedures which deal effectively with offenders;

- an approved system of communicating information about known abusers between agencies with a need to know.

The best safeguard is an environment of overall excellence. There are many excellent institutions - and people - caring for children who live away from home.

Bear in mind that the abuse of children in institutions is part of the wider issue of the abuse of children generally. The bottom line is drawn by the values and attitudes to children which characterise the society in which we live.

WHERE CHILDREN LIVE

About 200,000 of the 12 million children under the age of 18 in England and Wales are living away from their parent's home for at least 28 days. Many more in total, of course, experience living away from home before they are 18.

The Review's terms of reference directed it particularly to children's homes, foster care and boarding schools; it has also given some attention to children in the penal system and in health settings.

Children's Homes

Choice of placement for children looked after by local authorities – in children's homes, foster care or residential schools – is a fundamental safeguard.

Safeguarding residents is inseparable from the wider purposes of children's homes. Homes which meet the personal, social, health and educational needs of children are much more likely to be safe places for children than those that do not.

I last reported on residential child care in *Children in the Public Care* (1991). The Warner Report (*Choosing with Care*, 1992), the Support Force for Children's Residential Care and other initiatives by the Department of Health and the Welsh Office have concentrated attention on this under-valued sector. Other factors continue to destabilise it. It is still contracting under the pressures of financial retrenchment and ideological prejudice. At the same time the number of providers has increased. The 836 local authority homes in England at 31 March 1996 are now shared between 132 social services departments; there are in addition 202 private and 64 voluntary homes. There were 46 local authority homes in Wales in 1994 - now shared between 22 social services authorities.

Urgent action is needed to raise standards, but the sector now lacks enough providers of sufficient size to organise and achieve this from within. Government action is needed to implement a strategy to drive up standards all round.

Foster Care

Nearly 35,000 children looked after by local authorities in England and Wales were in foster homes on 31 March 1996. Foster care is in practice the preferred placement for these children, accommodating 2 out of 3.

Residential care costs on average 7 times as much, and the decline in its use has contributed to changes in the nature of foster care. The latter accommodates younger children than residential care, but the whole of its population is more vulnerable than it was. Many children entering foster care have already been abused, or show disturbed behaviour. Carers face more complex and stressful tasks. There is evidence of abuse in foster care, as elsewhere.

Local Authorities must follow existing regulations and guidance.

The Review recommends an inspection of the recruitment and support of foster carers, followed by a government code of practice.

Private foster carers should be registered by the local authority.

Boarding Schools

There are about 110,000 children in boarding schools in England and Wales. They range from the most privileged to the most disadvantaged children in society. 80,000 are in independent boarding schools registered by the Registrar of Independent Schools. Most of the remainder are children with disabilities or emotional and behavioural difficulties. About half of these are in schools provided by local authorities, and the others in schools which are approved by the Secretary of State or registered as children's homes.

The Children Act 1989 required independent boarding schools to safeguard and promote the welfare of pupils, and opened their arrangements for doing so to inspection. This responded to the concern aroused at the time by two cases of serious sexual abuse in boarding schools. It also came at the end of a period in which schools' arrangements for the welfare of children had steadily improved.

The Children Act requirement has worked well in general.

> The Review recommends that it be extended to the remaining residential schools, which accommodate numbers of particularly vulnerable children.

Problems can arise anywhere, and a small minority of schools cause more than temporary concern. The process for dealing with them needs speeding up.

Penal Settings There were 1,680 children under 18 in prison service establishments at 30 June 1995. 410 were remanded awaiting trial. Unconfirmed figures suggest that the total now exceeds 2,600, twice the number in 1993.

Prison is not a safe environment. HM Chief Inspector of Prisons has criticised overcrowding, with young and older offenders sharing accommodation, and the impoverished environment. The Review was particularly concerned by the prevalence of bullying, ranging from physical brutality to verbal intimidation, in spite of Prison Service strategies for countering it.

> The Review urges that the principles of the Children Act be incorporated into the rules governing children in prison service establishments.
>
> The Government should end remands to prison for boys under 17 forthwith.

Hospitals About 15,000 children in England and Wales spent periods of more than a month as in-patients in 1994/5. The majority were receiving treatment or surgery for medical conditions. Some were disabled and others had psychiatric conditions. Issues relating to safeguards and welfare arise as keenly in hospital as in other settings. The general safeguards recommended by the Review apply to health settings as elsewhere.

CHILDREN Certain children were identified to the Review as potentially vulnerable: young children, children looked after by local authorities, disabled children, children with emotional and behavioural difficulties, and children with parents overseas (mainly foreign children and the children of service families). Particular care is needed in promoting and safeguarding their welfare.

> A consistent legal framework should protect all children living away from home against all forms of assault, abuse and ill-treatment. Specific policies are needed to combat bullying and racial and sexual harassment.

Children who have been abused have a right to appropriate treatment.

The Review was greatly helped by young people. We obtained information from young people who are or have been looked after by local authorities, and from some disabled young people.

> Local authorities must pay particular attention to the educational and health needs of the children they look after, and ensure a better transition to independent living.
>
> They should make direct use of the experience of the young people they look after in developing policy, practice and training for services for children who live away from home.

RESPONSIBILITIES

Parents

Many children, including most of those in boarding schools, live away as the result of a decision by their parents in the overall interest of the child or the family. The exercise of parental rights and responsibilities is therefore particularly important to children living away from home.

Government assumes that parents placing a child away from home satisfy themselves that arrangements for keeping their children safe exist and are likely to prove effective. They have moral and in some cases legal rights to expect that the people and agencies to whom care of their children is transferred will prove trustworthy and competent. Parents should also be able to rely on the support of statutory systems of registration and inspection. Nevertheless, the decision about placement is ultimately their responsibility. It is not clear to the Review that parents are necessarily aware of the risks to their children's welfare that may exist, or that they are informed about all the safeguards which should be in place.

> All organisations which care for children living away from home should provide parents with full information about their arrangements for keeping children safe. This might include information about recruitment procedures for staff, codes of conduct for staff, anti-bullying policies, child protection procedures, discipline and control of children, complaints procedures, access to telephone, and arrangements for health and pastoral care. Parents should always know the identity and location of registering and inspecting authorities.

> The Review also recommends that the Government sponsors a programme on public health lines to increase the understanding of parents and relevant staff about the risks to children's welfare and the means of reducing them.

Government

> The responsibilities of parents are not clearly stated in the law for England and Wales. Government should define these in primary legislation; or issue a statement of them when next it legislates on matters that affect them.

> Departments of State and Agencies with responsibilities for children should include safeguarding and promoting the welfare of children in their principal aims.

The number of social services authorities in England and Wales has increased sharply, and services for children are dispersed among a larger number of providing agencies. A greater responsibility consequently rests on the centre to secure consistent standards nationally in protecting and promoting the welfare of children.

> The Department of Health/Welsh Office should identify a dedicated group to drive through the changes needed to raise the standards of residential child care.

> The Departments should review and re-issue in the medium term their guidance on the Children Act 1989.

There may be a case for rationalising the present system for registering independent schools, but this is a general issue for the Department of Education and Employment and is beyond the scope of this Review. That part of the sector with which the Review is concerned is itself very large and varied, around 700 independent boarding schools in England and

Wales providing some 80,000 places. The Registrar of Independent Schools should be empowered to deal speedily with serious concerns about the welfare of pupils. Swift and co-ordinated action is needed to deal with serious situations revealed by child protection investigations or inspections. Six months may be needed to put right an educational problem, but is far too long to wait if an institutional problem is harming children.

> The Secretary of State's powers of inquiry into children's services under Section 81 of the Children Act should be extended to include all boarding schools.

Department for Education and Employment and the Department of Health/Welsh Office should dovetail any revision of arrangements for regulating homes, schools and fostering in order to clarify responsibilities and remove overlaps and gaps. These are exploited by dubious providers to avoid complying with the intentions of legislation and to prolong processes of complaint and investigation.

Local and Health Authorities

Over 50,000 children are looked after by local authorities in England and Wales. Parental responsibility is borne by the local authority as a whole, and cannot be discharged effectively without the full participation of all the services to which local authorities have access, including health services. Political leadership is essential in demonstrating acceptance and guaranteeing fulfilment of these responsibilities.

> The needs of disabled children living away from home require an integrated approach by education, health and social services authorities. Education and social services authorities should unify systems for placing, financing, reviewing and supporting emotionally and behaviourally disturbed children in boarding schools. They should be assessed by social services authorities as children in need' under the Children Act 1989, and appropriate services offered to them and their families.

ISSUES

Abusers

The Review was precipitated by the past activities of sexually and physically abusive terrorists in children's homes. Such persistent abusers may be a small proportion of all those who harm children, but they create havoc with their lives. A single perpetrator is likely in a lifetime's career to abuse hundreds of children, who suffer pain, humiliation and torment, and incur permanent emotional damage.

Becoming associated with residential work as an employee or volunteer provides the abuser with a captive group of vulnerable children. Entrapping them involves deceiving and disarming adults also. Abusers may be good at their jobs, winning respect, affection or fear from their colleagues and admiration from the parents whose children they corrupt. They are adept at avoiding detection and disciplinary or criminal charges - in which they are inadvertently assisted by the assumptions and values of our social institutions. They are very dangerous people.

It is important in the first place to keep them out of work with children and, secondly, to investigate carefully any suspicions that arise about members of staff; even the best organisations are not immune to infiltration by determined abusers.

Below this extreme level are larger numbers of adults who fall into abusive behaviour in circumstances ranging from personal weakness to the influence of a malignant institutional culture.

Finally, there are children who abuse, who represent a serious danger to the safety of other children.

Keeping these risks in check depends upon selection of staff and of residents, assessment of need, choice of placement, supervision, training, management, inspection, alertness, openness, investigation, detection, disciplinary and criminal procedures, and treatment for abuser and abused. All these processes should focus on the safety and welfare of the children.

Staff

The recommendations about recruiting and selecting staff in Choosing with Care (the Warner Report) have been implemented by most local authorities. The Review believes that they should be applied in all settings in which children live away from home. Conformity should be a condition of registration, approval, accreditation and the award of contracts.

Communicating information between employers about people unfitted to work with children is complicated legally and procedurally. The Government should extend the legal protection of employers in such cases; the new system for criminal record checks should access other approved lists as part of its own checks.

Staff should be required to communicate concerns about the conduct of other staff towards children and afforded full legal and employment protection when acting in good faith.

Monitoring and Enforcement

The main purpose of statutory regulation is to protect vulnerable people. Its effect is haphazard unless it is properly monitored and enforced.

Parents can to some extent monitor arrangements for their children's safety themselves. More formal responsibilities are undertaken by managers, professionals, public authorities, inspectors and the Secretary of State. Those responsible for registering or approving institutions must be prepared to act on adverse monitoring or other reports. The current process of de-registration needs speeding up when children are in danger. Departments of State should be active in pursuing the public interest and the interests of children in cases brought to their notice.

Criminal Justice

Criminal justice is not working in a way which protects children against abuse. Convictions are few in relation to the cases investigated. Young children and disabled children are disadvantaged to the point of being deprived of justice. Child witnesses may be further harmed by the court process. Known perpetrators avoid penalty and are free to continue to threaten other children. Notification of people unfit to work with children, which depends heavily on convictions for criminal offences, loses much of its effectiveness.

The Review recommends that the Government implements the remaining recommendations of the Pigot Report;
and undertakes a comprehensive review of the arrangements for prosecuting offences against children in order to make them more effective.

ENDPIECE   The experience of the Review has seemed at times a crash course in human (predominantly male) wickedness and in the fallibility of social institutions. The fact that the bad is only a tiny proportion of the whole should not obscure the fact that it tarnishes the lives of many children. Yet there are excellent schools, children's homes and foster carers.

The main requirements for bringing all up to the level of the best are thought, planning, systems and skill. Many of the Review's recommendations need only these resources, but material resources are important too. We received telling submissions about the impoverished lives many children lead, and the shifts authorities were reduced to in maintaining services. Some of our recommendations need more money and more people: improving quality of service, making choice of placement a reality, getting children on remand out of prison, extending inspection. They must take their place among other priorities for increased public expenditure. The Review would argue, however, that the ultimate cost to society of not doing these things will be many times greater through the burden of ruined adult lives.

> The principal joy of the Review came from children and young people who have lived away from home. Their incisive insights helped us to see how things looked to children, and we admired their cheerfulness and resilience.
>
> Looking after them would be easier and much more effective if we really heard and understood what they have to tell us.

SIR WILLIAM UTTING   **Catherine Baines**   **Marian Stuart**

                                      John Rowlands   **Roz Vialva**

PRINCIPAL RECOMMENDATIONS

Principal Recommendations are both

- important in themselves, and

- affect large numbers of children

The Synopsis of each chapter refers to all our Recommendations. Many of these are important in themselves and have significant implications for particular groups of children.

Where Children Live

1   The Department of Health/Welsh Office should establish and resource a dedicated group to develop and implement a comprehensive strategy for residential child care (Chapter 2).

2   Local authorities should secure sufficient provision of residential and foster care to allow a realistic choice of placement for each child (Chapters 2 and 3).

3   Local authorities must pay particular attention to the educational and health needs of the children they look after, and ensure a better transition to independent living (Chapters 2 and 3).

4   Local authorities must observe the Regulations governing the placement and supervision of children in foster care (Chapter 3).

5   The Department of Health/Welsh Office should commission a Code of Practice for recruiting, selecting, training and supporting foster carers (Chapter 3).

6   The Department of Health/Welsh Office should secure legislation requiring local authorities to register private foster carers and making unregistered foster care a criminal offence (Chapter 3).

7   The Department of Health/Welsh Office should extend Section 87 of the Children Act 1989 (which requires independent boarding schools to safeguard and promote the welfare of children, and opens their arrangements for doing so to inspection) to all schools with boarding provision (Chapter 4).

8   Local authorities should unify their educational and social services arrangements for assessing and supporting children with emotional and behavioural difficulties and their families (Chapter 4).

Parents

9   Government should define parental rights and responsibilities in legislation (Chapter 6).

10 All organisations caring for children away from home should provide parents with all relevant information about their arrangements for safeguarding children before placement is made (Chapter 6).

11 Government should sponsor a programme to inform parents and relevant staff of the risks to the welfare of children living away from home and of ways of reducing them (Chapter 6).

Staff

12 All organisations in which children live away from home should apply the recommendations of *Choosing with Care* (The Warner Report) in selecting and recruiting staff and volunteers with substantial and unsupervised access to children (Chapter 13).

13 Government should examine the need to strengthen the legal protection of agencies communicating information about the suitability of individuals to work with children (Chapter 15).

14 All organisations accommodating children should instruct staff to raise legitimate concerns about the conduct of colleagues or managers and protect them against victimisation (Chapter 15).

Children

15 Local authorities should make direct use of the experience of the children they look after in developing policy, practice and training for services for children living away from home (Chapter 7).

16 Government should ensure that legal protection against abuse and harm is consistent in all settings in which children live away from home (Chapter 10).

17 Local and health authorities should assess and meet the need for treatment of children who have been abused (Chapter 10).

18 Departments of State with responsibilities affecting children should adopt and actively pursue the aim of safeguarding and promoting their welfare (Chapter 16).

19 The Department of Health/Welsh Office should in the medium term review and re-issue the Regulations and Guidance associated with the Children Act 1989 (Chapter 17).

20 Government should implement the remaining recommendations of the Advisory Group on Video Evidence (The Pigot Report), and undertake a comprehensive review of arrangements for prosecuting sexual offences against children (Chapter 20).

PART I: THE STARTING POINT

Chapter 1	# INTRODUCTION

'It would not be wise for anyone to approach this Report on the basis that it all happened a long time ago and that nothing like it could ever happen again.'
Andrew Kirkwood QC. *The Leicestershire Inquiry 1992.*

Background to the Review

1.1 The Children Act 1989 and its associated Regulations and Guidance introduced significant new safeguards for most of the children who live away from home. Additional action to protect them has been taken following the publication of *Children in the Public Care*[1], *Accommodating Children*[2], *Working Together*[3], *Choosing with Care*[4], the reports of the Support Force for Children's Residential Care[5], and circulars issued by the relevant Departments of State. Overall, a formidable body of directive and advisory guidance now exists, in addition to a substantial volume of research and other literature, including the reports of various inquiries. A reasonable person might suppose that, were all this advice and guidance implemented, children living away from home would be as well protected as it is possible to be in the world in which we live.

1.2 Information has since come to light, however, about serious and systematic abuse of children in children's homes over a period of many years before the Act came into force. It therefore becomes necessary to ask whether the safeguards instituted since 1991 are strong enough to prevent similar abuses occurring. It would be intolerable if the next century brought revelations of widespread abuse in some children's homes now.

1.3 Questions are also raised about how far the requirements of regulations and statutorily based guidance are met, and about the effectiveness with which they are monitored and enforced. Regulations and guidance which are not put into practice create a false sense of security which adds to the risk faced by the very children they are intended to protect.

Protection – from What?

1.4 The terms of reference of the review speak of 'abuse and other harm'. 'Abuse' is interpreted, for the purposes of the Review, as 'action or conduct by another person which causes physical or psychological harm'. The Review is therefore principally – but not exclusively – concerned with physical, sexual and emotional abuse by adults or other children. The circumstances in which the Review was established compel particular attention to the threat of habitual abusers.

1.5 Harm is usefully defined in Section 31(9) of the Children Act as 'ill-treatment or the impairment of health or development', and this enables the Review to extend beyond too narrow an interpretation of abuse. The terms of reference also allow adequate consideration of institutional and other impersonal factors. Matters which are the subject of fire, environmental health, and health and safety legislation, while obviously of cardinal importance in safeguarding children, are remote from the central purpose of the Review and are not discussed.

1.6   The Review did not consider that the phrase 'living away from home' in its remit was intended to include short absences for holidays or other purposes. We have accordingly assumed absence for 28 consecutive days to constitute 'living away', since this period is specified in parts of the legislation governing the registration of children's homes and private fostering. The term 'children' in the text takes the Children Act meaning of children and young people under the age of 18.

Developments since 1991

1.7   The Children Act 1989 came into force on 14 October 1991. It strengthened the safeguards for children living away from home both generally and in detail. The concept of the state working in partnership with parents improved the security of children in that majority of cases in which parents are committed to the welfare of their children. The new duty on the proprietors and managers of independent schools to safeguard and promote the welfare of boarders was a major advance. Existing regulations were revised and new ones promulgated to cover arrangements governing the placement of children in the public care and the conduct of the caring environment.

1.8   The Act was followed by further initiatives by the responsible Departments of State, often based on the recommendations of major reports. The Department of Health had already requested local authorities to review and report on both management and practice in their children's homes following the report by Allan Levy QC and Barbara Kahan into the use of 'Pindown' in Staffordshire Children's Homes[6]. In August 1991 it had asked local authorities to address immediately 3 major recommendations of *Children in the Public Care*[1] about inspecting local authority children's homes, producing plans for children's services, and improving personnel management and training policies. The Department subsequently issued circulars on planning, inspection, and permissible forms of control, and mounted an important initiative in training heads of homes.

1.9   Following the conviction of Frank Beck in 1991, the Secretary of State for Health set up a Committee of Inquiry under the chairmanship of Norman Warner with terms of reference which included examining 'selection and recruitment methods and criteria for staff working in children's homes'. The Committee published its report *Choosing with Care* in December 1992. The Department of Health issued an immediate letter asking employers to implement 22 recommendations dealing with the recruitment and selection of staff. Local authorities were asked in the following year to implement the remaining 19 recommendations addressed to them as employers.

1.10   The Department did not, however, accept one of the Warner Report's most important recommendations in the form envisaged. This was for the creation for 3 years of a small independent Development Action Group to secure and follow through the implementation of a programme of change for children's homes agreed by the Government. It established instead, for a period of 2 years, the Support Force for Children's Residential Care under the direction of Adrianne Jones 'to advise and assist local authorities in England and Wales to help to bring about necessary changes in management and personnel practices'. Ms Jones subsequently led the Examination Team on Child Care Procedures and Practice in North Wales which reported in 1996 to the Secretary of State for Wales, who accepted all its 41 recommendations and required the local authorities to report on their implementation.

1.11   Between 1992 and 1996 the Department of Health and Welsh Office published 18 Circulars (3 jointly with the Department for Education and Employment) bearing directly or indirectly on the safety of children living away from home. Education published 4 important Circulars of its own (See Appendix B). The Social Services Inspectorate has continued to issue major reports, and Local Authority Independent Registration Inspection Units (referred to as local authority inspection units hereafter) now produce a substantial volume of information about children's homes and independent schools. This is part of the prolific literature on child abuse and residential life produced by individuals, practitioners, researchers, voluntary organisations and pressure groups.

1.12 The initiatives in residential child care have occurred against a background of continuing contraction, fragmentation and stress. There has undoubtedly been progress in significant areas such as staff selection and the training of heads of homes. Overall, however, the sector remains in urgent need of development as a national service.

1.13 The character of foster care has changed as the number of children looked after by local authorities and the use of residential care have both continued to decline. Its range now extends from the traditional role of providing a family home to a semi-professionalised service catering for severely abused or disturbed children. The issue of safeguards for children in foster care has rightly come into greater prominence. Arrangements for private fostering remain a source of anxiety.

1.14 The fastest progress in improving safeguards since 1991 has probably taken place in residential education. The Children Act served to crystallise and disseminate much of the development that had occurred over the past 20 years in the more advanced part of this large and heterogeneous sector. Inspection of welfare arrangements by local authority inspection units has led to productive partnerships in some areas, not yet reflected in others where traces of mutual incomprehension persist. The Education Act 1993 revised the definition of schools required to register as children's homes, and in 1995 the Department of Health issued guidance to relax the frequency of social services inspection of some schools. The progress made in most parts of the sector serves to highlight deficiencies in the remainder. Some schools seem impervious to outside influence; some individuals cause great anxiety; some children in residential education are as vulnerable to abuse as any child in the public care.

Guiding Principles   1.15 The review is informed by the values of the Children Act and of the UN Convention on the Rights of the Child.

1.16

> ### The UN Convention on the Rights of the Child
>
> **– Articles particularly relevant to the Review**
>
> 12[1]: States Parties shall assure to the child who is capable of forming his or her own views the right to express those views freely in all matters affecting the child.
>
> 19[1]: States Parties shall take all appropriate legislative, administrative, social and educational measures to protect the child from all forms of physical or mental violence, injury or abuse, neglect or negligent treatment, maltreatment or exploitation, including sexual abuse, while in the care of parent(s), legal guardian(s) or any other person who has the care of the child.

20[1]: A child temporarily or permanently deprived of his or her own family environment, or in whose own best interests cannot be allowed to remain in that environment, shall be entitled to special protection and assistance provided by the State.

28[2]: States Parties shall take all appropriate measures to ensure that school discipline is administered in a manner consistent with the child's human dignity and in conformity with the present Convention.

34: States Parties undertake to protect the child from all forms of sexual exploitation and sexual abuse. (The Article mentions, in particular, inducement or coercion, prostitution and other unlawful practices, and pornographic performances and materials.)

37[c]: Every child deprived of liberty shall be treated with humanity and respect for the inherent dignity of the human person, and in a manner which takes into account the needs of persons of his or her age. In particular, every child deprived of liberty shall be separated from adults unless it is considered in the child's best interests not to do so and shall have the right to maintain contact with his or her family through correspondence and visits, save in exceptional circumstances.

39: States parties shall take all appropriate measures to promote physical and psychological recovery and social reintegration of a child victim of: any form of neglect, exploitation, or abuse; torture or any other form of cruel, inhuman or degrading treatment or punishment; or armed conflicts. Such recovery and reintegration shall take place in an environment which fosters the health, self-respect and dignity of the child.

1.17 Parents have the primary responsibility for safeguarding their children. Government supplements parental resources in safeguarding children living away from home, and intervenes only to secure and ensure protection from harm.

1.18 Clear direction from the centre on the implementation of statutory duties, clear statements of policy, and clear guidance on the principles of good practice are needed to secure consistent standards nationally. Directions and guidance should be as short and simple as possible, and allow scope for local interpretation and flexibility wherever possible.

1.19 Delegation of authority, power, responsibility and provision should be matched at every level by exacting comparable accountability. Action to implement the requirements of protective legislation, regulations and statutory directions should be monitored and, where necessary, enforced.

1.20 People and organisations paying for services should satisfy themselves that those services keep children safe.

1.21 Arrangements for protecting children living away from home should arise from the needs of the child rather than from the nature of the service he or she is receiving. Every setting in which children live away from home, however, should provide the same basic safeguards against abuse.

General Safeguards

1.22 The Children Act says that the first duty of a local authority to a child it is looking after is 'to safeguard and promote his welfare' (Section 22). A similar duty is laid on the proprietors and managers of independent schools which provide accommodation (Section 87).

1.23   'Safeguard' and 'promote' are equal partners in an overall concept of welfare. Safeguards are an indispensable component to the child's security, and should be the first consideration for any body providing or arranging accommodation for children. Safeguards form the basis for ensuring physical and emotional health, good education and sound social development. These are the proper objectives of all institutions providing care and education for children. I cannot emphasise too strongly the importance of these objectives for all children living away from home, the difficulty of achieving them for children in the public care, and the need for renewed and sustained effort in accomplishing them.

1.24   The Children Act was accompanied by numerous volumes of authoritative guidance to assist local authorities and others in its implementation. Several of these contained Regulations and Guidance on sectors with which the review is particularly concerned: Volume 3 on Family Placements, Volume 4 on Residential Care, Volume 5 on Independent Schools, Volume 6 on Children with Disabilities, Volume 8 on Private Fostering, and the practice guide to The Welfare of Children in Boarding Schools. It appears to be the practice of the Department of Health and Welsh Office to issue all circulars deriving from the Children Act under Section 7 of the Local Authority Social Services Act 1970, which requires local authorities to act under the general guidance of the Secretary of State.

1.25   Practice guidance from the Department of Health which is not issued under Section 7 is nevertheless 'something to which regard must be had in carrying out the statutory functions' (*Times Law Report 17.4.96: Regina v Islington Borough Council, Judgment 15.3.96*). The circulars issued by the Department for Education and Employment to local education authorities on the topics covered by the review are of similar status. Where such circulars are addressed or copied to independent bodies they are advisory only. They are delivered, of course, in a context of regulation and inspection which should normally ensure their careful consideration (aided by such emphatic formulae as 'The Department strongly advises').

1.26   Reference has already been made to the host of research and other literature which is available, especially about child abuse and residential care. The work of the Support Force for Children's Residential Care is particularly important in this context, and its published reports shed light on important aspects of this Review. The Social Services Inspectorates in England and Wales have published overview reports on residential and foster care which distil valuable advice from their programme of inspections. Their reports on individual authorities and voluntary organisations are also available to the public. The Social Services Inspectorate also inspects voluntary children's homes. Local authority inspection units inspect the children's homes provided by their own authority and by private proprietors, as well as the welfare arrangements of boarding schools; practice varies about the availability of their reports. OFSTED publishes reports of its inspections of boarding schools, but reports made by HMI and by local authority inspection units to the Registrar of Independent Schools are not published.

1.27   The adequacy of this regulatory framework, its implementation, monitoring and enforcement are addressed in Chapter 17.

Children at Home and Away

'The range and extent of the unkindness, cruelty, violence and wrongdoing to which children are subject is shocking.'
ChildLine – submission to the Review

1.28   How safe children are in their own homes provides a benchmark for what is achievable for the safety of children living away from home. The great majority of parents represent their children's best security, but there are few grounds for complacency about the safety of children living at home. Some parents are their children's worst enemies. Relations and acquaintances – as well as strangers – abuse and harm children. Most abusers are previously known to their victims.

1.29   The National Commission of Inquiry into the Prevention of Child Abuse[7] reviewed the current state of our knowledge. It estimated that

- at least 150,000 children annually suffer severe physical punishment,

- up to 100,000 each year have a potentially harmful sexual experience,

- 350–400,000 live in an environment low in warmth and high in criticism, and

- 450,000 are bullied at school at least once a week.

ChildLine counselled 90,000 children in the year ending 31 March 1996, 12% of them about bullying, 10% about physical abuse and 9% about sexual abuse. A written Parliamentary Answer earlier this year estimated that 110,000 men aged 20 and over in 1993 had a previous conviction for a sexual offence against children. This suggests – in view of the low reporting and even lower conviction rate for such offences – a truly alarming level of sexual offences against children by men. Women also commit sexual offences against children, but in much smaller numbers.

1.30   The effects of abuse as a child may in some cases be long lasting and persist throughout adult life, impeding mature sexual relationships and affecting mental health. American research suggests, for example, a degree of correlation between abuse in childhood and later mental disturbance. Particularly serious, from all points of view, are the instances of some children subjected to persistent abuse who then abuse others.

1.31   It may not seem realistic to expect life away from home to be safer than life at home for the generality of children. The law, however, expects it to be as safe: people caring for other people's children are required to exercise parental responsibility. *The Public Inquiry into the Shootings at Dunblane Primary School 1996*[8] acknowledged that *'Parents sometimes have to take a great deal on trust; and it is reasonable that they should be assured that the clubs or groups which their children attend have shown that they provide an adequate degree of protection against abuse. The children's safety is paramount.'* Those remarks apply with even greater force to children who are not just attending clubs or groups but actually live away from home.

1.32   Such children are more vulnerable than others on a number of grounds. All lack the immediate supervision of parents and the support of familiar environments in which there are other trusted adults they could turn to. Some who are away from home have already been abused and may have acquired the vulnerability of established victims. Some lack the personal defences of other children because of physical or learning disabilities. Those classified as 'difficult' or disturbed are less likely than other children to be taken seriously if they complain. Some children are in relatively isolated circumstances and almost wholly dependent on adult carers. Career abusers may target any of these children and their environments. Those who achieve power and influence within institutions may corrupt both staff and children.

1.33   There is no doubt, from the perspective of the Review, that the safeguards for some children living away from home should be strengthened. Every organisation providing accommodation for children must make their safety its principal objective. Public policy requires local authorities, in particular, to achieve standards of protection for the children they look after which are higher than may be expected from all parents. Giving the extra protection that particularly vulnerable groups of children need may, however, deflect persistent abusers to other groups of children living away from home. What is needed in addition, therefore, is for every setting in which children live away from home to provide the same basic safeguards against abusers.

The State of Safeguards Today

1.34   The briefest commentary possible is that safeguards are stronger than they were 10 years ago and of a higher order altogether than they were 10 years before that. This is due in large part to increased awareness and knowledge of what children away from home need to be protected against. This knowledge is widely, if unevenly, distributed among people with professional responsibilities to children. The work of voluntary organisations in particular, supplemented by press, radio and television, has raised awareness in the community. High levels of incomprehension and denial nevertheless remain. This is unsurprising: my contemporaries and I passed the first half of our professional careers in similar states of innocence and ignorance – less excusably, perhaps, than average members of the public today. Spreading knowledge responsibly – of both dangers and safeguards – for the general information of the public remains a vital task. It is important not to inflict unnecessary damage on the networks on which many families depend to provide full social lives for their children. Unreflecting trust, however, in adults who are presumed to be just like us in their concern for our children is itself a major danger.

1.35   Regulations, statutory guidance and other forms of advice provide a full and detailed web of safeguards. This report identifies gaps which need to be filled. Pointing out what ought to be done is the easier task, however; doing it, not just once but over and over again, every time it needs to be done, in all circumstances, under all the pressures of time, money, staff and unforeseeable emergencies – that is what is so difficult. That context of reality puts into a more understandable perspective some of the acts and omissions by managers and professional workers which are otherwise inexplicable. Bad decisions get made, however, even in favourable circumstances. Safeguarding children requires both managers and staff to be directed at all times to serving the primary purposes of their organisation, and to be trained and resourced to the highest levels attainable. The totality of that prescription is realised too rarely in the principal settings with which the Review is concerned.

1.36   Regulations and operational instructions are useless without monitoring and enforcement. Bodies with statutory duties and powers towards children have a special responsibility for monitoring their own performance. Departments of State need to know that what they require of agencies responsible for children is actually delivered.

Statistical information is important but ultimately inadequate for this purpose and needs the essential supplements of inspection and research. These disclose an inconsistent implementation of regulatory requirements. This is not perhaps surprising in view of the number of providers and the size of the sectors regulated. Some of its manifestations, however, speak clearly of incompetent or irresponsible practice, and of management which is haphazard, insouciant or unscrupulous.

1.37   The framework of statutory regulation – even as improved by the Children Act – has not prevented fraudulent and abusive practitioners operating at the margins of residential care, independent education and fostering. The changes recommended by the Burgner Report[9] and by this Review would close important gaps. Just as important, however, are the powers and policies of the bodies responsible for monitoring and enforcement. Cumbersome statutory procedures handicap the quick response needed to urgent welfare issues. Decisions to de-register institutions are quite properly subject to appeal. The costs of failure (political, managerial and, not least, professional) lead to a cautious approach when the needs of the children cry out for boldness.

1.38   The Support Force identified a number of factors associated with residential homes in which children have been abused:

- they often have a charismatic leader with apparent expertise;

- they can have a good reputation and be seen as being successful; and

- they deal with damaged and vulnerable residents with low self-esteem, usually children or young people whom the relevant authority has found hard to place and who are regarded as 'unreliable' witnesses.

Some problem schools showed similar characteristics: with the addition of a proprietor/head operating without a board of governors or trustees. It must be emphasised, however, that such factors do not cause abuse, that institutions which exhibit them may also demonstrate the highest ethical standards, and that much abuse will occur in places which do not match this prototype.

1.39   Groups more vulnerable than the average child living away from home are:

- Children in public care

- Children in private foster care

- Disabled children including those with learning or communication difficulties

- Young children

- Children with emotional and behavioural difficulties

- Homeless children

- Children of parents living abroad: expatriates, service personnel, foreign nationals.

1.40   Persistent paedophiles for whom abusing children is a lifelong career appear in various guises: as proprietors, heads of institutions, professional or ancillary workers, volunteers or helpers. Staff who are not habitual abusers may nevertheless resort to abusive conduct under stress or in corrupting environmental circumstances. Children may inflict harm on each other: physical, sexual and emotional. Some parents resume abusive behaviour when children return to them for holidays, or even pursue their children to the places in which they are presumed to be safe.

1.41   Finally, there is the impersonal harm wrought by malfunctioning systems and institutions: possibly less destructive of the personality than the harm done by individuals, but affecting whole cohorts of children in ways which might permanently damage their prospects of successful and happy adult lives. The factor common to this malfunctioning is the substitution of other goals – whether of policy, management, administration or professionalism – for the primary objective of promoting the welfare of children. Everything that goes on in organisations with that objective should be put to the test of whether it serves the interests of children. If it does not, either at first or second hand, it is likely to harm their interests directly or indirectly. The capacity to apply such a test depends, of course, on the organisation's understanding of what constitutes welfare. For many, this remains inextricably attached to the functions of the organisation or the roles of different professions. Only the best authorities and institutions are able to see and deal with children as whole people.

1.42   While the Review is confident that safeguards are stronger than they were, they operate in a society under the pressure of changing values, behaviour, communication and technology. They too need regular review and revision to ensure that they remain adequate to the task.

PART II: WHERE CHILDREN LIVE

Chapter 2   CHILDREN'S HOMES

SYNOPSIS

This chapter considers the current state of children's homes, the area which is of greatest current concern. It notes the good work done by many homes despite adverse circumstances. It concludes that residential care is an important option for looked after children and makes a number of recommendations for improvement.

The Review believes that safety is a function of overall effectiveness and that quality protects. It feels that residential child care as a national service has shrunk to below that which provides a reasonable choice for children. Choice is vital both in meeting needs and in safety. Local authorities should secure sufficient provision of residential and foster care to allow a realistic choice of placement for each child (paragraph 2.3). Continuing retrenchment is also at odds with the needs of looked after children even though residential child care is a costly alternative (paragraph 2.6).

The Department of Health/Welsh Office should set up and resource a dedicated group to devise and implement a national strategy for residential child care (paragraph 2.9).

Staffing is a chronic problem and should be addressed in the national strategy (paragraph 2.10). Problems are compounded by inappropriate placements, which can make the situation in a home impossible. The number of placements some children have is extremely damaging. Local authorities should review their placement policies and practice to ensure the safety of each child remains a continuing priority (paragraph 2.12).

Children are at risk in small unregistered homes. The Review urges speedy implementation of the Burgner recommendation that these be brought within the regulatory framework. The Burgner suggestion that local authorities should register and inspect voluntary children's homes is supported and other points about registration endorsed (paragraph 2.13–15).

Improvements in both health and education services are needed for looked after children. Local authorities should take a corporate approach to deal with a situation in which over a third of children in residential care are not receiving education (paragraph 2.16). They also have serious health needs which must be addressed in order to keep them safe. It is recommended that the Department of Health/Welsh Office should facilitate the action needed by local and health authorities to identify and meet the health needs of looked after children (paragraph 2.17).

'Strong belts and braces do not make a good pair of trousers.'
British Association of Social Workers – submission to the Review.

'I no longer feel alone. I no longer feel afraid of myself.'
Resident writing to the Review.

Children's Homes

2.1   This is the area of greatest current anxiety. Information has recently come to light about the systematic abuse of children in children's homes over a period which began many years before the Children Act came into force. The most pressing question is whether the safeguards instituted by the new Act and subsequently would have prevented such abuses. Answering this is inseparable in practice from the larger question about whether the system of residential child care is operating as effectively as it could and should. There is little doubt in the mind of the Review that the 'best' homes (or schools, or hospitals) are also the safest. Safety is a function of overall effectiveness. If the child is not safe, the home is achieving objectives neither for the child nor for itself as an institution. Quality protects.

2.2   It is not the task of the Review to publish a comprehensive primer on how to provide an effective residential child care service. The materials for this are easily accessible elsewhere. We lack neither the theoretical nor the practical knowledge to provide good residential child care. The persistent deficiencies in children's homes are symptoms of a lack of commitment by political and service managers to unpopular, expensive but necessary provision.

2.3   The Review must, however, offer comment on matters which bear directly on its terms of reference. It is probable that residential child care has shrunk as a national service to a level below that at which a reasonable choice of placement is possible for any child. Choice of placement is a vital factor in meeting the assessed needs of children. It is also important in simply keeping them safe. Shoe-horning children into vacancies in unsuitable establishments exposes them, other children, and even the establishment itself to the danger of unforeseen harm. Assessments, plans and reviews are a mockery if a reasonable range of services are not available to fulfil their purposes. Pre-occupation with occupancy levels in the authority's homes, or with keeping children within the geographical boundary, may further weaken choice. It is safer to err on the side of generosity of provision, even with an expensive service like residential care. Choice is safety. Local authorities should secure sufficient provision of residential and foster care to allow a realistic choice of placement for each child.

2.4   The survey undertaken by Price Waterhouse in 1992 for Warner[4] estimated that there were about 950 local authority homes, 170 voluntary homes and 180 private sector homes in England. Appendix C shows that at 31 March 1996 there were 836 community homes run by local authorities, 64 voluntary children's homes, 202 registered (private) children's homes and 84 registered residential care homes. About 40 independent schools were also registered as children's homes. 10,490 children were living in local authority homes in England at 31 March 1990, but only 7,596 six years later. The figures for Wales were 527 children in 1990 and 298 in 1994.

2.5   It is important to keep deterministic pessimism about residential care in check and to give full weight to the developments described in the previous Chapter. Berridge and Brodie[10] summarise these in the following terms: *'Most but not all were initiated directly by the Department of Health. They constitute an impressive series of strategies, which at last address some of the longer-term structural problems of the residential sector'.* Plans for children's services, statements of purpose and functions for homes, improved training for heads of homes, planning for children, inspection of local authority homes and renewed managerial involvement have provided strong stimuli to change. Individual authorities have evolved impressive strategies which they are progressively implementing. The practical results are that one resident could tell inspectors that *'The staff here have made me very happy and they have given me a lot of confidence'*, and another could tell the Review that *'All the staff at my home are nice and understanding towards me – and always have time for me'*.

2.6   Factors in the general background against which social services departments operate, however, continue to work against residential care and impede implementation of these strategies. The financial pressures on social services through the general restraint on local authority spending expose the high unit costs of residential child care to continuous critical scrutiny. General arguments in favour of alternative services are heavily weighted by consideration of cost. The Review acknowledges how difficult these matters are for bodies which are stewards of public funds and under additional financial pressure. The fact that the average cost of a residential placement is seven times greater than one in foster care is not a negligible matter when priorities for the use of limited budgets are being discussed. The continuing retrenchment in residential care is at odds, however, with objective analysis of the needs of the population of looked after children. That retrenchment, incidentally, means that local authorities now spend less in real terms on residential care than they did 10 years ago.

2.7   Local government reorganisation increased the financial pressures for some authorities by further sub-dividing the available cash. Creating large numbers of new social services authorities also produced other difficulties for the organisation and provision of residential child care. A service reducing in size is distributed across larger numbers of social services authorities: 22 in Wales compared with 8 before reorganisation, 132 in England (rising to 150 in 1998) compared with 109. Management and professional skills are more thinly spread. Few authorities will be able to meet the need for residential services from their own resources or even within their own boundaries. These could be short term problems, but there is little doubt that they must slow down the strategic developments already under way.

2.8   More seriously, the decline in critical mass at the level of the average local authority may invalidate the government's reliance on the local authority structure to produce overall improvements. That structure is now too fragmented to be a reliable means of securing the improvements nationally which every contemporary analyst has recommended. Moreover, the residential child care sector as a whole now lacks the capacity to initiate widespread improvements in standards. The major voluntary bodies have been forced by contracting demand to diversify into community-based work. The independent sector is therefore now largely made up of small suppliers. There is no grouping of services of sufficient strength – and not enough confidence or stability in the sector as a whole – to provide the basis and the motive power for the development required.

2.9   Warner's 1992 [4] recommendation for a Development Action Group to institute a programme of change for children's homes appears to the Review to possess even greater validity in the different circumstances of 1997. The changes that are needed in residential child care require the implementation nationally of a national strategy. The Department of Health's recent initiatives, and the agenda provided by the Support Force's excellent series of reports [5], provide the basis for such a strategy. What is needed now is a body with the authority and resources to drive it through from partial to complete achievement nationally. The Review accordingly recommends that the Department of Health/Welsh Office establish and resource a dedicated group to develop and implement a national strategy for residential child care. Such a strategy should naturally include the elements now in hand, and extend to the volume and nature of service needed, with plans for securing provision to the standards required.

2.10   The object of this recommendation is not to relieve local authorities of any of their responsibilities, but to help them discharge them fully. Local authorities are the principal agencies in this field, as purchasers of services and as major providers. Individually, however, they struggle with a range of difficulties which need a single, co-ordinated response. All local authorities, in the words of the submission to the Review from the Association of Directors of Social Services, *'experience significant difficulties in establishing and maintaining adequate staffing for what is a very demanding job'*. Submissions from voluntary and private providers echoed and reinforced the importance of this chronic problem, and the inability of individual organisations to solve it. Progress is made here and there by dint of determined and persistent effort. The overall impression is of progress too slow to redeem the sector as a whole. Yet it still has an indispensable national role, even at the modest level asserted in guidance attached to the circular Children's Services Planning (LAC(96)10): *'Foster care will be desirable for the majority. But adequate residential care has to be available to support foster care through respite and transitional provision, or as a possible longer-term solution in its own right for some young people.'* The staffing problems of residential child care are a national as well as a local concern, and need to be addressed in the national strategy.

2.11   The Association of Directors also called for *'serious recognition of the part played by placement policy and practice in ensuring the safety of children in the public care'*. These are matters for local authorities within the range of placements available nationally. The Review has already called for a range of provision that permits the exercise of choice as an essential safeguard for the child. Local considerations, policies and practices then take over. Dorothy Whitaker in her submission from the Social Policy Research Unit at York University commented that research *'revealed that the existing mix of young people is rarely taken into account when placing a child'*.... *'Some mixes are virtually impossible to manage.'* .... *'Under such circumstances the Home is in a virtually constant state of crisis and unsettledness.'* Reports by local authority inspection units comment critically on placements made without proper information provided to the home and on placements of children patently unsuited to a home's purpose and capability (*'Recent admissions all had records of serious violence, assaults on staff and arson'*).

2.12   Many representations were made to the Review about the number of placements some children received and the risks this unbelonging lifestyle exposed them to. ChildLine, for example, told us that one quarter of 840 looked after children who called its service had 4 or more placements (a few had at least 10); and commented, *'Given that these are youngsters who have already experienced family loss and disruption, these are shameful statistics'*. Placements outside the local authority may be necessary in the interests of an individual child, but special consideration is then needed for supervision and monitoring by the responsible authority. The Review received comments from Wales and Kent, for example, which suggested at least the possibility that children placed there by other authorities lapsed into a limbo out of sight, out of mind. One of the most alarming findings of the 1995 report by the Social Services Inspectorate into small unregistered children's homes[11] was that 14 local authorities who claimed not to be using such homes were in fact doing so. *'All too frequently it was left to junior management staff to make such decisions, often without reference to senior staff and sometimes in contradiction to the stated policy of their employing department.'* Local authorities should review their placement policies and practices to ensure that the safety of each child remains a continuing priority.

2.13 The Burgner Report in 1996[9] recommended that small children's homes be brought within the regulatory framework. The Government accepted that recommendation. The Review hopes that Government will proceed quickly with the necessary legislation, since the absence of regulation exposes children to unnecessary danger. In the meantime, local authorities must ensure that proper procedures for protecting children are followed. The SSI report referred to found nearly half the social services authorities were using these homes. *'There were some who had a history of financial misdealing......... There were others against whom allegations of both physical and sexual abuse had been made prior to them setting up small homes, and some of these have subsequently been convicted and sentenced. In all the cases given as examples, however, local authority checks had not been sufficiently robust to prevent them from placing children in the care of these people.'* Wide variations in standards were found: *'children are being placed by some local authorities in accommodation which, at the very least, is unsuitable and, in some cases, is placing them at risk'.*

2.14 The Burgner Report also suggested that the registration and inspection of voluntary children's homes should pass from the Department of Health to local authorities. I support this, having made a similar recommendation in 1991 and finding no cause to change it. The Secretary of State should not have to remain concerned with the detailed conduct of individual homes now that local authority systems for registering and inspecting children's homes have reached a reasonable level of effectiveness. I appreciate the reluctance of the voluntary sector to give up a valued link with a Department of State, but this is now an anomaly overdue for elimination.

2.15 Burgner noted the absence of a power comparable to Section 11 of the Registered Homes Act 1984, which enables a local authority to apply to a magistrate to cancel the registration of a home on the grounds of serious risk to the life, health or well-being of the residents. Similarly, there is no facility comparable to Regulation 20 of the Registered Homes Regulations, by which local authorities can serve notice on a provider if conditions of registration are not fulfilled, requiring compliance within 3 months. Burgner commented on the lack of a power for the local authority to take over management of a registered children's home in an emergency, and on the slowness of appeals to a Registered Homes Tribunal, which may extend the period in which residents are at risk. The Review confirms the importance of these matters and trusts that the Department of Health/Welsh Office will expedite their consideration of them.

2.16 The importance of health and education services for looked after children has been emphasised in a sequence of reports. The Review received vigorous representations about the inadequacies of both. The

Audit Commission pointed out that audit work shows that over one third of the children in residential care are not receiving education. A joint SSI/OFSTED report[12] found that 1 in 4 of those aged 14–16 *'do not attend school regularly and many have been excluded and have no regular educational placement.'* It concluded that *'The care and education systems in general are failing to promote the educational achievement of children who are looked after.'* *'Professional bodies attribute much of the deterioration in an already unsatisfactory situation to the greater readiness of schools to exclude difficult pupils who are already known to be 'in care'.'* Whatever the cause, it produces a scandalous situation in which the life prospects of these young people may be irretrievably damaged and their immediate safety put at greater risk. A corporate approach is needed by education and social services authorities to resolve it.

2.17   Professor Jo Sibert told the Review at a meeting in Wales that children looked after by local authorities were the most deprived group of children he had met, with serious health needs requiring expert attention from community paediatricians and psychiatrists. A submission to the Review estimated that 75% had mental health problems, some complex and severe, some with undiagnosed psychoses. The National Institute for Social Work emphasised the importance of health issues in relation to social behaviour (in such areas as sex education, AIDS, drugs and prostitution), and pointed to the roles of public health doctors, health visitors and schools in dealing with them. The Royal College of Nursing suggested that a named person in each authority should be responsible for the health of children living away from home. The Review supports the efforts of Warner and other reports to get more done to meet the health needs of looked after children. Progress is possible: we were encouraged by what was happening in Wales in the context of the report *The Health of Children in Wales*[13]. The overall situation is frustrating, however, as if people are hoping for some magic key to unlock the problem. The health needs of looked after children seem to the Review to be fundamental to keeping them safe. The Department of Health should facilitate the action needed by local and health authorities to identify and meet the health needs of looked after children.

Secure Accommodation

2.18   The Howard League report *Banged up, Beaten up, Cutting up*[14] found that local authority secure accommodation provided *'much higher standards of supervision and care than the prison system'*. Problems of bullying and self-harm were identified, but *'The major area of concern is the lack of properly trained staff'*. Local authorities provide secure accommodation as part of their children's services. It is approved by the Secretary of State and inspected by the Social Services Inspectorate. There were 29 units open at 31 March 1996, providing 274 places, of which 246 were occupied – the great majority by boys aged 14 and over. Inspection reports confirm the generally favourable view of the Howard League: for example, 'young people seen by inspectors confirmed that their experience of being admitted to the Unit had been positive', *'young people who deliberately harmed themselves.... received prompt treatment and appropriate support'*, and complaints were independently investigated.

2.19   The Howard League was less reassured about the Youth Treatment Centres, however: *'The investigations and re-organisation which took place between 1989–92 have still not resolved many of the problems'* (of unacceptable practices such as prolonged solitary confinement and the use of tranquillisers). An inspection of the remaining Youth Treatment Centre (Glenthorne) by the Social Services Inspectorate in 1996 reported more favourably. *'Young people who had been previously placed in a range of secure units commented favourably upon the standards of day-to-day care experienced in Glenthorne.'* Inspectors felt some concern about race and cultural matters and gender issues. They observed *'considerable skill and high levels of effort'* in diffusing difficult situations. *Single separation was not used as a sanction.'* Overall, inspectors found *'a much calmer atmosphere'* than at the last full inspection in 1993. The Youth Treatment Service Group established by the Department of Health in 1991 and chaired by Winifred Tumim was laid down in 1996. Its 4 Annual Reports offer valuable insights into the lives of staff and children in institutions coping with profound and complex behaviour disorders. Tom White continues as an external independent visitor to Glenthorne.

2.20 It would be wrong to end this section on children's homes without re-emphasising that good work is done by many in spite of adverse circumstances. One local inspection report from 1996 says, simply, *'There are many examples of outstanding care practices with this often troubled group of young people.'* Another report recorded: *'It would appear from our observations and the comments of placing agencies, coupled with our discussions and observations of both clients and staff that a sensitive and protective care base has been established.'* A third report, on a registered home, quoted residents saying it was *'like living at home rather than living in a home.'*

Chapter 3:   FOSTER CARE

SYNOPSIS

About two thirds of looked after children are in foster care but this has been neglected in policy terms until recently. The current interest in foster care is welcomed and the Review urges that priority should be given to safeguards in this.(The isolated nature of foster care means that children are at risk of abuse and it is clear that the safeguards intended in the Children Act are not being fully implemented.)A first priority must be to do so (paragraph 3.23).

A number of recommendations are made which aim to improve the level of safeguards in foster care.

The main recommendation is that arrangements for the checking and assessment of foster carers should be strengthened (paragraph 3.37). The Social Services Inspectorate should inspect current practice on the recruitment, selection, training and support of foster carers with an emphasis on the degree of protection these offer. The result should then be used to form the basis, along with expert advice, for Department of Health/Welsh Office guidance on the lines of the Support Force's Code of Practice for the Employment of Residential Child Care Workers. Other related suggestions of this Review – on the need for awareness training about male and female abusers, on assessing those related to the child or with whom he/she has a professional relationship and on the need for improved assessment documentation – should also be taken into account. (This recommendation responds to that made by Adrianne Jones in The Report of the Examination Team on *Child Care Procedures and Practice in North Wales*.)

Authorities and agencies should review their policies on family placements to ensure they take account of the dangers of peer abuse (paragraph 3.38).

Arrangements between carers and authorities would be improved if foster carers are treated as full partners who are entitled to all relevant information and if more emphasis is given to authorities' obligations in relation to support and training in foster care agreements (paragraph 3.39).

It appears that there may be more risk attached to long term foster care. Authorities should carry out an audit of their long standing carers in order to see whether there are any grounds for concern (paragraph 3.42).

They should keep clear records about allegations of abuse and have a clear policy on when carers would be removed from the foster carer register. Records should be taken into account in any further allegations, during regular reviews and in deciding what to put in references (paragraph 3.44).

Placing authorities should notify approving authorities of any allegations and their outcomes and foster carers who are removed from the local register as a result of investigations should be put on the Department of Health Consultancy Index (paragraph 3.45).

Because of the isolation of foster care, it is recommended that social workers should be required to see the child alone during each visit made under Section 6(3) of the Foster Placement Regulations. Regulation 6(1) should be amended to reduce the maximum period between visits to a child in a foster home after the first year of placement there from 3 months to 8 weeks (paragraph 3.46). Local authorities should assess any special or additional needs for the support of single foster parents and the children placed with them and consider whether to provide the child with an Independent Visitor.

Children in foster care should be given information to help them protect themselves. Social workers should provide or arrange this and discuss it with the child on his/her own (paragraph 3.48). Children should be given age appropriate sex education and have access to help and counselling (paragraph 3.49).

Apart from issues directly related to protecting children, the chapter discusses other issues relevant to the wider welfare of fostered children. Most importantly, the need for an adequate choice of placements so that these are appropriate to the child's needs and the foster carer's ability. Authorities should develop a strategy for dealing with emergency fostering with a view to minimising damaging breakdowns (paragraph 3.51).

Education and health matters also need to be given priority and proper after-care is vital (paragraph 3.52).

Another major proposal is that the Burgner recommendation that Independent Fostering Agencies should be brought within the regulatory framework should be implemented as soon as possible (paragraph 3.67).

It is not known how many children are privately fostered since statistics are not kept but it appears the number may be substantial. Children in private foster care are extremely vulnerable and at very considerable risk of abuse (paragraphs 3.68–81).

The current arrangements clearly do not work since very few private foster care placements are notified to local authorities. Attempts to improve the level of notifications appear to have very little effect. This situation should not be allowed to continue. It is recommended that private foster carers should be required to seek approval and registration. The law should be changed to make caring for children without registration a criminal offence. It should also be an offence for parents to place children with unregistered foster carers (paragraph 3.80).

It will be necessary to give the public notification of the proposed changes in the law and it is recommended that the Department of Health should mount a public awareness campaign about this (paragraph 3.81).

'A healthy foster care service is pivotal in ensuring the successful outcomes of all other child care services, including Child Protection, Youth Justice and Respite care. It is your family support.'
ADSS Report on the Foster Care Market.

Foster Care   3.1   There were some 31,700 children in foster families in England on 31 March 1996. Since 1991 there has been a slight decline, of 3,000, in numbers. In Wales between 1992 and 1994 there has been an increase in both the number of approved foster carers, from 1,565 to 2,095, and in approved places, from 2,416 to 2,926. Many thousands more children move in and out of foster care in the course of the year, giving an estimated total of 50,000. Since numbers in residential care have declined considerably, the proportion of children looked after by local authorities in foster care has grown to around 65%. The average stay in foster care is about 22 weeks but there is a wide range. Over a quarter of placements last for 4 weeks or less, whilst a similar proportion last over a year. According to the National Foster Care Association (NFCA) (*Foster Care in Crisis* [15]) there are about 27,000 foster families caring for children in the UK.

3.2   Children in foster placements tend to be younger than those in children's homes. 42% of children in foster placements are under 10 compared with only 8% in children's homes.

3.3   A substantial number of fostered children have some form of disability, including emotional and behavioural problems. A 1992 study by Parker, Loughran and Gordon (quoted by Berridge in his review of the research [16]) estimated that this amounted to a quarter of all those in foster care, though it is likely that some of these were in respite care. Despite some increase in specialist foster schemes – to cater for teenagers, children with a disability, those on remand and respite care – the service provided is still mainly short term temporary care.

3.4   With the decline in the overall number of children looked after, it is generally agreed that those in both residential and foster care have more complex needs than previously. For example, in one London Borough as many as two thirds of fostered children had been sexually abused, though only one third had been known to be so at the time of the placement. Foster carers are thus dealing with children with a wide range of complex needs.

Regulation of Fostering   3.5   The Foster Placement (Children) Regulations 1991, made under the Children Act, broadly retained the structure which was introduced in the 1988 amendments to the Boarding Out of Children Regulations 1955 but with some additions. The Regulations cover the approval of foster carers and annual reviews of the approval; the circumstances in which placements are made; how they should be supervised and how often they should be reviewed; the records to be kept and the frequency and nature of local authority visits.

3.6   The Children Act and associated regulations and guidance are detailed and provide a sound basis for improving fostering practice. There is evidence that there have been improvements in a number of areas since 1991. For example NFCA told us that more recently recruited foster carers are better prepared for the task and receive more guidance and support. There is also evidence that implementation of the regulations and guidance is variable, some authorities have made good progress, others much less so. It seems that very few are complying with all the requirements. A recent Association of Directors of Social

Services (ADSS) survey, to which 100 out of 140 local authorities in England and Wales responded, found that only 79 said they were able to comply with all the Foster Placement Regulations. Important gaps are: failure to visit and review at the required intervals; lack of clarity on whether the child has been seen on his/her own; poor record keeping; a lack of awareness of complaints procedures. There is clearly scope for improving safety by better application and observance of the existing arrangements.

3.7   It seems to be accepted that assessment of potential foster carers is relatively thorough – with interviews, home visits and talking to two personal referees. However few prospective foster carers are checked against the Department of Health Consultancy Index.

3.8   It is also accepted that children are at risk of abuse in foster care. Its isolation and private nature does make them more vulnerable. Some of the safeguards available in residential care are not suitable for care which is provided in a family home, such as unannounced visits and those from elected members. Another factor is that many of the children are very young, over 13,000 under 10 and many (1,200) pre-school age. That renders some other safeguards such as complaints procedures ineffective. The fact that much fostering is very short-term also adds to the problems.

Policy   3.9   Despite the predominance of foster care for looked after children, there is relatively little data on it. It has had a lower profile than residential care and less media and policy attention. Until recently, very little research or inspection work has been done in this area. It is now getting a higher profile than it has had for many years and there have been a number of useful pieces of work in the last two or three years (including *The All Wales Review of Fostering Services* [17]; *Social Services Inspectorate* (SSI) *National Inspections; ADSS Report on the Foster Care Market* [18]; NFCA's study of the organisation of fostering services [19] and David Berridge's *Foster Care: A Research Review* [16]). Research into fostering has been neglected: it was the main focus of only 13 major research studies in the last 20 years, whereas during David Berridge's survey of the field there were 10 studies of residential care underway. The main focus of policy interest has, however, been on the newer developments rather than short term care for younger children which is the mainstream of the service. There is little evidence about outcomes but studies, on the whole, show a generally positive view of the care provided, including the views of children obtained in the Camden survey of looked after children.

3.10   However, evidence to the Review from Sonia Jackson, Chair of Children in Wales, which was based on two research studies, said *'There was a strong view, ...particularly ...in the focus groups, that foster care had actually deteriorated since the Children Act. The emphasis on family preservation and contact and the shift in balance towards parents' rights meant more going in and out of accommodation and great instability. About half of our subjects had had multiple placements (more than five), one had had 39 and one 38 (checked from files). This instability was very harmful to their physical and mental health and to their education'.*

3.11   The SSI National Inspection Reports of 1994–95 and 1995–96 [20] identified some areas of concern about practice in foster care. The former noted a number of aspects which were generally done well. These included work that was focused on the welfare of children and that took their wishes and feelings into account. Most parents felt their children were well looked after and most of the children felt safe.

However it listed a number of areas in which improvements were needed. The 1995–96 Report concluded that *'The profile of fostering services within Social Services Departments' policies and children's services must be raised. Services plans should address how SSDs intend to develop a service that will adequately meet the needs of children looked after, both within the department and through arrangements with other agencies.'* It recommended that plans for development and resourcing should be included in Children's Service Plans. It noted the lack of routine aggregated data on children and carers and recommended the establishment of monitoring and quality control systems. It found that coverage in local authorities' children's services policies and plans were insufficient.

3.12   The ADSS Report[18] affirmed the importance of foster care but felt that it was under more pressure than ever before and that 'a crisis is in the making'. It argued that foster care should receive more attention from Directors of Social Services and that strategies needed to be developed to take the services forward which enabled them to cope with the changed, and increased, pressures involved. Strategic planning in this area was essential, yet it was too often managed and financed in isolation from residential care. It needed to be fully integrated if double standards were not to prevail.

3.13   The Report listed a number of reasons for concern:

- The difficulty of recruiting and retaining sufficient numbers of carers in order to cope with the higher proportion of children with complex needs who require long term specialist help.

- The lack of choice of placements for children (especially black and mixed race children, who are over represented in care), siblings, those with disabilities, and adolescents.

- The increase in black and mixed race children placed inappropriately without sufficient support and training for carers.

- The difficulty of finding placements near home so that contact with friends and family could be maintained.

- The placing of children with carers who were not matched to their needs leading to breakdowns and long term damage to the child.

3.14   There were differences of view about what the status and role of foster carers should be. The increased complexity and difficulty of the foster care task and the need to undertake training and to liaise closely with other professionals was thought to sit uneasily with the traditional voluntary service ethos. The legislative demands and requirements of the Children Act had also led to a need to raise quality standards but some local authorities were having difficulty in meeting these. The growth of Independent Fostering Agencies (discussed in paragraphs 3.55–67) had implications for local authorities – some carers were transferring to agencies and this increased both the cost and out of area placements. Competing demands on budgets (Community Care, NHS reforms) and structural changes such as a purchaser/provider split and the creation of smaller, single tier authorities were also complicating factors.

3.15   Foster carers also have a number of concerns. They feel that they are given insufficient training for the specialist needs of the children they are asked to look after and that the support, advice and assistance they receive is inadequate. They complain of being asked to take children outside their approved remit. They also regret their lack of involvement in the planning of the service.

3.16 In May 1997 the NFCA published a paper entitled *Foster Care in crisis: A call to professionalise the forgotten service.* [15] It called for a rethink of the traditional view that it was a volunteer service and advocated greater investment and improved status for foster care. It called for payment of carers for their skills and time, together with clear terms, conditions and tasks; compulsory training; development and enforcement of national standards for all aspects of child care; mandatory regulation and inspection of all foster care agencies; and preparation of detailed care plans for every child in public care. It argued that *'the cost of failing to invest in foster care is high'* and that *'Long term, the economic and social costs of failing to provide adequate care for children and young people when they need it, will be considerably greater than the short term investment required'*.

3.17 There is a considerable degree of overlap between the concerns of the interested parties and some of these have a bearing on safeguards, though the safety of children in foster care has not been the driving force behind this work. The increased difficulty in caring for the children and young people now being fostered means that carers need more training and support. There is considerable variation in the financial and support arrangements provided by local authorities as well as in how far they involve foster carers in policy making. There is conflict between the traditional voluntary approach and a growing awareness that the task demands an increasingly professional approach. This carries with it significant implications for employing authorities and foster carers alike. A more professional approach would involve participation in preparation and training, and greater expectations of record-keeping and other activities by foster carers. It would imply closer arrangements for supervision and support from employers as well as a more coherent and consistent approach to remuneration. There may be some loss of privacy for the carer and her family and resource consequences for authorities. In view of the vital contribution of foster care the work already undertaken by ADSS is welcome, as are the recommendations for further policy initiatives on this front. The Review believes that there is a danger that safeguard issues may not get the prominence they deserve in this – particularly given the overall pressure to increase numbers of carers through improved recruitment and retention. We would not wish to express a view on the preferred outcome of the current policy debate about the future direction of foster care, but would emphasise the importance of ensuring that safeguarding children in foster care should be at the forefront of those considerations.

Practice   3.18 The Review believes that all children should be able to expect the same overall level of protection against physical, emotional or sexual abuse or neglect whatever their circumstances. Fostering is an essentially private activity; it is hard to assess in general terms or to gauge how effectively safeguards for the protection of children are working, including the extent to which foster care has been affected by the Children Act. The inspection work undertaken by SSI did, however, identify a number of areas where there were significant concerns, including many where the minimum requirements set down in statutory regulations were not being complied with. A significant proportion of children had not been assessed comprehensively and did not have individual care plans. Reviews and supervision of children did not always meet statutory requirements. Little attention was given to involving parents in the day to day care of their children and there was very limited contact with fathers. The content of foster placement agreements varied in the extent to which they contained the details required by regulations.

Poor record keeping led to difficulty in knowing how decisions were made and whether the child had been seen alone. There was little information about the health histories of many children. The inspections also found that children and parents were not made sufficiently aware of complaints procedures.

3.19   Some further points of concern in relation to safeguarding children emerge from the inspection reports on individual authorities. Records do not always give the outcome of an investigation of abuse and the nature of the investigation is often not clear. There is a considerable difference in the support, training and supervision given to foster carers both between authorities and in relation to different types of foster carers. Those who have been more recently recruited get more, as do short term foster carers. Longer term carers are relatively neglected. Family placement/fostering officers are quite well regarded, field social workers much less so. They are said to be inexperienced, their practice variable and fostering low on their list of priorities.

3.20   The All Wales Review of Local Authority Fostering Services[17] identified a range of similar problems. Reviews of children were *'not met uniformly within some authorities'*. Reviews of carers were *'unlikely to be up to date'*. Several authorities had *'no central system of information gathering on the level of completion of reviews'*. And *'monitoring, as in the measurement of overall service inputs and impacts, is undeveloped in most departments'*.

3.21   Adrianne Jones in *The Report of the Examination Team on Child Care Procedures and Practice in North Wales*[21] reported that since 1991 there had been significant reductions in the proportion of children in residential care in Clwyd and Gwynedd and consequential increases in the proportion in foster care. On 31 March 1995, Clwyd had 77.6% in foster care and Gwynedd 75%. These figures were said to be much higher than for other authorities in England and Wales. The report commented that *'support systems for foster carers remain significantly under-resourced'*. It also noted *'a widening gulf between the practices employed in the recruitment and selection of workers for residential establishments and those in operation for foster care'* and recommended that *'Consideration be given by the Welsh Office, in conjunction with the Department of Health, to establishing a review of the recruitment, selection and support of foster carers'*. Welsh Office Circular 35/96 remitted that recommendation to this Review.

3.22   The ADSS Report[18] indicated that local authorities were having difficulty meeting the requirements of the Children Act in raising quality standards.

3.23   The Children Act and accompanying regulations provided an appropriate framework for safeguarding children and a first priority must be to ensure that children can rely on the safeguards provided. In particular, authorities should ensure that they are visited at the required frequency; that their reviews are conducted regularly and thoroughly; that foster carers are also reviewed as required, with proper account being taken of all relevant past history of complaints and allegations; and that proper and accessible records are kept. However, in our view, those safeguards – even if properly implemented – do not go far enough. Because of the vulnerability of children in foster care, particularly those who are very young, further measures are needed.

3.24   A number of letters were received from young people with experience of foster care. Some of these were grateful for the warmth, help and tolerance they had experienced. Some felt their carers had discriminated against them in favour of their own children. Others had experienced abuse and had not been believed when they sought help. The recommendations of this Review are aimed at building on the positive contribution that foster care makes while improving the safety and security of the children and young people it serves. It does not intend to imply criticism of foster carers either individually or collectively.

Abuse in Foster Care   3.25   Abuse clearly does happen in foster care and it seems the general view that there has been an increase in the number of allegations against foster carers though there is no firm data to confirm or deny this. An NFCA study in 1995 (published in the January 1996 issue of Foster Care) found that there were allegations of abuse in 4% of foster homes. (Others told us that the figure may be closer to 5%, particularly in large urban areas.) 22% were deemed founded and in 20% of cases it was not possible to determine either way. Only 22% of children were removed during the investigation and in 15% of cases it was thought likely that the carer would continue to be used, even though the complaint was substantiated. However, NFCA told us that a more recent survey found 305 cases considered to be abusive out of 13,333 (a rate of just over 2%). As NFCA said *'Any case of abuse is one too many and all foster carers have a responsibility to provide a safe placement for children'*.

3.26   Although ChildLine receive fewer calls from children in foster care than in residential care (1.1% compared with 10%), they say that they are more likely to call about physical and sexual abuse (though less likely to call about bullying). They are concerned that fewer younger children call from care than on their general service (under 4% compared with 9.5%) and that this may be because they are more likely to be in foster care and may be prevented from seeking help because of lack of information and access to a telephone. Recent figures show a significant decrease in the number of children in foster care ringing their special line about sex abuse – 3% compared with 14% four years ago.

3.27   There have been a number of cases over the years involving foster carers who have abused children in their care. It should be remembered that Frank Beck and other multiple abusers were foster carers. Moreover a substantial number of children can be harmed by one foster carer over the course of a long fostering career.

3.28   There are also risks from the children in the foster family. An NFCA study (published in the October 1995 issue of Foster Care) found that 11% of allegations concerned the foster parent's own child (average age 14). But on the other hand the risk clearly works both ways as in 14% of cases the alleged perpetrator was the fostered child (average age 13).

3.29   Although foster children are exposed to fewer carers than those in residential care, the very nature of foster care means that they are isolated and vulnerable. They have less choice of people to turn to if there is a problem and they may be reluctant to complain since to do so would put the placement at risk. Nearly half the children in foster care are also very young (under 10) and are therefore particularly vulnerable.

3.30   It is increasingly becoming recognised that women may abuse sexually as well as in other ways, and it is important that foster care officers and field social workers are aware of this and remain on their guard for the sort of warning signs which would give rise to concern with a male carer. Allegations from children should be dealt with thoroughly rather than assuming that 'women do not do things like that'. Vigilance is particularly important since it appears that some female abusers start the abuse when the child is very young and the majority of very young children are in foster care.

3.31   It seems that where allegations do arise there is concern to ensure that the foster carer is handled appropriately and sensitively, and given proper support – as is right and proper. We were less sure that the needs of the child were handled as sensitively.

Recruitment of Foster Carers

3.32   Special care must be taken in the recruitment and approval of those who foster children. While the arrangements for recruiting foster carers have in the past been more thorough than those for residential care staff, there is a need to improve them in a number of ways. The Review is aware of the importance which local authorities attach to maintaining, or increasing, the number of foster carers available to them and of the tension felt in pursuing what may appear an intrusive process in determining whether the prospective carer should be recruited. This may apply particularly where the person will not be a paid member of staff but a volunteer, providing help for largely altruistic reasons. But it is vital that, in attempts to recruit more carers, authorities do not lose sight of the paramount need to ensure the safety of the child. Care needs to be taken from the advertising stage onwards – for example abusive carers have been known to choose foster children from advertisements which include pictures and descriptions of the child. And providing too clear a description of the sort of carer wanted provides those with ill-intent the opportunity to present themselves accordingly. There can be no 'right' to look after a child, particularly a very vulnerable one, and all well-meaning applicants can be expected to appreciate this. We consider it vital that prospective foster carers should be subject to a fuller range of checks and references.

3.33   Those who assess prospective foster carers should be expected to have a good knowledge about child care, including a sound knowledge about child abuse and its effects, but they may not know enough about sex offenders to look for the right pointers. All staff involved in assessment should receive awareness training about both male and female offenders who abuse in a family context. This should cover the type of questions to ask in order to determine whether the applicants have appropriate attitudes to children, especially in relation to sexual matters, and whether they have a clear concept of proper boundaries of behaviour.

3.34   Carers and their partners (whether married or cohabiting) should be checked thoroughly. Their personal histories should be explored and full CVs provided so that gaps can be checked. References should be sought from present or past employers as well as from those named by the prospective carer. Proof of identity such as birth and marriage certificates should be seen and then the prospective carer should be checked against the Department of Health Consultancy Index as well as with the police. Home visits should be undertaken to ensure that accommodation is appropriate. The present documentation used in assessing foster carers (forms F1 and F2) is not sufficiently geared to safeguarding children and should be reviewed with that in mind.

3.35   In general it is helpful if a child can be fostered by a relative or family friend. Some use of discretion is appropriate in these cases in relation to the normal physical expectations of a foster home, for example in allowing less bedroom space. There may however be a tendency for assessment to be less comprehensive, particularly where the proposed family placement is with another member of the original family. However, if the child is being placed because of sexual abuse within the original family this may lead to further difficulties where there is a family culture of weak boundaries, worrying attitudes, and sexual abuse. We recommend that checks should be similarly thorough where prospective foster carers are related to the child.

3.36 There have been a number of cases where someone with a professional relationship with a child has abused them and gone on to become their official foster carer. A study in 1990 by Bebbington and Miles quoted in Berridge[16] found that a quarter of foster carers were working in child care or related activities, such as nursing, social work and teaching. Special care should be taken in assessing the placement of children, particularly those who are very troubled and vulnerable, with someone in these circumstances, and there should be no assumptions about suitability. Approving authorities may wish to consider asking an independent authority/agency to provide an assessment.

3.37 The recruitment and selection of appropriate carers is particularly vital in foster care, given its isolated nature, as is the need to ensure that they are given the training and support they need. The Review supports the recommendation made by *The Report of the Examination Team on Child Care Procedures and Practice in North Wales*[21] that these aspects of foster care should be reviewed. We recommend that SSI should undertake an inspection to establish current practice on the recruitment, selection, training and support of foster carers, with a particular emphasis on the degree of protection these afford the child. The findings, together with the recommendations of this Review, should form the basis of a study, involving also experts on offending behaviour, which produces a Code of Practice on the lines of the Support Force's Code of Practice for the Employment of Residential Child Care Workers[5]. The Department of Health/Welsh Office should issue the Code of Practice under Section 7 of the Local Authority Social Services Act 1970.

Information for Foster Carers

3.38 A major safeguard for fostered children is to have well chosen, well-informed foster carers who know that they can call on help and support when they or the children they look after need it. Unfortunately this is not always the case. Foster carers sometimes feel that social workers have been less than open with them about the background of the children they foster and there have been a number of instances where this has had tragic consequences for the fostering family. Where such families are taking on children who have been abused, or who may have been abused, they have a right to be given full information. We recommend that authorities should treat foster carers as full partners who are entitled to all relevant information, and that there should be no excessive preoccupation with confidentiality. It is in no-one's interest if a placement is made which results in the children of the foster family being abused by the fostered child or in the fostered child being abused by the children of the foster family. The possibility of peer abuse needs to be seriously addressed at the time of placement and its risk minimised, even if this means taking a more restricted view of potential fostering solutions for some children. Residential care may be the better option in some of these cases. We recommend that local authorities and agencies undertake reviews of their policies on family placements to ensure they take account of the dangers of peer abuse.

3.39   Where foster carers take on very disturbed children they have every right to expect that they will be given appropriate training to enable them to understand and respond appropriately to the child's behaviour. This is especially important where they are asked to do so after some years of experience of fostering less troubled children. It should not be assumed that they should be suitable for the task and a proper assessment should be made of this, particularly where sexually abused children are involved. They should be given full support, information and training. This should include how to protect themselves and their families against the sort of misunderstandings which may lead to allegations against them. The NFCAs guidance in *Safe Caring* [22] is particularly helpful about this. In order to ensure that carers and authorities have a clear understanding of each other's roles and responsibilities, particularly in respect of training and support, we recommend that greater emphasis should be given to the obligation to specify these arrangements in foster care agreements (Item 1 of Schedule 2 to Regulation 3(6)b of the Foster Placement (Children) Regulations 1991).

Long Term Foster Carers

3.40   From the evidence the Review received it appears that there may be more risk attached to longer term foster care, particularly where the foster carers have been looking after children for a number of years. NFCA identified this as an area which was *'exceptionally vulnerable'*: it said that *'Although not widespread, it is our experience that there is very limited oversight of these care arrangements due to resource constraints. Annual reviews of long term carers are not given priority'*.

3.41   There may be a number of reasons for the higher risk in long term foster care, including the reduced level of supervision and external involvement, increased confidence that the situation is 'settled' and needs no intervention, and confidence in the carers themselves. Such isolation makes it difficult for the child or young person to signal where things are going wrong, particularly if they were placed at a very young age. The lack of support for the carer may also be a factor in triggering abuse.

3.42   It is vital that authorities do not 'take their eye off the ball'. There have been a number of cases where carers have won considerable confidence and respect but where this has masked abuse. It is quite possible, indeed quite likely, that there are some like this still caring for children as this Report is written. Enquiries, when they eventually unearth abuse of this kind, usually also uncover a background of past allegations that were not taken seriously or where the outcome was inconclusive. Authorities should carry out an audit of their long standing carers, including an examination of their records, and should undertake police checks where these have not previously or recently been carried out, in order to see whether there are any grounds for concern. It should be possible to do this at the next periodic review or before another child is placed. It is also recognised that many carers may feel hurt at the need for this, but it is hoped that they will understand that in order to protect children and the excellent reputation of foster carers generally, it is important to identify as quickly as possible any who might be abusing their position.

3.43   Paragraph 10.15 suggests that Independent Visitors might carry out exit interviews with children. This may prove an effective way of identifying problematic placements at an earlier stage than hitherto. It would enable the reasons for placement breakdown to be explored with the child rather than too ready acceptance that this is due to difficult behaviour.

Records 3.44 Local Authorities should keep clear records about allegations of abuse and have a clear policy on when carers would be removed from the foster carer register. Records of allegations made against each foster carer should be kept on one sheet at the front of their file; information should include how the matter was investigated and the outcome. The records should be monitored and there should be an established policy on what accumulation of allegations should lead to a review of the carer's continued use. Local authorities may wish to have an informed assessment made of the allegations and the abuser at that stage to avoid the risk of removing a carer unnecessarily or unfairly or may prefer to have a set of criteria, known to the carer, which would result in her being removed. The records should be referred to in the case of any further allegations and should be taken into account in deciding what to put in any reference provided. They should be one of the aspects automatically scrutinised when regular reviews of foster carers are undertaken.

3.45 Although foster carers can only be approved by one authority at a time, it is common for more than one authority to use the same foster carer either at the same or different points in time, and carers may also move onto the books of Independent Fostering Agencies. It is important that all parties that might wish to place a child should have access to all relevant information in making their decision, and it is recommended that placing authorities should notify approving authorities of any allegations and their outcomes. We recommend that foster carers who are removed from the local register as a result of investigations should be put on the Department of Health Consultancy Index.

Dealing with the Isolation of Foster Care 3.46 Given the isolation of foster care it is important that there is regular external involvement with the child. It is vital that the social worker visit the child at least at the required intervals. It is also important that the child knows how to contact them in between if necessary. Children should see their social worker often enough to build up a rapport and trust so that problems can be shared. Regulation 6(3) of the Foster Placement (Children) Regulations 1991 should be amended to make it mandatory that the social worker sees the child alone for at least part of each visit. This should preferably be outside the foster home. In view of the concern expressed about those in long term foster care, it is also recommended that Regulation 6(1) be amended, so that after the first year, visits should reduce from a minimum of one every 6 weeks to one at least every 8 weeks rather than the present reduction to three months.

3.47 NFCA's *Foster Care in Crisis*[15] points out that almost 90% of foster children live in placements which are two parent households. This compares with less than 50% of children generally and only a quarter of children who come to be looked after. The presence of two adults generally provides an extra safeguard, not least in dealing with tensions and difficulties that arise. Local authorities should assess any special or additional needs for the support of single foster parents and the children placed with them. They should consider whether to provide the child with an Independent Visitor and should seek to ensure that either the carer or the Independent Visitor is female.

3.48 All children need to have an understanding of what is normal behaviour, for themselves and others, particularly where their early experience has been abusive or neglectful. This is even more important in the foster care situation where the child will have fewer peers and other adults with whom to confide than in residential care.

Information should be introduced from as early an age as practicable and should be provided regularly as the child gets older. It should be the responsibility of the social worker to provide this, or to arrange for it to be provided by someone suitable other than the foster carer and to ensure that the child has a chance to discuss it during the part of the visit when they are on their own. It should not be left to the foster carer to pass on this information.

3.49   Foster children should also be given age appropriate sex education. Agreement should be reached between the social worker and the carer about how this can best be provided.

Choice and Placement

3.50   Apart from the question of abuse, it is clear from the findings of recent work, particularly SSI inspections, that the welfare of fostered children is not being adequately protected in a situation where there is little or no choice of placement. The 1995–96 National Summary Report[20] said *'There had been no choice of placement in the majority of cases, and this meant that children's needs were not being fully met'*. Inappropriate placements are likely to result and increase the probability that these will break down. This further undermines the children's confidence and trust, leading to a deterioration in behaviour and to a worse prognosis for the future. Inappropriate placement might also put the child at risk of abuse if the carer cannot cope, or if it sets off child on child abuse which could have been avoided. The major decline in the number and size of children's homes and a failure to increase the pool of foster carers has led to a dearth of alternative placements particularly when an emergency arises. In such circumstances it is more likely that foster carers deemed suitable for a young child may be persuaded to take on a difficult adolescent without the preparation needed to cope successfully. A further breakdown in relations with adults will further undermine the young person's trust and self-esteem. It may also lead to the foster carer withdrawing her services even for more suitable future placements.

3.51   The high level of placement breakdowns experienced by a significant proportion of looked after children is unacceptable. It takes a heavy toll on the children's future prospects and leads to long term costs for society as a whole – through criminal and self damaging behaviour, mental health problems, family breakdowns and parenting problems. It also takes a heavy toll on those who try to care for them. Authorities should develop a strategy for dealing with emergency fostering or other placements that is less damaging for the children and carers involved. They should maintain an excess of places over demand for emergencies and should follow up placements in these as quickly as possible by a considered appraisal of the child's needs. It is appreciated that this is likely to have resource implications but the cost of maintaining small emergency units, or keeping some emergency foster carers, would be far cheaper in the medium to longer term to society as a whole. The obvious benefit to the child is finding a family willing and equipped to provide him or her with a secure and lasting environment.

3.52   Other areas in which children's interests are not adequately safeguarded at the moment are education and health. The low expectations of educational achievement from fostered children (and those looked after generally) and higher rates of exclusion mean they are not given the help and encouragement they need to succeed, with all the implications that follow for employment and life in general thereafter. Health concerns also may not be adequately addressed, particularly where there are several moves. Public services need to act corporately and each play their part in the successful parenting of children who are looked after. The educational and health services should be active in helping the foster carer to provide the best care for the child and to ensure that the carer has some positive help in rectifying problems and difficulties rather than feeling unsupported.

3.53   Paragraphs 10.8–9 discuss the need for support, treatment and counselling for children who have been abused. This affects children in foster care as much as other looked after children – and the relative isolation may make the need even greater.

3.54   Appropriate after care is an important safeguard since young people leave care at a very vulnerable stage of their lives. The need for adequate after care is discussed in paragraphs 8.54–64.

Independent Fostering Agencies

3.55   There is no legal definition of an Independent Fostering Agency. They are agencies which are independent of local authorities. Some have acquired the status of charities, some operate under a 'not for profit' policy and others are profit-making partnerships. Most operate as 'not for profit' organisations. They have developed since the passage of the Children Act. Initially they consisted of groups of experienced foster carers previously approved by local authorities. More recently they have sought to recruit their own carers.

3.56   They are not subject to registration or inspection by local authorities or SSI. There are no agreed standards or criteria with which they must comply. Instead the responsibility rests with each local authority placing a child to satisfy itself that the placement is suitable and likely to safeguard the child's welfare. The Department of Health issued a circular in 1994, LAC(94)20, which clarified the legal position with respect to the delegation of duties under the Foster Placement (Children) Regulations 1991. Voluntary agencies may undertake some local authority functions such as approval of foster carers, reviews and termination of approval, placements and their supervision and termination. Agencies which operate for profit can play a much more limited role. Consideration was given to extending this but has not been proceeded with following consultation in which concern was expressed about doing so without inspection and regulation.

3.57   An increasing number of children are being found foster care placements through Independent Fostering Agencies. It is not known how many Independent Fostering Agencies there are but NFCA is aware of 49 in England and 1 in Wales. An SSI study [23] conducted in 1994 estimated that about 400 to 500 children, or 1.5% of those in local authority care, are placed with them – often out of area.

3.58   At the time of the SSI study 19 agencies were known to the Inspectorate but, since there was no requirement to register, there were likely to have been more. 10 of the 19 responded to a questionnaire and formed the basis of the information. They were responsible for 417 children. 68% of the children were of secondary school age, 30% were under 10 and 34 were under 5, all but one of whom had been placed outside their home area. In some cases the inspectors thought that the children were amongst the most troubled children they had seen in foster care and in others they found it hard to believe that placements could not have been found nearer their homes. The study illustrated some examples of good practice, such as effective work being done to maintain appropriate cultural links for a mixed race teenager, and good working relations and mutual respect with local authority staff. However there were many causes for concern. These are summarised in paragraphs 3.59–63.

3.59   There was a concentration of Independent Fostering Agencies in some areas. Of the known agencies at that time, 8 were located wholly or mainly in Kent. (This has since doubled.) 5 of those 8 responded to a questionnaire and revealed that 251 children, out of 417 covered by these agencies, had been placed by outside local authorities in Kent. This leads to problems for that area, for the placing authority in providing supervision and for the children and families concerned – increasing the difficulty of maintaining contact and the likelihood of losing contact with friends and having to change schools.

3.60   There was not much evidence of service level agreements between local authorities and the agencies, with only one agency in the study having a fully developed agreement. Most local authorities said they placed on an ad hoc basis when suitable placements could not be found from within their own resources.

3.61   There was concern about standards of recruitment. There was a wide variety of practice in relation to police checks – and some reluctance on the part of local authorities and police to respond to requests. Some checks fell well short of what is required by the Regulations. There had been media coverage at the time of the study about a placement made by a London Borough with an Independent Fostering Agency foster carer with a record of convictions previously unknown to the authority.

3.62   There was confusion over whether Independent Fostering Agencies could provide their own foster carers. This was linked to confusion over legal status (voluntary organisation/not for profit organisation), though it was hoped that this had been clarified by LA Circular (94)20. There remained the issue of the extent to which they should undertake the preparation and approval of foster carers and of the extent to which responsible authorities should repeat assessments of carers undertaken by the agencies. SSI pointed out that *'Legally speaking, foster carers remain local authority foster carers even though they are supported and trained by an independent agency'*.

3.63   A wide range of fees were charged – one agency charged £430 per week whilst another charged £1000 for an equivalent service. Independent Fostering Agencies were, however, often able to offer placements for children with emotional and behavioural difficulties at short notice and provide them with some form of education. This made them attractive to local authorities since, although more expensive than their own foster carers, the placements were cheaper than residential care.

3.64   It should be remembered that these concerns stemmed from information derived from a limited number of agencies who had made themselves known to NFCA and been prepared to participate in the SSI study. The activities of other agencies operating in this field are likely to be much more worrying. For example, a television programme on the subject showed an 'agency' could consist of a person operating from a car and with a mobile telephone.

3.65   The ADSS Report[18] also expressed the concern of local authorities that they are losing foster carers to Independent Fostering Agencies. Carers are attracted by better remuneration and the higher level of support they receive from the better agencies. This means that local authorities may have to buy back the services of the same carers they have used in the past but at much higher rates.

3.66   Evidence from the Welsh Local Government Association reflected similar worries. It mentioned that many children placed in the independent sector come from local authorities at some distance and that the host authority incurred costs, for example those associated with the preparation of court reports. It said that *'It is also evident that neither the Care Authorities nor the fostering agencies are informing host authorities of such placements as required by the Regulations. There is a clear need in terms of the safety of children for these agencies to be registered, for standards to be established regarding the quality of care etc., and for the relationship between them and the host authority to be worked out'*.

3.67   The Burgner Report[9] considered the case for regulation in this area and concluded that *'In any regulatory system the interests of the child must be paramount; minimising bureaucratic controls, though a desirable objective, has to take second place'*. It suggested the broad outlines of the type of statutory regulation that would be appropriate covering registration and inspection but thought that decisions on where to locate this function would depend on those relating to more general regulation issues. Wherever the function is located we are convinced that this area cannot be left outside the inspection and regulatory framework if children are to be properly safeguarded and recommend accordingly that the recommendation in the Burgner Report be accepted and the arrangements brought within it as soon as possible.

Private Fostering   3.68   The legal framework for private fostering is set out in Part IX of the Children Act, Section 66–70 and in Schedule 7. The relevant regulations are The Children (Private Arrangements for Fostering) Regulations 1991. Any person proposing to privately foster a child under the age of 16 for a period of 28 days or more is required to notify the local authority. The authority then has a responsibility to look after the general welfare of the child. They do not approve or register private foster parents and Volume 8 of the Children Act Guidance says *'A proper balance, therefore, needs to be maintained between parental private responsibilities and statutory duties towards private foster children.'* Agencies have to ensure arrangements are satisfactory and private carers are suitable. Prospective private foster carers must give permission for police checks to be sought. Local authorities have to visit and may ban individuals from taking on the role. The disqualification of certain persons from private fostering are set out in the Disqualification for Caring for Children Regulations 1991 (see paragraphs 14.36 –39).

3.69   It is not known how many children are privately fostered since the central collection of statistics was discontinued in England in 1991. At that time official statistics showed 2,000 in this category whilst the African Family Advisory Service estimated there were 6,000 West African children. In Wales, in 1994, 29 children were recorded as being in 27 private foster homes.

3.70   Many of the children have West African or Chinese parents but there are a range of others, including foreign language students, children attending independent schools for whom arrangements are made during school holidays and those who, for educational reasons, stay with friends or neighbours when their parents move. There continues to be considerable anxiety about private fostering on a number of fronts – including lack of awareness of the need to notify local authorities; low standards of care; the potential for abuse and the predominance of transracial placements.

3.71   The Race Equality Unit in its report *Black Children and Private Fostering* [24] said that children fall into several different categories:

Children with difficulties at home, or mobile parents, or educational needs which cannot be met by school residence who live with non-related friends or neighbours.

Children, mainly from European countries, attending language schools and staying in a family for more than 28 days.

Children attending independent schools for whom private arrangements are made during the school holidays.

'Back-door' pre-adoptive placements, often from overseas, whose prospective parents have not given notice of intention to adopt and therefore cannot be a 'protected child' under adoption law.

West African or Chinese children placed for varying lengths of time, mostly in transracial situations. These constitute the majority and cause greatest concern, particularly the former. Chinese placements are often because parents work late in the evening when child care is not available but firm links tend to be maintained and they are often placed near the family. West African children may have parents who are students, or working, or travelling to and from West Africa, or who are permanently there but want their children to benefit from UK education, health care and other facilities.

3.72   There are substantial differences between the types of arrangements involved. Parents may make arrangements for friends or neighbours, whom they and their children know well, to look after their children for a period for example if they have to move house because of a change of job but do not want their children to move school until important examinations are taken. They are able to make their own judgements about safety and can be expected to be in continued contact with the children and the carers. That is very different from a situation where a child is left with a carer who is unknown to the parent, possibly only after the most cursory enquiries or meeting, and where the contact with the child and carer may then be minimal and the arrangement last for a considerable period of years; or from the situation where a child is sent from abroad to a language school where contact with home may be minimal, where the child may be as young as ten and the arrangement last for up to a year. Yet in all these cases there are risks, albeit of differing degrees.

3.73   Private fostering is clearly an area where children are not being safeguarded properly, indeed an unknown number are likely to be seriously at risk.

3.74   An SSI inspection in 1993 [25] found that information about private fostering and the requirement to notify local authorities was not known by the general public, leading to significant under-notification. Arrangements were not in place in all Social Services Departments and there was confusion and some ignorance of the legislation, regulations and guidance. It concluded that '*Private fostering covered a wide range of situations in which potentially vulnerable children were being placed in the care of strangers, without any checks being undertaken as to their suitability to care for children,*' and that '*The way in which some placements were being made raised some very real concerns about the welfare of the children*'.

3.75   The Racial Equality Unit said that most placements were transracial and that black children were being brought up in predominantly white rural areas with little recognition of their cultural needs and identity. Standards of care may be low and many carers are poor. A large number have been not accepted as foster parents by local authorities and in some cases rejected and some had had their own children removed from them in the past. Parents were often a long way away and visited infrequently, or were out of the country, in prison or had not continued payments. It was not unknown for children to be moved without the parents being informed or to 'disappear'.

3.76　There have also been cases where private foster carers, who have looked after a child from an early age, with minimal contact with the family, come to regard the child as their own. In these cases the custody of the child becomes a source of contest between carer and parent. In other cases the child is 'returned' to a culture, perhaps abroad, which he or she is totally unfamiliar with and unprepared for.

3.77　The SSI Report recommended that Social Services Departments should be proactive in seeking out private foster placements through publicity campaigns and by alerting health and teaching professionals. Local authorities could then fulfil their statutory responsibilities to these children. However, attempts to improve the situation at a local level have not been very successful. Where local authorities have tried to raise awareness of private fostering requirements, through poster campaigns and advertisements in local papers, it seems that they received very little response. Researchers in this area have found that parents are very reluctant to talk to them since they are wary of any official involvement. While some may be unaware of the statutory arrangements, others are clearly wishing to flout them.

3.78　This is not a situation that can be tolerated. These must surely be amongst the most vulnerable of children living away from home. They may be placed at a very early age, sometimes, it seems, without contact with their parents, or anyone else with a responsibility for their welfare, for a number of years. Their position contrasts starkly with that of children who live with their parents, but go each day to a childminder or day care service. Childminders and people who provide day care services have to be registered with the local authority and be inspected at least once a year. Local authorities have to keep a register of childminders and providers of day care which parents can consult. That registration system is based on the person being 'fit' to look after young children and their premises being suitable.

3.79　Broadly the options are: to leave things as they are; to de-regulate on the grounds that the current regulations are unenforceable; or to enforce regulation on the basis of the risk to children. We do not recommend retaining the status quo, as it seems the worst of all worlds to give an appearance of safeguards while in practice they are not complied with. Deregulation would effectively abandon children to their fate when it is clear that there is a substantial risk and that cannot be right. We would also be concerned that any area left unregulated would be a 'honey pot' for abusers frustrated as a result of safeguards elsewhere in the system. Nor is it right to burden social service departments with commitments they cannot realistically fulfil; this counts against the third option as the law now stands.

3.80　It is a fundamental tenet of this Review that all children living away from home should be safeguarded and those who are privately fostered should be no exception. They should have the full protection of statutory regulation. As the present arrangements do not appear workable as they stand, it is proposed that private foster carers should be required to seek approval and registration from a local authority before taking on any children as is currently required in the case of childminders and providers of day care services. To do so without registration should be a criminal offence. It should also be an offence for parents to place a child with unregistered foster carers. Local authorities should vet private foster carers in the same way as other foster carers and should visit children in line with the current Regulations. Private foster carers who are removed from the register because of concerns about abuse should be notified to the Department of Health Consultancy Index.

3.81   The public should be notified of the proposed change in the law by a public awareness campaign mounted by the Department of Health and given notice of the need to comply with the existing Regulations. The Department should monitor the situation to see whether there is any need to modify the Regulations.

Chapter 4: SCHOOLS

SYNOPSIS

This chapter describes boarding and residential schools, noting the new duty introduced in the Children Act requiring proprietors of independent boarding schools to safeguard and promote children's welfare and local authorities to inspect their arrangements for discharging this duty. There are two main categories of school: those attended by 'ordinary' children and those approved by the Secretary of State for Education and Employment to take children with statements of special educational needs. Most of the 110,000 children who go away to school are in independent boarding schools. A sizeable number attend maintained special residential schools. There have been more reports on abuse in maintained special schools than in independent schools.

The new duty has improved welfare in independent boarding schools. Maintained and non-maintained residential special schools are outside its scope, so their welfare arrangements will not be subject to regular inspection. The principal recommendation for the schools sector is that the scope of Section 87 be extended to apply to maintained boarding schools and LEA, grant maintained, and non-maintained schools approved to take children with statements of special educational needs (paragraphs 4.28, 4.47–4.50).

It also suggests these improvements to Section 87 procedures:

- Inspection reports to be publicly available on the same basis as those on children's homes (paragraph 4.25);

- Local authority inspection units to give priority to making the format and content of reports more accessible to a lay audience (paragraph 4.25);

- Local authorities to be responsible for following up recommendations (paragraph 4.27).

Independent boarding schools should ensure that their brochures include information on safeguards. The Independent Schools Information Service's guide to choosing an independent school should include a section on safeguards (paragraph 4.10).

The Review supports the Service Children's Education Authority's proposal that payment of the Boarding School Allowance be conditional on parents seeking advice from the Authority (paragraphs 4.8–9).

It concludes that foreign children may not be particularly vulnerable. It welcomes the imminent launch of an umbrella body for guardianship agencies (paragraph 4.19).

It welcomes the Department for Education and Employment's intention to review the registration system for independent schools. Any review should be based on the principle that boarding schools should not accommodate children without preliminary examination of the welfare aspects. Any new Notice of Complaint procedure should allow for immediate cancellation where children are in danger (paragraphs 4.29–4.31).

It welcomes the fact that maintained and non-maintained residential special schools are required to have a governing body with a duty to make arrangements for safeguarding and promoting the welfare of pupils, and recommends that independent special schools should be required to have similar bodies (paragraph 4.40).

Children with emotional and behavioural difficulties need additional safeguards to be provided through the statementing process and assessment as children in need. The principle that the statementing process involves close co-operation between education, social services and health interests appears not to work consistently or universally in practice.

The Review recommends that local authorities unify the process as much as possible so that education and social services departments each make an appropriate contribution. This should be supported with a separate budget. Disabled children, who are defined as children in need in the Children Act, will have their needs and those of their parents assessed. It recommends that children with emotional and behavioural difficulties who are placed in a residential school for social and educational reasons should also be assessed as potential children in need (paragraphs 4.42–4.44).

The Department of Health's and the Department for Education and Employment's statistics on numbers of schools required also to register as children's homes are markedly different. It suggests that the two Departments look into the effect of the Children Act definition and take steps to make the regulatory framework simpler and more effective (paragraphs 4.52–4.53).

It comments on the dearth of information about the effect of Section 85 of the Children Act which requires educational establishments to notify local authorities of any child they accommodate or intend to accommodate for 3 months or more. It suggests that the Social Services Inspectorate should set up an inspection to obtain information about this (paragraph 4.54).

'We class schools, you see, into four grades: Leading School, First-rate School, Good School, and School. Frankly' said Mr Levy, *'School is pretty bad.'*

(Evelyn Waugh: Decline and Fall)

' The overall impression is that the school is well managed and the children who board are well cared for.'

(Inspection report)

[Registration] simply means that the school has met the basic legal qualifications for the number of children, suitability of teachers and certain health, building and other requirements.'

(Independent Schools Information Service: Choosing Your Independent School 1997)

Schools

4.1 Happy well cared for children are likely to do better at school. A good school is as concerned about the welfare as about the education of its pupils. This is important for all schools, but boarding and residential schools [1], where children do not see their parents every day, need to take particular care to safeguard and promote their welfare. While there is currently no widespread anxiety about extensive abuse or other harm in schools, episodes causing concern are sufficiently frequent to call for continual vigilance over this very large sector. There are particular concerns about schools catering for children with special educational needs [2] (SEN children), especially those which admit children with emotional and behavioural difficulties (EBD children).

4.2 Section 87 in the Children Act introduced a welfare and inspection provision for independent boarding schools – a direct response to scandals in two such establishments which hit the headlines while the Bill was going through Parliament. This section places a duty on proprietors and people responsible for running such schools to safeguard and promote the welfare of pupils and requires local authorities to inspect them in order to satisfy itself that children's welfare is being so safeguarded and promoted. The question for the Review is whether this new provision provides an effective further safeguard to protect children from abuse or other harm in all boarding and residential schools. Answering this question has to take into account the fact that the term 'boarding school' covers a wide range of educational establishments. (Appendix D summarises how the different categories of school are regulated.)

4.3 It is not just privileged children whose parents choose to pay substantial fees for their children's education, who go away to school. Sizeable numbers of SEN children also do so, with the costs being met from the public purse. There are about 110,000 places in boarding and residential schools, 85,000 in boarding schools and 25,000 in special schools. About 10,000 children in boarding schools are paid for by the Ministry of Defence's Boarding School Allowance. There are nearly 2,000 boarding and residential schools, the majority being independent schools, followed by a sizeable number of maintained [3] special residential schools. (See Appendix C for more details on statistics.)

---

[1] Boarding schools are those required to be registered with the Registrar of Independent Schools and residential schools are those approved by Secretary of State for Education to take children with statements of special educational needs -- called special schools in this Report.

[2] Section 312 of the Education Act 1996 states 'A child has "special educational needs" for the purposes of this Act if he has a learning difficulty which calls for special educational provision to be made for him'. This report refers to these children as SEN children.

[3] LEA and grant maintained.

4.4   Some types of children appear more vulnerable: disabled or EBD children; children with parents overseas; foreign children. Some types of school may be associated with greater risk: schools with no external oversight from a board of trustees, governing body, or advisory group; schools catering for EBD children; special interest schools attended by children particularly gifted in music, drama, dancing or sport.

Boarding Schools

4.5   There are two categories: around 730 independent ones registered with the Registrar of Independent Schools (25 in Wales) and nearly 40 maintained ones (only one in Wales). The main difference between the two is that maintained boarding schools are not subject to welfare inspections under the Children Act. Another important difference is that parents whose children go to a maintained boarding school only pay for the costs of boarding with the educational component being free. In other respects maintained boarding schools appear to be like independent boarding schools.

4.6   Boarding schools have changed a lot in recent years. There are fewer of them and nearly all take day pupils as well. Many children are weekly boarders and even those who are not will go home several times a term, with their parents also visiting the school frequently. Children are now less likely to start boarding at age 8 or 9 and more parents decide on a boarding education at secondary school stage. In a paper commissioned by the Review, Derek Turner wrote *'Even in the "great" Public Schools in the late 40s and early 50s, the physical welfare could be appalling and the regimes of corporal punishment, fagging and the like presided over by senior pupils, were scarcely less brutal than those instituted or tolerated by Victorian headmasters. ... Over the two or three decades following the Second World War, without either self-regulation or government legislation, and largely as a result of stronger middle class family values...the great majority of boarding schools experienced a quiet but very significant revolution in their treatment of children and young people in their care.'*

4.7   Parents who choose a boarding education for their children are wholly responsible for deciding on the school and in the majority of cases for meeting all the costs. It is left to them to judge whether a particular school is the right one for their child. The Independent Schools Joint Council (ISJC) commented that boarding schools see themselves as accountable to parents above all and many parents show strong feelings of loyalty to the school they have chosen for their child.

4.8   The Independent Schools Information Service (ISIS) told the Review that its role is to help parents choose the right school for their child. Their Directory of schools produced annually contains useful information about boarding as well as advice on what to look for and questions to ask when visiting schools. Schools' own brochures are another source of information, even though they will naturally present the institution in the best light.

4.9   The Service Children's Education Authority told the Review that its function in this country is to advise armed forces' parents about schools, their curriculum and their pastoral care and to ensure that Boarding School Allowance represents value for money. (It also manages some 55 schools in other parts of the world.) They provide lists of questions for parents to ask when visiting schools, but parents are not obliged to consult the authority before deciding on the school for their child. The Boarding School Allowance is payable provided the parent chooses a school on the 'admissible list' – currently defined as schools which have been attended by an armed forces child in the past. This criterion may be tightened. The authority has two OFSTED registered inspectors on its staff, who aim to visit all these schools on a regular basis. Parents make very few complaints about welfare issues to the authority, but it has had concerns about poor standards of care in some schools attended by armed forces children. These have been difficult to resolve, because the authority has no formal responsibility or role. The authority told the Review that it is asking the Ministry of Defence to make the Boarding School Allowance payable on condition that parents seek advice about choosing a school from the authority. We support this suggestion.

4.10   ISIS and a headmaster of a preparatory school told the Review that parents rarely asked specifically about safeguard issues when visiting schools or making enquiries about them. Parents concentrate on the educational aspects and, presumably, assume that schools will, naturally, have procedures to prevent the appointment of people to teach or care for children who are likely to abuse or harm them. The Review's study of inquiry reports and other material suggests that this is misguided. Schools should ensure that their brochures and other material are explicit about the arrangements for safeguarding children. The Service Children's Education Authority and ISIS should also ensure that their material includes advice on the questions parents need to ask about safeguards.

4.11   An ISIS report on a 1995 survey of parents[26] showed that nearly all parents who responded were happy with their decision to send their child away to school: *'The regime experienced by our children is much improved to the one we both experienced as children: a wider choice of subjects…but above all a caring atmosphere. The pastoral care is better developed and our sons were and are now less separated from the realities of the outside world.'*

4.12   What do children think about boarding? Children in one preparatory school visited by the Review found it easier to think of the advantages than the disadvantages. Advantages included: always having peers available to play with, lots of different activities on offer out of school hours and being able to be more independent. Disadvantages included: having to get up at a set time, being restricted in the amount of television they could watch, not having as much 'tuck' as day pupils. Those children seemed to feel well cared for and safe. They had some concerns about bullying – how incidents might be handled and who to go to –, but felt that the issue was taken seriously by the school. Bullying is discussed in more detail in Chapter 9.

4.13   The Review read a sample of inspection reports produced by local authority inspection units some of which specified what they learnt from talking to the children. While we cannot draw firm conclusions from this random selection, it would appear that where children's views were specified, they felt reasonably safe. *'Although the children have access to an "outside listener", he is not mentioned as a significant figure. Information of other external sources are evident around the school.'* (Inspection report 1996)

4.14   ChildLine said (submission) that from their experience of running the Boarding School Line between January and July 1991 (1,012 calls) and after analysing calls made to their general line during 1995/96 *'Many callers felt abandoned by their families – particularly the case when parents were overseas'.* More callers in boarding school were bothered about bullying compared to callers from other settings (16% of calls compared to 12%), but the proportion who were bothered about this was significantly higher at 20% in 1991 when the Boarding School Line was operating. ChildLine comment that *'bullying behaviour can be very hard to tackle. Anti-bullying work requires constant attention. There is excellent guidance available on how to prevent and minimise bullying... . Each school should appoint a senior teacher with responsibility to promote the school's anti-bullying programme. Young people themselves are the most underused resource.'* School Life [27] has a clear anti-bullying strategy at number four on the list for a pupils' 'best buy' school after (in this order) amount of personal space, privacy, support for homesick pupils. The ISJC told the Review that boarding schools are probably more conscious now about the harmful effects of bullying and make every effort to minimise the risk and deal quickly with incidents when they do occur.

4.15 It is important for children to have plenty of choice about who to go to about problems or complaints. The children the Review met said that they would talk to their parents, a friend, their tutor, or another teacher in that order. Inspection reports also indicated that children said they would go to parents, friends or houseparents. The ISJC (submission) said that *'schools like to think that there are few problems which cannot be handled [by teachers], they do accept that there will always be occasional situations in which children cannot bring themselves to unburden to a teacher and for whom some other avenue is needed. ...nowadays there is normally so much contact with the family that it is not necessary to look further than this obvious escape route... . ...for the small minority of children for whom this is not true or who find it difficult to confide in their parents it has been strongly recommended that other safety valves should be provided, whether by making private telephone calls possible and by displaying the ChildLine number or by arranging other means of access to a trusted adult...'.*

Foreign Children

4.16 The Review initially felt that foreign children were a vulnerable group. Theoretically they are: they are many miles from home in a different country and often living in a different culture. ISIS's Annual Census 1997 showed that nearly 8,000 foreign children started attending boarding school of whom some 1,500 came from Hong Kong and 1,700 from other parts of the Far East. ISIS estimate that at any one time there are between 15,000 to 20,000 foreign children attending schools in this country.

4.17 We received no information to confirm that this group was more vulnerable than other children living away from home. Discussions with ISIS and Gabbitas Educational Services – one of several agencies which recruit guardians[4] for foreign children – suggest that all agencies, especially the schools, are anxious to ensure that foreign children settle down here and benefit from a British education. Children nearly always go home for holidays and will have no hesitation in telephoning their parents if they are unhappy.

Guardians

4.18 Gabbitas Educational Services told the Review that their agency provides a helpline for children in addition to recruiting guardians. These people will typically accommodate children at half term and other weekends and attend school events. They fall outside the remit of the private fostering regulations unless the child stays with the guardian for more than 28 days and is aged under 16 – see paragraphs 3.68–3.81. It would appear that the legislation regulating these arrangements may not always be well understood. The Department of Health circular LAC (93)24 [28] says *'The use of "guardians" to look after, or have some responsibility for, children accommodated by independent schools whose parents live overseas... has no basis in the Children Act. It is important that*

---

[4] The term 'guardian' has no legal force. The boarding school sector uses it to describe people who act 'in loco parentis' for children whose parents live abroad.

schools should clarify with parents whether such accommodation [i.e with a guardian] is arranged by a parent or the school. The provisions of the Children Act governing independent schools (or private fostering) will apply, regardless of the existence of a "guardian".' One inspection report commented *'Although the school has modified its policy on guardians since the last Inspection, it is still felt that the school is placing itself and possibly the children at some risk. ...The school may wish to consider whether the responsibility for...children placed with guardians is ultimately theirs and, if so take more action to safeguard the welfare of children in their care'.*

4.19 An umbrella body for guardianship agencies (AEGIS – the Association of Educational Guardians for International Students), which will produce a Code of Practice and set up an accreditation system, is about to be launched. This is a welcome development which the Review commends. It would be desirable to ensure that parents always appoint a guardian from an agency accredited by AEGIS and conforming to a Code of Practice.

Associations of Schools

4.20 The ISJC is a federation of 10 different associations to which independent schools belong. It runs an accreditation system which includes regular inspection every 10 years, or every 7 years for schools which belong to the Headmasters' Conference which operates a separate system. Inspection reports are sent to the Registrar of Independent Schools and OFSTED. The Council represents the views of independent schools to Government and other organisations. Nearly 500 of the 730 or so independent boarding schools belong to one or other of the 10 associations and benefit from advice on particular issues such as recruitment and selection procedures, child protection and inspection. The Council's accreditation system is a worthwhile addition to the framework of statutory regulation as it provides another view on the schools. It cannot serve as a substitute for statutory inspections by OFSTED and local authorities, which have no direct involvement with independent schools.

4.21 Maintained boarding schools may belong to the Boarding Schools' Association whose subsidiary – the State Boarding Information Service (STABIS) – provides information about these schools and promotes their interests. This provides a mechanism for this smaller category of schools to share information and concerns.

4.22 The Review postulated that schools catering for specialist interest – sport, drama, dance, music – might be a category which placed children at more risk. Derek Turner wrote that *'These schools face unusual challenges in ensuring that their pupils receive both a rounded general education and the long hours of instruction and practice needed to produce a ballet dancer, pianist or swimmer. These dual pressures can have deleterious effects on the pupils' personal and social development. There are dangers of both passive failure to safeguard welfare and active abuse'.* We received no evidence to confirm our hypothesis. One inspection report said *'The children are expected to spend considerable amounts of time on dance tuition and practice, in addition to a normal academic programme, leading inevitably to a very full schedule. The children commented that although the timetable was disciplined and without much "leisure" their world was ballet and performing, making this regime totally acceptable.'*

Effect of Section 87

4.23 Section 87 of the Children Act, which requires schools to promote and safeguard the welfare of children and local authorities to inspect the welfare arrangements, has been taken up positively by the independent sector as a whole. The change has reinforced the increasing importance schools give to welfare issues. Many of the inspection reports read by the Review have been thorough and rightly have focused on issues such as personnel procedures as well as the more obvious child protection ones. Many have also shown considerable insight into the world of boarding schools. *'The College gives pastoral care a high priority, using a proactive approach and making eminently suitable arrangements for the pastoral care of all pupils.'* (Inspection report 1996) *'We acknowledge that the 3 Housemistresses have experience in their roles and all have received some training in this. We consider that further training in counselling and residential care is required to equip them to carry out their responsibilities in loco-parentis.'* (Inspection report 1993)

4.24   There are three issues about the operation and scope of Section 87: the status of the reports which appears to affect the exchange of information between OFSTED and local authorities, the arrangements for follow-up of any recommendations, and the fact that the provision does not apply to maintained boarding schools.

4.25   These reports are the property of the Registrar of Independent Schools and not publicly available, though the school receives a copy. There seems to be no good reason for treating these reports differently to other reports produced by local authority inspectors, though some would not be easy for the lay person to follow. It should become standard practice for parents to be told about these reports, which they can read, if they so wish. Local authority inspection units should give priority to ensuring that the format and language used is accessible to the lay reader.

4.26   One of the themes to emerge from this Review is the difficulty facing different agencies and individuals in sharing information. HMI reports on independent schools are not sent to the school; the Registrar writes with the main findings and recommendations and the inspectors give oral feedback. Local authority inspection units appear not to receive information about the content of these reports as a matter of routine. The Registrar usually sends copies of Inspection Unit reports to OFSTED, so that HMI can study these before their inspections. Ideally this should be a two way process and the Review hopes that arrangements can be made by OFSTED in discussion with the Local Government Association and the Welsh Local Government Association for this practice to be adopted.

4.27   Local authorities have no responsibility for following up any recommendations. This is a matter for the Registrar, which is not a good use of his expertise. These reports deal with welfare matters and should properly be pursued by local authorities.

4.28   The introduction of Section 87 has been good for children in independent boarding schools. There is no justifiable reason for excluding the much smaller maintained boarding school sector from its scope. Some of these schools in particular are used by armed forces' children, whose parents are likely to be abroad. One inspection report, when summarising the discussion with the children said *'The availability of the telephone in this House is very important as out of 18 boarders 14 have their parents overseas. A number of these boarders told us that they have difficulty receiving incoming calls from their parents as the only telephone is in constant use.'* The Review was told that some Independent Registration and Inspection Units and schools have agreed that 'informal inspections' will be carried out. It is encouraging that some schools already recognise the benefits of inspection. The Review recommends that it is introduced for all of them. (Extending the scope of Section 87 to special schools is dealt with in paragraphs 4.47–4.50.)

4.29   The Review has reservations about the registration system for independent schools. Designed in earlier days, its criteria and procedures are difficult to adapt to contemporary expectations about the welfare of children. We understand that the Department for Education and Employment is considering a review of the whole registration system, and welcome this.

4.30   Appendix D shows that registration has two stages – provisional and final. Provisional registration is granted on receipt of an application form containing basic information about the proposed school including details about members of staff as well as the names of the children. The Registrar checks the names against List 99 and will request a criminal record check. Final registration follows satisfactory HMI and welfare inspections, but this can take years. While there are sustainable arguments on educational grounds for allowing a school to open before it has been inspected, this does not apply to welfare. It is not acceptable to continue to allow schools proposing to offer boarding facilities to open without some preliminary examination of the welfare arrangements. Local authority inspection units have considerable experience of doing this when registering children's homes and find that it helps to identify weaknesses at an early stage when it is simpler for proprietors to put things right. The Review urges the Department for Education and Employment to adopt as a basic principle that such schools do not admit children to board without such a preliminary examination.

4.31   The process for dealing with a poorly performing school is protracted: the Registrar when he invokes the Notice of Complaint procedure has to give the school at least six months to put matters right, unless he decides that the matters complained about cannot be remedied. This sort of timescale is unacceptable when the safety and well-being of children is in question. This quotation from LAC (95)1 [29] illustrates why this procedure is unsuitable when the welfare of pupils in an entire school is threatened: *'A Notice of Complaint is normally served only in extreme cases where a school has consistently failed to act on the advice and recommendations contained in official letters from the Registrar over a period of time. If a school does not act to remedy complaints it can be removed from the Register.'* The Review recommends that the Secretary of State provide the Registrar with powers to cancel registration immediately when children's welfare is seriously endangered and to give shorter periods of notice to remedy deficiencies in policies or procedures for safeguarding children such as the lack of an effective child protection policy.

Special Residential Schools

4.32   There are three groups: maintained (226 (20 in Wales) with 13,300 places), independent (76 with 3,450 places) and non-maintained [5] (68 with 3,830 places). Appendix D sets out the regulatory system for each group. Maintained special schools are not covered by Section 87. The position for the non-maintained group is somewhat obscure, although it would appear that local authorities have power to inspect under Section 62 of the Children Act. The size of the maintained and non-maintained groups has remained fairly static in recent years and this is unlikely to change.

4.33   All special schools may apply for approval to take SEN children and in granting approval the number, age and gender of children and the type of disability are specified. The disability categories are: severe learning difficulties, severe learning difficulties associated with

---

[5] Schools run by a voluntary organisation.

autism, moderate learning difficulties, speech and language difficulties, hearing impairment, physically disabled, emotional and behavioural difficulties. Schools have to obtain fresh approval if they want to change the disability category they wish to cater for and/or the number, gender or age of children. There are also some 80 independent schools catering wholly or mainly for SEN children which have not been approved. These admit children on the basis of individual consent given by the Secretary of State.

4.34   Most schools have fewer than 100 residential places, take boarders and day pupils and take boys and girls. Some schools approved for EBD children take boys only and a few girls only.

Views of Children 4.35   How do SEN children view life in a residential school? The National Children's Bureau, commissioned by the Review, talked to disabled children in two residential schools. Those children mostly felt safe and had regular contact with at least one of their parents. They also said there were other adults they felt they could go to, though they seemed not to know about any formal complaints procedure. They did not feel they had been abandoned by their parents. One of the striking things to emerge from these discussions was the rich and varied friendships the children had with children of their own age. The Bureau concluded *'The general impression was that they saw living away from home as a positive option. Noticeably, we sensed that the majority of these children and young people had stable lives and a sense of permanency, with long-term primary carers and relatively few moves. This no doubt contributed to their sense of security and happiness.'* This contrasts with the 10 'life stories' in *Gone Missing?* [30] where adults with experience of living away from home as children speak of feelings of being abandoned, not being able to see their parents and being abused. Their experiences mainly predate the Children Act and it is to be hoped that SEN children now in residential schools will not recount such tales of neglect and unhappiness to a future researcher.

4.36   Children with communication difficulties need help to tell people they are being ill-treated. Parents will quickly identify abuse or neglect, but find it difficult to make regular visits. One parent wrote *'What I have observed both as parent and school governor has alarmed me a little. I now ask questions I suspect my daughter would raise if able to speak'*. These children have to rely on other adults or other children. The Bureau's report refers to one child aged 15 who *'explained that a child with no speech had said that a member of staff had hit him. The 15 year old felt he should support the other child because he was able to speak'*. Jenny Morris told the Review (personal communication) that more work was needed on how to communicate with this group of children about what makes them feel safe. The Council for Disabled Children listed as one of its particular concerns *'the importance of developing professional awareness of **how** to communicate with children with disabilities'*. (See also Chapter 8 on disabled children.)

4.37   Parents of SEN children who go away to school will not have made the decision on their own and they may be ambivalent about their child going away. The Council for Disabled Children in its submission described one mother who *'recognised that a child who cannot write; who has limited telephone skills and who was placed 330 miles from home will have a poor chance of complaint'*. It is noticeable that, whereas children in boarding school are more likely to be about 50 miles away from home, children in special schools can easily find themselves at the other side of the country, often for longer than the usual school term. The distance alone makes it difficult for parents to maintain regular contact. Disabled children and children with emotional and behavioural difficulties may be more vulnerable than other SEN children. Their parents may be the children's best safeguard, but may find it difficult to discharge this role to their satisfaction without some support.

Governing Bodies 4.38 Under the Education (Special Schools) Regulations 1994 governing the approval process – see Appendix D – maintained and non-maintained schools must have a governing body, whose composition is specified. One of the conditions for obtaining approval from the Secretary of State requires the governing body to *'make such arrangements for safeguarding and promoting the welfare of pupils at the school as have been approved... .'* The primary responsibility for safeguarding children in the school rests with the governing body, whose membership has to include a parent representative. Those responsible for inspecting and monitoring all these schools must also look at their governance and be prepared to pursue weaknesses.

4.39 The Regulations governing the approval of independent schools to take SEN children make no provisions about governing bodies. Instead they place a duty on the proprietor to take steps to safeguard and promote the children's welfare and require the school prospectus to give *'particulars of the arrangements for pastoral care'.* Circular 3/94[31] advises: *'It may not be appropriate for all independent schools to have governing bodies on the lines of those required in the maintained sector, with LEA and parent representatives. But where responsibility for the school rests should always be clear, and proprietors may find it valuable to have access to a formally constituted advisory body comprising persons who are expert or suitably qualified in the areas in which the school operates.'*

4.40 It is welcome that the Regulations governing maintained and non-maintained special schools are specific about the welfare responsibility vested in the governing body. While the requirements about the proprietor's welfare duty and the content of the prospectus in independent schools are implicit acknowledgments of the importance of care, there should be more oversight. The Review recommends that the Secretary of State for Education and Employment amend the Regulations governing the approval of independent schools that take SEN children to have governing bodies with a similar composition to that specified for maintained and non-maintained special schools.

4.41 All these schools can become isolated. The Boarding Schools' Association is currently considering the possibility of opening its membership to special schools. Reading inquiry reports and other documents about maintained special residential schools suggest that these are not seen as integral parts of the educational provision within a local authority, so that they can all too easily become isolated, closed and remote. The Review hopes that the Boarding School Association will open its membership to independent special schools, as this would provide support and advice to this group. Major voluntary organisations and Local Education Authorities should make sure that they have structures to provide these residential schools with effective external management. Governing bodies can become too isolated and it is inappropriate to expect them to provide such external management support.

Children with Emotional and Behavioural Difficulties 4.42 These children are a particular cause for concern. They are more vulnerable because dealing with them is often challenging and stressful and they are less likely to be believed when they complain about abuse or neglect. They need additional safeguards. The Review considers that the statementing process and the provisions for assessing children in need should be used to provide these.

The Statementing Process

4.43   The legislation and guidance on the statementing process are rightly based on the principle of close co-operation between education, social services and health interests to ensure a seamless operation. The Education Act 1996 (Section 322) gives social services a duty to provide help whenever requested to do so by the Local Education Authority and Section 27 of the Children Act places a comparable requirement on the education authority should social services ask for help. *The Code of Practice on the Identification and Assessment of Special Educational Needs* [32] makes several references to this – '*[The Children] Act allows an integrated approach to the educational, health and welfare needs of children with special educational needs... . It also requires schools to co-operate with social services departments if a child is "in need". The advice appended to the statement must (emphasis added) include social services advice.*' Circular 9/94/ LAC (94) 9 [33] – issued jointly by the Department for Education and Employment and the Department of Health – gives clear advice on joint working particularly between education and social services: '*Residential education may be needed for reasons directly related to the child's learning difficulties. In other cases, a child's learning may be hampered by family circumstances.*' ; and later on '*The LEA and SSD need a clear working agreement to consider cases where there are shared interests. Joint standing panel arrangements generally work well. ... If a joint standing panel is set up... , those attending meetings should be authorised to discharge functions and so have delegated power as individuals to make decisions about placements and funding.*'

4.44   The Review finds little evidence that this is working as consistently or universally as might be expected from reading the clear messages in the legislation and guidance. There are still anecdotes about social services and education arguing about which budget should be used to pay for a child whose statement of special educational needs says this is needed for social rather than educational reasons. This leads to delays and the uncertainty makes children more vulnerable. It is all too easy for institutions to use structures to delay action. This must be addressed so that these children when placed in a residential school are properly safeguarded.

4.45   The Review recommends that local authorities unify the statementing process as far as possible so that education and social services can fulfil the aim of the legislation and guidance by each making the necessary contribution. These arrangements should be supported with a single budget.

Children in Need [8]

4.46   The Children Act (paragraph 3 of Schedule 2) gives social services power to assess a child in need at the same time as any assessment is made under the Education Act 1996. Disabled children are defined as children in need in the Children Act, which ensures that their needs and those of their parents for services are assessed. But so far as the Review could establish, EBD children may not be classified as children in need, and may therefore remain unknown to social services. Research carried out by Grimshaw and Berridge [34] in 4 residential schools found that of the 67 children in the study 61% had never been

---

[8]   The Children Act defines a 'child in need' in Section 17 as one who 'is unlikely to achieve or maintain, or to have the opportunity of achieving or maintaining, a reasonable standard of health or development without the provision for him of services by a local authority...; his health or development is likely to be significantly impaired or further impaired...; he is disabled.' The Act defines development as 'physical, intellectual, emotional, social or behavioural development and "health" means physical or mental health.'

in care, 32% were in care and 9% were on the child protection register. The factors affecting placement of these children in a residential school are as likely to be social as educational. The statementing process addresses assessment of their educational needs. Agencies involved need to ensure that the social needs of this group of children are also properly assessed. The Review considers that the best way to do this is for them and their parents to be assessed as potential children in need, as provided for in the Children Act.

Inspection   4.47   Appendix D shows that maintained and non-maintained special schools approved to take SEN children are outside the scope of the Section 87 provisions and not subject to inspection of their welfare arrangements. From its study of inquiry reports and reviews produced in accordance with guidance in Part 8 of *Working Together*[3] the Review concludes that maintained schools in particular can also allow an abusive regime or abusing member of staff to flourish. A report of an independent inquiry into one such school for children with emotional and behavioural difficulties, where the head expected staff to abide by his rules and systems, found that there was a culture of institutionalised abuse. The head told the inquiry that there had been 3 education inspections in 17 years, only one of which was a formal one. In another school a care worker was able to abuse boys over 9 years before being convicted and receiving a 6 year sentence.

4.48   The position for inspection of non-maintained special schools by local authority inspection units is more confusing. Section 62 gives local authorities a duty to satisfy themselves about the arrangements to safeguard and promote the welfare of children in these schools, but it says nothing about frequency or to which agency any report might be made. Guidance in Volume 4 advises local authorities to follow the general guidance on welfare in independent schools in Volume 5. The Review did not establish how well local authorities understood the inspection requirements for these schools. Some treat them like independent schools and, as this extract from an inspection report shows, this can be encouraging: *'the standard of care provided to pupils, the quality of the accommodation and the range of facilities…*[are] *of a very high standard. Inspectors especially commend the school on the work done by staff to ensure and maintain appropriate levels of independence, security and dignity to very vulnerable children.'* (Inspection report 1996). It would be sensible to make this category of school subject to the Section 87 provisions.

4.49   Independent schools approved to take SEN children are inspected under Section 87, which has helped to draw attention to poor standards – *'High turnover of both pupils and staff. Food, clothing and health care poor. Appointment system totally inadequate: several members of staff have had previous convictions (including two who had served periods of imprisonment)'.* (Inspection report 1996). The Review has already said (paragraph 4.28) that children in independent boarding schools have benefited from Section 87.

4.50   The Review recommends that Section 87 of the Children Act is extended to apply to maintained and non-maintained special schools, thereby placing a duty on the proprietors and managers to promote and safeguard the welfare of pupils and on local authorities to inspect their arrangements.

Health Care in Schools   4.51   The Review received very few observations on the adequacy of health care in schools or whether there were particular health problems for children living away from home in schools. The Royal College of Nursing, however, referring to *The Health Needs of School Aged Children* [35] wrote 'At present independent and boarding schools do not provide the same health care programmes that state schools provide. All children and young people need access to...services provided by the school health service... . This service is vital...to provide confidential advice about sexual health, drugs, alcohol, smoking and other issues relevant to young people. ...In some schools that standard of medical and health cover is excellent in others it is non existent. Children and young people in boarding schools should have access to the same community paediatricians and nurses as their contemporaries. This is particularly important as boarding schools take increasing numbers of children with special needs...'. Inspection reports on independent boarding schools read by the Review show that these usually cover the arrangements for pupils' access to a GP, storage of medicines and related matters and some refer to discussions between the doctor and school staff about general health issues. One report mentioned weekly meetings between the GP and the head and that school was also reported as having recently set up a psychiatric counselling department. In the case of special schools OFSTED's teams of registered inspectors will also examine the school's policy on providing sex education. The Review offers no view on the need for further action.

Independent Schools also Registered as Children's Homes

4.52   The Education Act 1993 amended the Children Act definition of this type of school to make dual registration as a children's home a requirement when the school was open to accommodate more than 3 children for 295 days or more in a year. While it was sensible to define these institutions according to the number of days children live in the school rather than the number of boarding places, the information collected by the Review suggests that it is difficult to apply the current definition. The statistics collected by the Department for Education and Employment show 41 such institutions, whereas the Department of Health statistical returns show a mere 14. It is thus impossible to answer precisely a question about the number of schools registered as children's homes. The Review's examination of reports supplied by local authority inspection units confirmed that several authorities identified from official sources as having this type of institution said that they did not.

4.53   These schools are likely to cater for children with disabilities or children with parents overseas or foreign children. It is essential that they are properly regulated, but it would appear that the current regulatory provisions make this difficult to achieve. The Review suggests that the Department for Education and Employment and the Department of Health re-examine the current definition in the Children Act and take the necessary steps to make it simpler and effective.

Section 85   4.54   This section of the Children Act requires educational establishments accommodating or intending to accommodate children for 3 months or more to notify local authority social services departments. The local authority has then a duty to satisfy itself about the welfare of the child. The Review was unable to obtain any information about the operation of this provision. It therefore recommends that the Social Services Inspectorate carries out an inspection to find out about its effectiveness.

Chapter 5: OTHER SETTINGS

SYNOPSIS

This chapter discusses the position of children in the penal system and children who spend weeks or months in hospital.

The Penal Setting

It concludes that prison is no place for children, particularly unconvicted children, and that it is impossible to meet the ordinary needs of children there. It makes a number of important recommendations.

Prison Service policy to keep children in discrete accommodation is not being achieved. The incidence of sexual assaults on children in the penal setting is unclear and research is recommended (paragraph 5.5).

Nor is the anti-bullying policy consistently implemented. The problems of bullying, suicide and self-harm are considerable. Prison Service strategy on self-harm and suicide is impressive but requires unremitting concentration to maintain effectiveness. Improvement in the environment, more educational and leisure provision and a reduction in bullying would help.

Children, particularly those who are disturbed, have special health needs. The Review believes the National Health Service should be responsible for the health care of children in penal settings (paragraph 5.8).

The fact that boys aged 15 and 16 are still being remanded to prison is a serious failure of public policy which should be put right as quickly as possible. The secure accommodation intended to end such remands has not been provided, indeed between 1990 and 1995 there was a slight contraction in the number of places, though the number has increased since then (paragraph 5.9). Implementing Section 60 of the Criminal Justice Act poses practical difficulties. These must be addressed especially the question of any need for more public expenditure to pay for any additional secure accommodation. The Review recommends that action is taken to bring this section into effect to end the remand of boys to prison establishments (paragraph 5.11).

It is recommended that the Department of Health/ Welsh Office consult the Local Government Association and the Prison Service about the support social services authorities provide to children in penal settings and their families (paragraph 5.12).

A major recommendation is that the principles of the Children Act in promoting and safeguarding children should be incorporated in penal system regulations. Allegations of abuse or other harm should be investigated by the criminal and civil arms as in other settings (paragraph 5.13). A major commitment to welfare as well as containment is needed (paragraph 5.14).

The Review supports the recommendation of HM Inspector of Prisons that a National Director be appointed for the young offender estate (paragraph 5.15).

A number of babies live in prison. Child protection procedures are needed in the two prisons that lack them (paragraph 5.19).

Health Settings

In 1994/95 12,500 children spent between 30 and 90 days in hospital and 2,000 were there for over 90 days. Most younger children were in paediatric units with adolescents being psychiatric units.

The main recommendation is that the Social Services Inspectorate should carry out an inspection to obtain information about the operation of Section

85 of the Children Act, which requires health authorities to notify local authorities about a child who has been or is intended to be in hospital for more than 3 months (paragraph 5.30).

The Review makes two other suggestions: psychiatric units should ensure that they have robust systems to prevent visits by undesirable people (paragraph 5.27); the Department of Health/Welsh Office should explore with health authorities ways in which recruitment and selection procedures should be monitored (paragraph 5.32).

The Penal Setting

5.1   This Review coincided with a thematic inspection by HM Chief Inspector of Prisons of provision for young offenders and juveniles. His report may appear before this, and will comment with all the authority of his office on the material produced by careful empirical work. The Review's concern is to examine the arrangements for safeguarding children under the age of 18 in penal settings against abuse and other harm, in the context of all children living away from home. It applies to them too the principles of the Children Act and the UN Convention on the Rights of the Child.

5.2   At 30 June 1995 there were 1,680 prisoners aged 17 and under in Prison Service establishments. 200 of these were detained under Section 53 of the Children and Young Persons Act 1933 for very serious offences. 790 were serving periods of detention in Young Offender Institutions. 280 awaited sentencing. 410 were on remand. The Review has unconfirmed information that the current total exceeds 2,600 – twice the figure recorded at 30 June 1993.

5.3   Prison Service policy is for children and young people to be kept in discrete accommodation such as Juvenile Units in Young Offender Institutions. This is plainly not being achieved in the prison population. The Review received anecdotal information of children on remand being allocated to wherever a vacancy could be found, in overcrowded conditions, in local prisons, sharing accommodation (even cells) with adults, leading nomadic lives without access to educational or leisure facilities. There must be considerable doubt about whether the UN Convention on the Rights of the Child is complied with.

5.4   The condition of young people in the penal system was graphically described by the Howard League for Penal Reform[14]. The commissioners visited 16 prisons. They found poor physical conditions and remand prisoners spending too much of the day in their cells. *'There is no proper protection from abuse and manipulation for younger teenage prisoners.' 'Despite recent improvements at Cardiff Prison, the general standards of care in Welsh prisons remain a matter of great concern.' 'All of the 86 young prisoners interviewed by commissioners gave detailed and consistent accounts of bullying whether or not they had been the victims.' 'The Prison Service anti-bullying strategy is not widely implemented.' 'Physical control and restraint is used routinely .... Restraint measures are potentially dangerous.' 'There were record levels of suicide and self-harm in 1994.'*

5.5   The problem of violence against young offenders is discussed in the section on bullying (paragraphs 9.41–49). The Review's limited reading left it uninformed (other than anecdotally) about the incidence of sexual assaults on children in the penal setting. It recommends research on this subject to complement the considerable research on bullying.

5.6   Suicide and Self-Harm[36] was the report of a review by HM Chief Inspector of Prisons, which stimulated development of the current Prison Service strategy. Self harm arises from the effect of an impoverished and violent environment upon existing personal problems. *'Self-injuries and attempted suicides in young offender institutions are not just a problem of individual pathology, but are also a problem of coping behaviour'* – particularly with bullying, boredom and isolation (Liebling and Krarup[37]. Young offenders made up 1 in 5 of the prison population but 1 in 2 of those involved in self harm – the majority of the incidents occurring in local and remand centres. Imitative self-harming behaviour was a problem among young men and young women. The Review was told, however, that the suicide rate for young offenders was only marginally higher than the rate for older prisoners, although both were rising.

5.7   The Prison Service strategy (revised in 1994) adopts a whole prison approach to preventing suicide and self harm. All staff are encouraged to share responsibilities in the programme. In addition, every institution has a multi-disciplinary team focusing on suicide awareness. The Samaritans contribute to the strategy and its implementation. Selected prisoners are trained to act as Listeners to vulnerable prisoners, and the support of the prisoner peer group is mobilised. Both the strategy and the commitment to it are impressive, but unremitting concentration is needed to maintain its effectiveness in the face of the stresses and strains on the Prison Service. Improvement in the environment in which children are confined, more educational and leisure provision, and a reduction in the menace of bullying would undoubtedly help.

5.8   Children – particularly the disturbed group of children who end up in custody – have special health needs. Young offenders appear to the Review to need a package of services which is more concentrated than, and perhaps different in some other respects from, the medical and nursing services available to all prisoners. *'A psychiatric disorder is recognised in a third of all young offenders between the ages of 16 and 18 years'*[13]. 49 of 65 young offenders in the establishment researched by Skett, Braham and Samuel[38] were using drugs; one third were using cannabis daily. The Review believes that the National Health Service should be responsible for the health care of children in penal settings.

5.9   Boys aged 15 and 16 should no longer be remanded to prison. HM Chief Inspector declared (1990) *'We firmly believe that generally no male aged 17 or under should be remanded in prison. When this is the case there must be clear guidelines on location, support, counselling and treatment.'* Section 60 of the Criminal Justice Act 1991 ended such remands, but its implementation was deferred until sufficient secure accommodation could be made available to absorb the numbers previously remanded to prison service establishments. As plans for more secure accommodation matured, the numbers of children remanded to prison grew to keep the gap between aspiration and fulfilment obstinately open. Indeed, there was a slight contraction in the number of places actually available in secure accommodation between 1990 and 1995. Since then, a Department of Health/ Home Office funded programme has produced a considerable increase in the number of places, but there still remains a gap between aspiration and fulfilment.

5.10   This represents a serious failure in public policy which should be put right as quickly as possible. Prison is no place for children, especially for unconvicted children. It is almost impossible to meet the continuing ordinary needs of children there. Their special circumstances seriously distract from its main task a Prison Service coping with almost unmanageable problems.

5.11   Implementing Section 60 poses a number of practical difficulties, not least of which is the large increase in the number of 15 and 16 year old boys remanded to prison over the last 3 years. More secure accommodation, which is more expensive than prison, may be needed. Paying for any increase would require more than a simple transfer of money from one place to another. This would have serious implications for public expenditure but additional funds must be found. Other ways of dealing with this group of 15 and 16 year olds might also be considered. Nevertheless, the Review must recommend that Section 60 of the Criminal Justice Act be brought into effect in order to end the remand of boys to prison service establishments.

5.12   The Review recommends that the Department of Health/Welsh Office consults the Local Government Association and the Prison Service about the support social services authorities provide to children in penal settings and their families. Links with the community are arbitrarily severed for people in prison, and young offenders suffer particularly from the loss of immediate support from family and friends.

5.13   The Review understands that the Children Act does not apply to children convicted or remanded in prison service establishments because the regulations governing penal institutions supervene in that as in other respects. The Rules governing Young Offender Institutions incorporate a number of provisions for the safety and security of inmates: limiting, for example, the use of force by prison officers, excluding the use of restraints for children under 17, and making disciplinary offences of fighting, stealing and threatening or abusive behaviour. These fall short in total of what the Children Act seeks to ensure for children under the age of 18. Indeed, the term 'welfare' is likely to receive a much narrower interpretation in a penal setting than the comprehensive meaning derived from the effect of the Children Act. The Review recommends that the regulations governing provision in the penal system for children under the age of 18 should incorporate and give effect to the principles of the Children Act in promoting and safeguarding the welfare of children. Allegations of abuse or other harm should be investigated by the police and social services as they would be in other institutions.

5.14   Indeed, it seems important to the Review – as a matter of public policy – that the Prison Service adopts the explicit aim of safeguarding and promoting the welfare of children as the basis for its approach to rehabilitating young offenders. These young people represent varying degrees of danger to the rest of us, and their arrival in the penal system provides one of the last chances of turning their lives round before they become a permanent and threatening deadweight on the community. The investment needed in education, health care, social skills and employment training is likely to be justified only by a comprehensive commitment to welfare as well as to containment. This should also weigh with the Department of Health/Welsh Office/Local Government Association in the consultation recommended above. Implementing the overall aim would require a renewed approach to staff training; we were encouraged that the Prison Service had developed a programme with the Trust for the Study of Adolescence for training staff working with juveniles.

5.15   The Review supports the recommendation of HM Chief Inspector of Prisons, in his report on Onley Young Offender Institution, that a National Director be appointed for the Young Offender Estate. The case for a senior manager to focus organisational activity in social services departments on the needs of children was argued by Levy and Kahan[6], which recommended *'a named person at senior management level with responsibility (a) for ensuring that care and attention is given to the education, career development and working life of children in care, and (b) for the consideration of any policy or practice issues'*. Similar considerations apply to the Prison Service, especially in relation to achieving consistent implementation of all its policies for young offenders.

5.16   Prison is not the first place one expects to find babies, but a number of small babies live there. Four prisons have a total of 68 places in Mother and Baby Units. In two the babies may remain until they are 9 months old, and in the others until they are 18 months. Both policy and practical difficulties cluster about them. A multi-disciplinary inspection team from the Department of Health in 1990 summarised the problem: *'The place of babies within the institutional setting of a prison creates an immediate tension between their complex and individual needs and the institutional requirements of an adult prison.'*

5.17   *'Members of the first inspection team (1990) recalled that they were dismayed by the conditions prevailing in the Mother and Baby Units at the time'* (SSI Inspection report[39]). The Prison Service promulgated new aims and objectives for the Units after that first inspection. Links were established with health and social services authorities, multi-disciplinary working established, training instituted for prison staff, and a professional approach to child care adopted.

5.18   The second in a programme of 3 inspections occurred in 1992. Two of the 3 prisons which then had units had worked through the recommendations of the earlier report. There was now a need for Area Child Protection Committees to address child protection procedures in prison. Overall, progress was sufficient to enable the inspectors to draw out standards of quality for Mother and Baby Units.

5.19   The last inspection in 1995 confirmed both the effort invested in reaching satisfactory standards and the problems inherent in caring for small children in prisons. It is difficult to sustain progress in a milieu with such different, over-riding priorities. The Prison Service was invited to review its programme for the Units and the further action needed. This Review's concern with safeguards leads it to reinforce the inspection team's view that written child protection procedures were needed in the 2 prisons which lacked them.

Health Settings

'If by excluding people with certain clearly definable characteristics we could be sure of excluding those who might harm vulnerable patients, then it would be worth taking the risk which such a policy would entail of incidentally excluding some people who would have made good nurses. The problem lies in determining which, if any, of Allitt's characteristics are clear indicators of possible danger.'

(The Allitt Inquiry)

5.20 Nowadays few children spend long periods in hospital. When children are admitted as in-patients, parents or other family members are encouraged to stay with their child throughout their stay in hospital. This provides the best safeguard. Nevertheless there have been cases where children have been abused in hospital. *The Allitt Inquiry*[40] on one of the most recent and most notorious cases showed how easy it was to appoint a nurse without adequate checks who then went on to abuse and kill children. There have also been incidents where strangers have snatched babies from maternity wards. Health authorities and trusts have to make sure that there are robust systems, rigorously enforced and monitored, to keep children and young people safe while in hospital.

Numbers 5.21 In 1994/95 there were about 1.3 million completed hospital in-patient episodes involving children aged 18 and under in England and Wales. About 41,100 of those episodes lasted more than 15 days (see Appendix C). The majority of episodes (26,500) lasted for less than 30 days, 12,500 for between 30 and 90 days and some 2,100 for over 90 days. Most of these episodes involved children aged under 5 – 27,200. Only 7,700 related to children aged between 5 and 14 and 6,200 to children aged between 15 and 18. These older children, while less likely than the younger ones to have in-patient treatment, were more likely to be in hospital for longer. Nearly all under 5s' episodes were in paediatrics and that was also the case for the 5 to 14 year olds. For the 15 to 18 year old group the episodes were more likely to be in the psychiatry or learning disability specialties.

5.22 The pattern for England and Wales was similar except that there were significantly more over 90 day episodes in Wales compared to England – 9% of the total compared to 5%.

5.23 The Department of Health has issued general guidance for NHS employers on criminal record checks[41] and on the role of the occupational health service[42]. NHS managers are responsible for ensuring that it is properly observed. The Department of Health does not monitor this. Most human resources departments in health authorities and trusts would be familiar with this body of guidance, except possibly in the case of smaller NHS Community Trusts, which might manage respite care hospices. Their personnel departments tend to be smaller and might therefore have less specialised knowledge about this. Some trusts had recruited personnel staff from outside the NHS and these people might also be less aware of this guidance. A nurse responsible for managing a children's hospice in Wales told the Review that parents always asked about procedures to protect children from abuse.

Paediatric Units 5.24 These are where most children are treated. Some are admitted for respite care where the child needs to be looked after by a nurse rather than a care assistant. Some may be in the unit for a matter of months.

5.25 Guidance in *The Welfare of Children and Young People in Hospital*[43] says that managers should ensure that, in allowing parents and other visitors unrestricted access to the ward, they do not jeopardise children's safety. Staff are expected to know the legitimate visitors and, therefore, be alert to the presence of strangers. A consultant paediatrician told the Review that all paediatric units now have systems including electronic devices to prevent access by intruders. It would be impossible for a stranger just to walk into a unit.

Other Units

5.26   A few children may be accommodated in specialist units – eg those recovering from severe burns or spinal injury – and there may be no paediatric advice available within the same hospital. Staff responsible for managing such units, especially if there is no paediatric unit in the hospital, may be less aware of the need to take steps to safeguard these children.

Child and Adolescent Mental Health Services

5.27   This may be an area of concern. Looked after children especially those in residential care are identified as a group whose mental health needs are known to be greater than those of the general population of the same age. This also applies to other groups already identified by the Review as being more vulnerable when living away from home: namely children with learning difficulties and children with emotional and behavioural difficulties. Although the NHS Executive has embarked on a programme of work to improve these services, the literature read by the Review suggests that they are patchy and not always well co-ordinated. Therefore it is reasonable to assume that children being treated as in-patients may be placed a long way from their families and, if they are looked after children, away from the responsible local authority. Some units may be managed by mental health trusts, which may be less aware of the importance of ensuring that the children are safe, though they will be familiar with the general guidance on criminal record checks and the occupational health service. It is as important for these units as for paediatric units that there are robust systems to prevent undesirable people gaining access to the children.

5.28   The Children Act and the Mental Health Act both apply in certain circumstances to children in hospital.

5.29   Section 85 of the Children Act gives health authorities and trusts a duty to notify the relevant local authority when a child has been or is likely to be in hospital for 3 months or more. Once notified, the local authority has a duty to take reasonable steps to satisfy itself that the child's welfare is being properly safeguarded and promoted and consider whether any further action is needed. Volume 4 in the Children Act series contains general guidance on this section, but the Review has been unable to find out how well it is being observed by NHS Trusts or local authorities. We were told that the number of social workers based in hospitals has gone down, so that NHS personnel could find it more difficult to establish close working relationships with social services colleagues. Under child protection procedures each hospital will have a clinical nurse with a child protection responsibility, which could be extended to take on this duty. Local authorities said that they rarely received notifications.

5.30   While it is likely that in many cases the children spending more than 3 months in hospital and their families are known to social services, the Review considers it essential to find out more about the operation of this section of the Act. As a first step the Social Services Inspectorate should carry out an inspection.

5.31   The Mental Health Act in many ways provides children who are admitted compulsorily to hospital with better protection than the Children Act provisions which apply to children taken into care. The guiding principles underlying such compulsory admissions are that the child is to be kept fully informed, and his views and wishes *must* be taken into account at all stages. Anyone detained under the Mental Health Act has the detention reviewed by managers and has access to Mental Health Act Review Tribunals with the whole being subject to general oversight by the Mental Health Commission. Exercise of powers in the Mental Health Act involves professional judgment rather than application to the courts.

5.32　The Review has concentrated on children spending 3 months or more in hospital where there is legislation designed to ensure that their welfare is being properly safeguarded and promoted. That is not to deny that children spending less time in hospital may also be at risk of abuse and other harm. *The Allitt Inquiry*[40] observes *'We have been advised that people who are determined to harm children can do so even on wards where the highest standards of care are maintained and where levels of staffing and provision of equipment are fully adequate. It takes only two minutes alone with an infant to cause death or serious injury'*. It is important that there is some external scrutiny of hospitals' recruitment and selection procedures. The Review was told that there were existing mechanisms in place which could be improved to ensure the checks recommended in guidance are being done. It is clear to the Review that potential sex offenders, especially persistent abusers, will always be able to find a loophole in a system and exploit it to gain access to children. We recommend that the Department of Health/Welsh Office pursues this with the NHS.

PART III – COMMON THEMES I:PARENT, CHILD AND ABUSER

Chapter 6: PARENTS

SYNOPSIS

This chapter discusses parental rights and responsibilities. It suggests that the Government enshrines these in primary legislation or issues a statement of its understanding of them (paragraph 6.2). It recommends ways in which parents can help to keep their children safe when they are living away from home.

It notes that the majority of placements used by children living away from home are now subject to some form of regulation and inspection. There is also a greater willingness in public policy to intervene in support of families or to protect children, without departing from the integrity and autonomy of the family.

Children living away from home lose the day to day protection exercised by a parent. It is the responsibility of parents to satisfy themselves that arrangements for keeping children safe exist and are effective. In order to do this they need to possess the necessary information. A list of pointers they should look for is given (paragraph 6.5). Organisations, including local authorities, which accommodate children should provide parents with the information they need (paragraph 6.6).

Knowledge of the risks children may face has developed quickly and parents lack the understanding to ask the right questions. So too may staff. The Review believes it important that both should be as accurately informed as possible. It recommends that the Government sponsor a programme along public health lines to increase their knowledge of the risks of living away from home and how to reduce them (paragraph 6.7).

6.1   Public policy is founded on the conviction that family relationships and family values are essentially private. So private, indeed, that public policy hesitated to pronounce upon what they are or should be. Parental responsibility was eventually described in statute as *'all the rights, duties, powers, responsibilities and authority which by law a parent of a child has in relation to the child and his property'* (Children Act 1989, Section 3(1)). The Introduction to the Children Act (HMSO 1989) said *that this concept of parental responsibility 'emphasises that the duty to care for the child and to raise him to moral, physical and emotional health is the fundamental task of parenthood and the only justification for the authority that it confers'.*

6.2   The Children (Scotland) Act 1995, the private law aspects of which came into force on 1 November 1996, makes brief but helpful statements of parental responsibilities and parental rights in its first two sections. Interestingly, for the purposes of this Review, they contain both a responsibility and a right, *'if the child is not living with the parent, to maintain personal relations and direct contact with the child on a regular basis'*. These provisions do not apply, of course, in England and Wales. Perhaps they should. The Government should follow the example of the Scottish Act and enshrine a statement of parental rights and responsibilities in primary legislation. As an alternative, it could issue a statement of its understanding of the responsibilities and rights of parents when next it legislates on matters that affect them. Such a statement should not be prescriptive. It should indicate the assumptions the state makes about the role of parents when it formulates policies which affect them and their children.

6.3   The exercise of parental rights and responsibilities is, as the Children (Scotland) Act makes plain, of particular importance to children living away from home. Most children are away from home by a decision or with the consent of their parents – a decision usually made in the overall interests of the child or of the family as a whole. Such children lose, for long or short periods, major features of their particular relationship with a parent: in particular, the reinforcement of emotional and physical security through the continuous attention and sustained oversight that a parent on the spot typically exercises. The rights and responsibilities of a distant parent remain unimpaired, however, unless a court has intervened.

6.4   Parents deciding to place a child away from home are therefore responsible for satisfying themselves that arrangements for keeping their children safe exist and are likely to prove effective. They have moral and in some cases legal rights to expect that the people and agencies to whom care of their children is transferred will prove trustworthy and competent. Parents are able under the Children Act (Section 2(9)) to arrange for another person to act on their behalf in discharging part or all of their parental responsibility. And anyone who has care of a child *'may ... do what is reasonable in all the circumstances of the case for the purpose of safeguarding or promoting the child's welfare'* (Section 3(5)). Parents should also be able to rely on the support of statutory systems of registration and inspection. Nevertheless, the decision about placement is ultimately their responsibility. In making it parents should possess all the information they need about the arrangements for keeping their children safe.

6.5   **Pointers for Parents to the Safety of Children living away from Home**

Recruitment procedures for staff with substantial and unsupervised access to children (eg, do they conform to Warner [4] principles; are recommended checks made?)

Codes of conduct for staff

Equal opportunities policies

Effective anti-bullying policy

Child protection procedures conforming to expectations of the Area Child Protection Committee (with, eg, senior designated teacher)

Policy for child discipline, including measures of control

Complaints procedures

Access to telephone

Registering authority (name, address, telephone number)

Inspecting authority (last report available from ...)

Arrangements for health care

Arrangements for pastoral care

Other issues specific to setting (prison, foster care, psychiatric unit, etc)

6.6   Many institutions and agencies which provide care and residential education offer such information as a matter of course. Organisations which accommodate children should provide parents with information on such matters – adapted to the particular setting – before placement is made. This includes local authorities in all the usual circumstances in which they accommodate children. The concept of partnership with parents seems to require that local authorities provide parents with sufficient information to assure them that their children will be kept safe in local authority care.

6.7   One of the problems parents face in formulating questions about keeping children safe away from home is that they lack authoritative understanding of what the risks are. Knowledge of these has developed so quickly that many staff are similarly disadvantaged. It seems important to the Review that both parents and staff should be as accurately informed as possible, so that their appreciation of the risks is realistic and avoids the twin pitfalls of denial and over-reaction. The Government should sponsor a programme along public health lines to increase the knowledge of parents and relevant staff of the risks to the welfare of children living away from home, and ways of reducing them.

6.8   The Children Act sets out and puts into practice the principles to be followed in England and Wales for promoting the welfare of children in partnership with their parents. These extend well beyond the narrow but fundamental area of protecting vulnerable children. *Working Together* [3] describes in detail the recommended approach to the complex processes of child protection. Other issues about safeguarding children are covered in regulations, circulars and other guidance which are examined in more detail elsewhere in this report.

6.9   The position has now been reached in which the majority of the placements used by children living away from home are subject to some form of regulation or inspection. The Children Act itself, for example, extended the duty of the state towards children living in health and educational establishments. There is now a greater willingness in public policy to intervene in support of families or to protect children, without departing from the principle of the integrity and autonomy of the family.

Chapter 7:   WHAT YOUNG PEOPLE TOLD US

SYNOPSIS

The Review was greatly helped by young people. The voice of authentic experience spoke more clearly than any other. This chapter records what they had to say. Their comments about being looked after were not as negative overall as their suggestions for improvement may suggest.

'There is a lack of faith in the effectiveness of current safeguards for children and young people. They are seen as not being impartial, confidential or independent of the systems, creating the feelings of vulnerability.'
FirstKey – Report to the Review

'A child is a child, not just a case.'
Carer, in conversation with the Review

What Young People Told Us

7.1   The Review was greatly helped by young people. First*Key* set up structured meetings for us with young people from 20 local authorities who had current and recent experience of being looked after. Children in Wales, through Voices From Care and the Children's Society Advocacy Unit, arranged for us to meet young people in Wales. The National Children's Bureau enabled the views of groups of disabled children to be communicated to the Review. We met children being looked after by the former County Council of Leicestershire, children at a preparatory school, children being looked after by the London Borough of Camden with their carers, and children in a special school. Others wrote to and telephoned us following an article in Who Cares? and advertisements in magazines and on local radio. The information we received from all those young people is of great significance to the Review. The voice of their authentic experience spoke more clearly to us than any other.

7.2   The views of the disabled children are incorporated in a later section. What is set down here is selected, on the basis of its relevance to the terms of reference of the Review, from what was said by young people with recent experience of being looked after by local authorities. Quotations are from the First*Key* report to the Review.

7.3   Entering the care system causes bewilderment, displacement and loss. The new entrant is peculiarly vulnerable at that point to bad influence by predatory adults or delinquent peers. What is needed then and thereafter is a trusted adult who knows the system, answers questions, listens to anxieties, cracks problems, guides and supports. Children lose control over what happens to them: little – if any – choice of placement, location, school, social worker or who one lives with. *'The key to a child or young person feeling safe in care is the quality and stability of the relationships they form with significant adults they can trust.'*

7.4   With experience they acquire cynicism about whether things can go well for them. Inertia takes over because it is too difficult to change things. *'Young people felt that they were not routinely listened to or involved in planning and decision making.' 'There were no positive comments made about the system of statutory reviews'*: participation is a matter of turning up to hear what the adults are going to decide for them. Worst, however, was the continual moving, often with little notice, so that one dared not feel settled anywhere – again, a condition which exposes one to exploitation by others.

7.5   The danger most often referred to was that from other children: particularly bullying, physical abuse and theft. Little was said about staff reaction to this. Generally, foster care was experienced as safer than residential care on this score; the dangers there were of being cut off and abandoned. For some, foster care was worse than being in a residential home; they found none of the benefits of being in a family, and had lost any of the advantages of communal living.

7.6   Less was said about danger to personal safety from staff, although occurrences of both physical and sexual abuse were mentioned to the Review. The environment of residential homes could present problems from burglars and other unauthorised visitors, or from harassment at school (racial, or from being known to be 'in care') or in public places. Abusive families continued to be a danger. Generally, the Review found that the children we talked to, and their carers, had clear and valuable opinions about what kept them safe and what exposed them to danger. Some local authorities have discussed these matters with children and carers, and we commend this to others. One fundamental point is the provision of information: to the carer in such detail that not only the big problems are known but also the personal matters that affect the children most closely; to the child, enough to prepare him or her for an environment threatening in its comprehensive newness.

7.7   Confidence in the complaints procedure is low. It is difficult to access privately from residential care, and much more so from foster care. How can it be confidential? *'I had to complain first to the head of the home, then the member of staff complained about got to know about it.'* And how can it be impartial if it's run by the social services department? Few had independent advocacy available. And it all takes too long.

7.8   The small group of Camden children knew why they were being looked after and what their care history was. They were familiar with their care plans and with complaints procedures. They understood what 'feeling safe' meant and how to share fears for their safety with a responsible adult. What upset them most was the sense of crisis and emergency that surrounded changes of placement.

7.9   The young people at the meetings facilitated by First*Key* seemed unaware that child protection investigations were carried out into allegations of abuse in residential homes. If they were, they were not seen as particularly effective. A management response was more likely: *'all that happens is that you are shipped from placement to placement because social services do not want to deal with the embarrassment'*. The Review believes that social services departments must give full weight to the child protection aspect of investigations when abuse is alleged in residential settings and foster care.

7.10 Other recommendations by these young people are applied to discussions and proposals under specific subject headings in this report. It is important to register that their comments about being looked after were not as negative overall as these suggestions for improvements necessarily suggest. Many talked about good experiences and good residential and foster carers, even if there were strong suggestions of chance and transience about them. Others who had not had the best of times acknowledged that the alternative of life in an abusing family would have been much worse.

7.11 The common theme to our discussions with young people was their very reasonable desire to be treated as people and as individuals – which is what the Children Act intended – and the reality that local authorities needed much more than avowed good intentions to achieve this. The inadvertently oppressive nature of professional systems was exposed by the Camden child who said, very simply, *'I don't like people making decisions about me and they think they know what's best for me just by reading my file.'* Young people in their turn said that they were not always easy to deal with, and that having clear boundaries was part of feeling and being safe. They did, however, point to the additional complications and frustrations of their lives in comparison with how they saw their contemporaries living. Ironically, one of the details of a bureaucratic attempt to keep them safe was seen as a humiliating provocation: the insistence on police checks before permission would be given for a sleepover at a friend's meant that such arrangements were in practice impossible.

7.12 What impressed the Review overall was the potential of these young people to contribute to overcoming the difficulties they and their contemporaries face. We acknowledge that they may not be completely representative of the population of looked after children. Nevertheless, their ability gives us a great deal of confidence that looked after children can not only share decisions about their own future as individuals but also contribute to the better working of the systems that govern their lives. Former children from care function successfully as members of teams of inspectors. The Review believes that children who are or have been looked after by local authorities can offer advice on policy and service developments and assist in the training and selection of staff.

Chapter 8: VULNERABLE CHILDREN

SYNOPSIS

This chapter discusses some groups of children who are particularly vulnerable: disabled children, children with emotional and behavioural difficulties, young children, those far away from home, lost children and the leaving care group. It also discusses the effect of Section 20 of the Children Act. It does not seek to identify or comment on all such groups.

In discussing the position of **disabled children**, the Review concludes that they are extremely vulnerable to abuse of all kinds, including peer abuse, and high priority needs to be given to protecting them and ensuring that safeguards are rigorously applied (paragraph 8.21).

It recommends that statistics should be collected to enable policy makers and planners to assess need, establish trends and develop services accordingly (paragraph 8.23).

It discusses the need for co-operation between education, social services and health authorities and for a specific commitment to work together to protect disabled children (paragraph 8.24). There should be greater interchange between disability and child protection services and clarity about who is responsible for child protection procedures when a child is disabled (paragraph 8.25).

It also advocates involving disabled people in policy making and helping children to protect themselves and have means of gaining help from others when needed (paragraphs 8.27–8.29).

Communication is vital. Staff should be taught to communicate with children. Where a child has been abused, police, social services and health should provide personnel who have been trained to communicate with those with learning disabilities (paragraph 8.32). Further work is needed in developing non-verbal means of communication and systematic approaches to interviewing and discussing emotional issues (paragraph 8.33).

There should be a good representation of women amongst carers and always one or more children to confide in (paragraph 8.34).

The need for appropriate placements, effective anti-bullying policies and adequate after-care arrangements is stressed (paragraph 8.35).

The emotional needs of **children with emotional and behavioural difficulties** make them susceptible and their behaviour means they are less likely to be believed. The agencies responsible for them may not be disposed to ask too many questions of institutions that seem to be successfully containing particularly difficult children. And they may be exposed to abuse under the guise of innovatory treatment. The Review believes that the existing protection for these children should be extended and improved (paragraph 8.37).

Young children are less able to protect themselves and to complain. Regulatory bodies need greater awareness of this in considering the position of younger children in foster care, preparatory schools and hospitals (paragraph 8.38).

Children who are far away from home such as those with families in the Armed Forces and foreign children who come to this country to be educated may be more at risk. Registering authorities need empowering to react more quickly when complaints are made. There needs to be continuing care to ensure that these children are not targeted by abusers or otherwise harmed. Schools with more than 10% of pupils from abroad might revert to annual welfare inspections. The accreditation of 'guardianship' agencies should be accelerated and their use by parents and schools encouraged. Arrangements for a foreign child aged under 16 to live with a private family for 28 days or more comes within the scope of private fostering regulations, which should be applied (paragraph 8.41).

Placing authorities should retain protective oversight of all the children they are responsible for, and children placed by social services, educational and health authorities some distance from their homes must not be overlooked (paragraph 8.42) .

Homeless children – **lost children** – are most vulnerable of all. The histories of young homeless people make uncomfortable reading. Physical and sexual abuse is common.

The Review supports recommendations 1–13 of the Bridge Consultancy report *In Care Contacts – the West Case* about children who absconded from local authority care and remained untraced. All instances of running away should be treated seriously. Authorities should take all the steps of a responsible parent and not forsake responsibility until the child's 18th birthday. Returning children should be interviewed by someone independent of the home to find out what precipitated their departure. One of the worst features of past scandals is that children who ran away were continually returned to the abuser's 'care' (paragraph 8.45).

Refuges play a useful role and there is a case for recognising them in service plans, and for extending them – perhaps as a regional resource – to other centres of population: ideally as part of a more strategic approach to the problem of homeless, 'missing' and disturbed youth (paragraph 8.47).

Section 20 of the Children Act empowers social services authorities to provide accommodation for a child if it would safeguard or promote the child's welfare. They may do so for a child under 16 only if the parents do not object. Letters received by the Review following articles in the Mail on Sunday were critical of the provision and the way it was operated. The Review believes the provision is sensible and doubts that amending the Act would provide better outcomes. It recommends that the Department of Health commissions a project to assemble and analyse information about services for troubled young people with a view to producing a national strategy (paragraph 8.53).

The care system provides many children with better support than is available to them anywhere else. But **children leaving care** are deprived of it at the most critical stage of their lives.

The schemes which endeavour to prepare young people for leaving care are commended but the Review was concerned that some authorities appeared to be encouraging premature 'independence' (paragraph 8.62).

The Department of Health/Welsh Office should amend Section 24 to convert into a duty the local authority's present power to assist a child it has looked after, and to make clear that the 'care' authority is responsible for after care (paragraph 8.64).

8.1 Paragraph 1.39 lists certain categories of children who are more vulnerable than others to abuse and harm when they are living away from home. This chapter discusses some of these in more detail. We also draw general attention to the situation of boys in all-male establishments and girls in institutions in which they are in a small minority, particularly when those institutions are staffed largely by men.

8.2 The Review considers a number of other groups below. It does not attempt to identify and comment on all: for example, the 2,125 young people serving in the Armed Forces in 1995, or unaccompanied asylum seekers (486 in 1995). The latter are covered by Unaccompanied Asylum-Seeking Children (CI(95)17), [44] which defines them as children in need with *'an absolute right to be protected from neglect and/or abuse of any kind and this must be the primary consideration'*. The Review understands that systems are in place to refer these children and that most become looked after by local authorities.

Disabled Children

8.3 Children with disabilities are more likely to be living away from their families than other children - sometimes for fifty two weeks a year. They are to be found in long term foster care and in respite care; in a variety of registered homes, not all of which specialise in children's services; in residential schools of various kinds; and in hospitals. On the basis of the limited information available, largely from abroad, it seems that they are more likely to suffer abuse of various kinds than other children living away from home.

8.4 Statistics concerning disabled children are poor and much information relies on studies. The Council for Disabled Children's evidence provided us with some background data, derived from a 1989 study by OPCS. This indicated that there are 360,000 disabled children under 16 in the UK (3% of the child population), 189,000 of whom have very severe disabilities. 5,500 live in residential care and 16,000 children with disabilities and special needs attend residential schools. Of those living in residential care, 33% had major health or behaviour problems; 33% had problems at home (eg parent unable to cope without additional support); 15% had been sexually or physically abused.

8.5 Many live away from home. Jenny Morris's *Gone Missing?* [30] also drew on the 1989 OPCS Study of Disabled Children. She said that secondary analysis of its data by Loughran, Parker and Gordon, 1992, showed that disabled children are eight times as likely to be in the care of local authorities and constituted 28% of all children in care. 37% of those in local authority care in a residential setting are disabled. She referred to a study by Hirst and Baldwin that found that three times as many disabled as non-disabled children were attending a residential educational establishment. She said *'There was evidence that residential school provision sometimes masquerades as education but is in fact social care.'* Anecdotal evidence points to an increase in 52 week placements in residential schools.

8.6 Section 17 (10) of the Children Act includes disabled children within those classified as 'in need' and says a child is disabled *'if he is blind, deaf or dumb or suffers from mental disorder of any kind or is substantially and permanently handicapped by illness, injury or congenital deformity or other such disability as may be prescribed'*. The Act integrated services for disabled children with those for other children in need thus providing them and their families with the same level of protection as other looked after children. They had previously not had this unless they were 'received into care'. Schedule 2 of the Act requires local authorities to keep a register of disabled children.

8.7   The Act rationalised and extended the legal framework for safeguarding the welfare of children living away from home in institutions in which disabled children may be cared for, such as private and voluntary homes, independent and maintained schools, private and NHS hospitals. It did so by giving the proprietor of the non-state facilities a duty towards the child and the local authority a responsibility, which varies with the type of institution, to take steps to check that the duty is complied with and the welfare of the child safeguarded. It did not, however, go so far as to give the same powers of regulation and inspection in those cases.

Evidence about Abuse   8.8   There are no reliable figures on incidence/prevalence of abuse against disabled children and there have been few studies. What information there is comes mainly from studies in Canada, the USA and Australia. An American study (Crosse, Kaye and Ratnofskey)[45] found that the overall incidence of abuse of disabled children was 1.7 times higher than for those without a disability. They were twice as likely to be emotionally neglected and physically abused. It also estimated that some impairments had been, or were likely to have been, caused by abuse – 147 per 1000 abused children. A Canadian study (Sobsey and Varnhagen)[46] estimated a 50% increased risk to disabled children. There is also some evidence that the degree of disability also influences the level of risk so that more severely disabled children appear more vulnerable. The presence of multiple disabilities appears to increase the risk of both abuse and neglect.

8.9   In the UK the information is limited. A small snapshot study by NSPCC[47] was carried out between March 1991 and February 1992. 28 teams or projects reported cases involving 84 children, 34 of whom had learning and/or physical disabilities. 77% were male and 87% of perpetrators were male. The largest group of perpetrators were peers (48%), followed by staff (42%). 71% had been abused by more than one perpetrator and 26% of perpetrators had a previous history. 39% resulted in a criminal prosecution. In Margaret Kennedy's 1990 study of deaf children[48] she found 192 suspected cases of abuse and 86 confirmed instances of physical and emotional abuse, with 70 cases of suspected sexual abuse and 50 confirmed ones. She concluded that not only were disabled children more likely to be abused but this was likely to last for longer than with non-disabled children.

8.10   Investigations of abuse show that there may be a single perpetrator or more than one. Abuse may become a collective activity with pupils in turn seducing and abusing other children. Peer abuse is clearly a significant and difficult problem.

Vulnerability   8.11   There is increasing recognition of the vulnerability of disabled children to abuse. A number of factors are relevant. Adults interviewed by Helen Westcott[49] who had been abused as children identified these as *'physical and social isolation; lack of choice; lack of physical and psychological resources to defend oneself; physical immobility; and the ability to 'switch off' one's body at will'*. (The latter because of frequent intrusive behaviour by professionals and adults.)

8.12   Their disability may make it more difficult for them to distinguish abuse from appropriate care, particularly if this is difficult to separate from legitimate intimate care or where it appears the norm since their peers are also being abused. It may also affect their capacity to resist or avoid abuse.

8.13   They are easy targets because their disability may impede their ability to complain and they may, in any case, be inhibited from doing so because of a fear of a loss of service as a result. The Council for Disabled Children told us that '*Parents of disabled children are frequently well aware of the risk of abuse. But many feel compelled to use services which many feel to be inadequate or unsafe because there are no alternatives.*'

8.14 Disabled children may have many carers. Help is needed with intimate personal care, with carers often working on a one to one basis in private settings. The children are thus exposed to greater risk. A study by Ruth Marchant at Chailey Heritage, a non-maintained special school where children with severe disabilities live, found that of the 20 children there some had over 40 carers and few had less than 8. The average was 18 including carers at home, in respite care, link families and school. They are also more likely than non-disabled children to be receiving services from a range of agencies in the health, education and social services fields.

8.15 As well as all the other types of abuse referred to in this report, they are also vulnerable to extra types of abuse, such as over-medication, poor feeding and toileting arrangements, lack of stimulation. Children with challenging behaviour present particular problems if methods of control are difficult to distinguish from abuse.

8.16 Communication difficulties may make it difficult to tell others if they are unhappy, hurt or afraid. Those communication difficulties also make it difficult for them to appear credible witnesses in court if they do manage to identify and accuse an abuser.

8.17 These factors taken together increase their vulnerability and make them targets for abusers, particularly since the risk of disclosure is low and the risks of a successful prosecution even lower.

8.18 Many are living away from home voluntarily so they do not have the same safeguards as those in care. Jenny Morris[30] described this as '*in care in the sense that they spend most of their time in some kind of residential provision rather than in a family environment. But often they are not "in care" in the sense that the social services authority has assumed parental responsibility for them.*' As a result they have less chance of a family life through fostering and adoption.

8.19 Some have extended stays in hospital and there is no national monitoring to establish whether this is notified to social services authorities (let alone whether the information is available to the right people there). Paragraph 5.30 recommends that this area should be the subject of an inspection by SSI. Some children and young people live in residential homes which are registered under Part 1 of the Registered Homes Act 1984 which do not provide the level of safeguard provided by children's homes, for example only the proprietors and heads of home are subject to criminal record checks.

Improving Protection for Disabled Children

8.20 A number of suggestions have been made for improving the protection afforded to disabled children. It is important to have an explicit commitment to child protection together with very clear definitions of good practice. Environments should be open to criticism and scrutiny and have a high internal awareness of risks of abuse. There should be close contact with families, communities and adults and there should be respect for children's ethnicity, religion and individuality. Chailey Heritage has developed this further, based on the right to be valued as an individual, treated with dignity and respect, loved as a child first and to be safe. Their approach includes a charter of children's rights and guidelines for good practice in intimate care, for working with children of the opposite sex, for handling difficult behaviour and on consent to treatment.

8.21   Disabled children and young people provided us with their own very helpful agenda for keeping them safe.

Employ the right kind of staff:

– with a good sense of humour

– with a good attitude towards children

– who try to understand children

– who do not shout at children

– who have been closely vetted

Allow children and young people to have a range of positive experiences

Give them a choice about which adults to approach for support

Help them become independent and confident

Develop a culture of openness

Make sure all, especially younger ones, know what their rights are

Ensure that there is a difference in atmosphere between school and home

Ensure that people of all ages can mix – do not separate younger and older children

Be protective and look after them

Install security cameras

Install security alarms

Employ security guards.

The Review hopes that our recommendations, when implemented, will properly address their concerns. As people caring for children become more alert to the danger of abuse and as protective measures have a deterrent effect, abusers may show an increased tendency to target those who are most difficult to protect. We consider it vital that all the safeguards available to other children should be applied rigorously in the case of disabled children. They should be entitled to the same range of protective measures as other children whether they live in a residential care home, foster care, spend 52 weeks a year in schools or spend substantial periods of time in hospitals or nursing homes. Because of their increased vulnerability extra vigilance is required. They should be able to have confidence that staff looking after them in any of these contexts have been carefully selected and vetted and that they are fully aware of the need for protection. Managers should ensure that procedures are in place to ensure they are effective. In addition to the measures mentioned elsewhere in this report we have a number of additional recommendations.

Statistics   8.22   Jenny Morris[30] pointed to the inadequacies in the statistics for monitoring the Children Act in providing information about disabled children living away from home. This was partly due to problems of definition and uncertainty as to whether emotionally and behaviourally disturbed children were included (as they were in the OPCS study), and partly due to the range of types of residential placement involved, many of which were likely to be out of authority. Statistics do not identify the number of disabled children 'accommodated' by local authorities or subject to care orders. There are no data on disabled children living away from home. Local authorities do record 'Reasons for being looked after' and these include three categories relating to disabled children:

- child with learning difficulties alone to meet his/her family needs

- child with physical/sensory disability alone to meet his/her family needs

- child with both the above.

But there are 17 other categories, some of which may also apply to disabled children.

8.23   The needs of disabled children are therefore obscured and this is unhelpful to planners and policy makers. It is hard to see how services for disabled children and young people can be managed in a strategic way in the absence of statistics that enable planners at national or local levels to take an overview of what is being provided and for whom. There should be a review of the current statistical information leading to the establishment of a coherent set of data which can be used to assess and develop services at local and central levels. Since disabled children may find themselves in social services, health or educational establishments this needs to be a co-operative exercise between those services. It is important that statistics on abuse should also include information on disability. This will enable a picture to be built up of the relative risk to disabled children and would help spot any trend for abusers to target them more.

Co-operation Between Services

8.24   Active co-operation between education, social services and health authorities is particularly necessary for disabled children. All should ensure that their policies include a specific commitment to protect disabled children and that they work together to achieve this. We agree with the evidence from the Council for Disabled Children that *'Effective prevention of potentially abusive situations... will depend on integrated assessment systems and common staff training and development procedures about child protection matters across health, education and social services.'*

8.25   The Council told us that it was aware of *'a significant gap between the expertise of disability-specific services and the experience on child protection issues in local authority teams'*. It said that this may lead to both under-reporting of actual or potential abuse and also to inappropriate concerns about abuse because the management of a child with challenging behaviour has been misunderstood. It called for a greater interchange between disability and child protection services, with common training and greater awareness of their respective contributions to protecting children with disabilities. We agree. This problem is compounded in cases where services for disabled children are dealt with alongside adult disability services. Area Child Protection Committees should have local policies and practice in relation to disabled children. There should be clarity about who is responsible for child protection procedures where the child is disabled.

Inspection and Regulation

8.26   We believe there is scope to extend existing inspection and regulation in order to provide greater safeguards for disabled children in schools. Chapter 4 recommends the extension of Section 87 of the Children Act to all maintained and non-maintained special schools.

Involvement of Disabled Children

8.27 The Council for Disabled Children said that it *'would welcome greater evidence in care plans and reviews for disabled children looked after by the local authority that disabled children and young people were involved in planning their own treatment'*. The Review also considers this very important and believes that disabled children and/or adults should be involved in policy making.

8.28 We believe that children should be helped to protect themselves. Child protection posters and telephones should be accessible but this is not enough. More thought should be given to how a disabled child accesses protection systems. Children should be given information on appropriate behaviour to help them recognise grooming and abusive behaviour, and encouragement to be assertive. This would not only be helpful in countering abuse but also in dealing with the bullying and teasing to which they can also be subjected. They need sex education. Craft[50] and Middleton[51] found that lack of sexual, personal and social education creates problems which are further compounded if isolation and rejection increases the need for affection and attention, which makes such children particularly vulnerable to adults' attention and favours.

8.29 They should also know how to complain and what to do if they are worried about inappropriate actions. They should have access to a choice of people inside and outside the establishment they can communicate with. Inspectors should find meaningful ways to listen to children's views. Independent visitors do not seem to be much used. There may also be a need for specialist advocacy/best friend service for disabled children independent of service providers.

Abuse and Disabled Children

8.30 It seems that there is still a reluctance to accept that disabled children *are* abused. Action is needed to raise the awareness of abuse of disabled children. Awareness must be raised as a deterrent, to assist in the early identification of abuse and to create an atmosphere in which victims are not easily discredited. Marchant and Page[52] demonstrated the possibility of using the observations and skills of parents, staff and whatever communication aids the child uses to assess the occurrence of abuse, to identify potentially abusive behaviour early and to avoid it if possible. There should be clear procedures to ensure that changes in behaviour are monitored and possible significance understood, bruises mapped and recorded. There is a need for urgent advice to staff about professionals who abuse, including what to do if they suspect a colleague. Numbers of carers should be minimised and safe caring codes adopted. Those who do not comply with them should be challenged.

8.31 Professionals sometimes feel that it is better not to pursue suspicions of abuse as it would be too upsetting for the child and family. This adds to their vulnerability as easy targets, and means that perpetrators remain free to abuse and that the child does not get the therapy he/she needs.

Communication

8.32 Communication is a major issue – both in relation to the identification of abuse and to subsequent action. Some of the communication systems used do not include the necessary symbols for the disclosure of abuse. There is a need to provide the communication skill *before* the abuse rather than try to achieve it afterwards. Staff must be taught to communicate with children. Child protection officials should familiarise themselves with non-verbal communication systems and know how to contact suitable interpreters/facilitators or Human Aids to Communication (HACs) for investigation interviews and court related work. All relevant staff should work in partnership to investigate where abuse is suspected. Where a child has been abused interagency co-operation is vital. Police, social services and health should provide personnel to make up a child disabilities team, all of whom would be trained in means of effective communication with children with learning disabilities. A facilitator (as recommended by the AMA in *Special Child: Special Needs*[(53)]) may be needed.

8.33 Ways to communicate with disabled children should be developed, and those in authority in social services, the police or the criminal justice system should be prepared to facilitate this so that the potential to give evidence and to be taken seriously is maximised. To present as a competent witness and be able to explain the allegation is vital, since to fail in this is to create a group of ready made victims. Positive working relations between all agencies should be developed with voluntary exchange of information to provide an effective way of protecting children. Further work is needed on developing non-verbal means of communication, systematic approaches to interviewing and discussing emotional issues with children with complex needs.

Other issues 8.34 Some have suggested limiting the role of men in caring for disabled (and non-disabled) children because, although a minority of staff, they are responsible for the majority of the abuse. We do feel that having a good representation of women amongst carers, whatever the setting – particularly in positions of influence – would provide disabled children with some element of safeguard and we believe that they should always have one or more women that they can confide in.

8.35 A number of issues of relevance to disabled children are considered elsewhere in this report – notably health, education and issues of control. So too are choice of placement, bullying and after-care, but a brief comment is added here. Choice is even more of a problem for disabled children and their parents since no alternative care or support may be available. This means that parents and/or local authorities have to leave the child in what they know is a potentially harmful situation. It is unacceptable for extremely vulnerable children to be in this position and vital that concerns about safety are properly addressed. Disabled children are particularly vulnerable to bullying and teasing and strong anti-bullying policies should be in operation in all settings in which they live. There is very little after-care for young disabled people, many simply move on to adult residential services. Little is known about what happens to those living away from home at this stage. These gaps in service add to vulnerability and mean that safeguards are likely to be lacking at an important and difficult period of these young people's lives.

Emotional and Behavioural Difficulties

'The pupils in all these schools are among the most vulnerable members of the community.'
Circular 3/94 – The Development of Special Schools

8.36 Children with emotional and behavioural difficulties are vulnerable in a number of ways. Their emotional needs may make them more than usually susceptible to the flattering attention of improperly motivated adults. Their behaviour may lead people to dismiss any complaints they make as fantasies or lies. The agencies responsible for them may not be disposed to ask too many questions of institutions which appear to be containing particularly difficult children. And they may be exposed to abuse under the guise of innovatory treatment. According to Grimshaw and Berridge[34] *'Under the Children Act 1989, these are certainly children "in need" entitled to a co-ordinated response from the agencies within local authorities.'* In the experience of the Society of Education Officers, *'it is those pupils attending residential schools for their learning, emotional or behavioural needs that have been seen to be most at risk'.*

8.37   These are not merely theoretical considerations. They emerge as matters of fact from inquiry and other reports with sufficient weight to support the recommendations in Chapter 4 that Section 87 of the Children Act be extended to all residential schools, and that local authorities unify to the fullest extent possible the arrangements for discharging their educational and social services responsibilities for these children. The Review does not imply special failings in the institutions of the educational and social services providing for these children. Indeed, it wishes that the successes of this sector in residential schools, therapeutic communities and children's homes, and the skill and dedication of their staffs, were more widely understood and appreciated. We wish simply to extend and improve the protection these children currently have.

Other Vulnerable Children

8.38   Young children are less able both to protect themselves and to complain about their treatment. Regulatory and inspectorial bodies need greater general – but not oppressive – awareness of this in considering the position of younger children in foster care, preparatory schools and hospitals.

8.39   Another group is those children who are separated from parents by extreme distances, so that their main source of support and succour seems impossibly remote: children whose parents work abroad, for example, the children of families serving in the Armed Forces, and the foreign children who come to this country to be educated. Of the new pupils entering schools included within the Independent Schools Joint Council in 1996, 1,626 had parents living abroad, 1,669 were the children of parents in the Armed Forces, and 7,392 were foreign.

8.40   In practice, ease of communication and travel mitigates much of the difficulty, particularly for foreign children. Well documented problems have occurred, however, in schools where the children of service families make up a substantial proportion of the complement of pupils. Inspectorial bodies do not need reminding of this; registering authorities need empowering to react more quickly when complaints are made. Foreign children have not in practice been established as more vulnerable to abuse and harm than their British contemporaries. One small 'fringe' school set out to attract – and abused – foreign children some years ago, but no other examples of similarly corrupt institutions have come to the Review's attention.

8.41   Nevertheless, continuing care is needed to make sure that these children are not targeted by abusers or otherwise harmed. It might be prudent, for example, for schools with more than 10% of pupils from abroad to revert to annual welfare inspections where a more relaxed regime is currently permitted by LAC(95)1[29]. According to a recent inspection report on one school, 59 out of 217 boarders had permanent addresses outside the UK. The accreditation of 'guardianship' schemes should be accelerated and their use by parents and schools encouraged. Arrangements by any educational body or parent for foreign children under 16 to be accommodated by a private family for 28 days come within the scope of the private fostering regulations, and these should be applied.

8.42 Children may also be placed at some distance from their homes by social services, education and health authorities. It is important that placing authorities retain protective oversight of the children they are responsible for.

Lost Children 8.43 Homeless children are the most vulnerable of all. Reliable statistics are difficult to obtain. Surveys have been carried out and valuable reports published by voluntary organisations and children's charities. Barter[54] reports earlier studies in her survey of 200 children under 16 who used Centrepoint. She confirms the value of preventive work and of refuges, but the mobility of these young people makes service co-ordination difficult and there are in any case grounds for doubting the motivation and resourcing of agencies to cope with the problems disclosed. *We don't Choose to be Homeless*[55] bluntly declared *'Social Services Departments are, in the main, failing to fulfil their responsibilities to homeless 16/17 year olds under the Children Act.'*

8.44 The histories of young homeless people, and their present and future plight, make uncomfortable reading. Craig and others[56] interviewed 161 homeless young people aged 16–21. One third had first become homeless before the age of 16, and half had first run away from home before that age. One in 3 had also been physically abused severely and repeatedly over a considerable length of time, often involving multiple perpetrators across more than one care arrangement. Childhood sexual abuse, often associated with physical abuse, was reported by 1 in 4. Women were particularly vulnerable both before and after becoming homeless. *'Many of our homeless young people report childhoods lacking in affection, surrounded by indifferent often violent adult figures'. 'A history of having run away from home under the age of 16 was associated with lifetime risk of mental illness or substance abuse disorders.'*

8.45 The Bridge Consultancy in *In Care Contacts – the West Case*[57], drew attention to children who absconded from local authority care and remained untraced. The Review supports its recommendations 1–13 for action concerning young people who run away from residential care. These should apply to all children looked after by local authorities. I had stressed in my 1991 report the importance of treating all instances of running away from care with proper seriousness. Local authorities should take all the steps that responsible parents take in such circumstances. They should not forsake responsibility for the disappeared child before his or her 18th birthday. Returning children should be interviewed by someone independent of the home to find out what precipitated their departure. Many of the children who run from care were earlier running from their parents and are still running from their past. But they may also be running from the present: one of the worst features of earlier scandals is that children who ran away from abuse were continually returned to the abuser's 'care'.

8.46 There are currently 3 refuges operating under Section 51 of the Children Act. Together they fulfil functions ranging from breathing space for stressed families to early rehabilitative work with isolated and distressed children. The Centrepoint/NSPCC experience is that 80% of its temporary residents are on the run from parents and the remainder from care. Local authorities are apparently as capable as natural parents of reacting in an aggrieved or rejecting manner.

8.47 Refuges can stop children disappearing from the care system, and they play an obviously useful role in restoring enough stability to dangerously volatile situations to enable some planning for the future. There are arguments for recognising them in service plans, and for extending them – perhaps as a regional resource – to other centres of population. Ideally, however, this should occur as part of a more strategic approach to the problem of homeless, 'missing' and disturbed youth.

Section 20 of the Children Act

8.48   After the Review was established, the Mail on Sunday ran a series of articles critical of the manner in which some social services authorities interpreted and implemented their power under Section 20 to provide accommodation for a child if it would safeguard or promote the child's welfare. They may do so for a child under 16 only if the parent does not object. Reporting of the Review in this context led to my receiving 78 letters from parents, grandparents and others, nearly all of them critical of this provision or of the way in which the officers of the authority operated it. The common feature of these situations was that the relationship between parents and child was in difficulty to a point at which help was sought from statutory sources.

8.49   The provision in the Act seems eminently sensible. It gives valuable flexibility to accommodating children in a variety of circumstances in which their welfare needs promoting and safeguarding. It provided, in the majority of the cases quoted to the Review, a breathing-space for parents and child in which plans could be made and work done. This seems a more satisfactory arrangement than the older legislation permitting parents to bring a child before a court as beyond their control, in which the parties were compelled to continue in adversarial mode and the child usually ended under supervision or in care. The Review doubts that amending the Act would provide better outcomes; the law is inevitably something of a blunt instrument in resolving problems in the delicate and varied relationships between parents and children.

8.50   In any case, parents were less concerned about the Act than they were about the local authorities (and, in particular, the social workers). A theme running strongly through the correspondence was of dissatisfaction with what was experienced as the weakness of the local authority's action. It seemed to adopt the child's view of the situation. Parental views were not listened to or were over-ridden. Authorities seemed unaware that exploitative adults were weaning children away from parents by telling them that they had a right to go into care, where they could do what they liked and would be provided with ample personal cash. Disaster might have been averted if only the social workers had taken a stronger line from the beginning.

8.51   Disaster was indeed the outcome of some of these situations, and great damage and unhappiness a feature of all. The Review was not authorised to examine them further. One social services department wrote of its own volition outlining a carefully thought out and professional approach. In general, the very challenging circumstances described would have tested the skill and resources of the most competent organisation. They disclosed educational difficulties, problems of physical and mental health and malevolent external forces combining to place relationships between parent and child – some of them already stressed – under intolerable strain. A strong line is not likely to be the most productive approach if earlier strong lines have failed, but parents understandably expect measures to be taken to protect young children against the worst consequences of their actions.

8.52   I have no doubt that practice in this area could be improved, but there is no evidence nationally to support the view that local authorities accommodate children unnecessarily. English authorities provided 2,610 young people aged 16 and over with accommodation under this Section in 1994/5. The complaint more frequently encountered is of the difficulty of persuading local authorities to take needy children in. What impressed me about the majority of the correspondence is that these were complex cases referred at the point at which problems were becoming chronic. In some the onset of difficulties was acute, but many might have been picked up at an earlier stage by educational or health agencies. The local authority powers were no more than a longstop in many of these cases. Some further investigation is needed of the adequacy and co-ordination of local services for troubled young people living at home, and their families, in circumstances in which a harmful breakdown of relationships is threatened.

8.53 Such an investigation might take place in the context of a larger piece of work. The plight of troubled, missing, lost, absconding and homeless youth causes much anxiety. The information available might now be pulled together and analysed with a view to producing a viable strategy for tackling the interlocking problems. We need to understand not only what causes them but also how local and national agencies can engage in more effective preventive and remedial work. I recommend that the Department of Health, with inter-departmental support, commission such a project.

Leaving Care

'Social services don't always help. They do not check where you are going to live, you have only one chance, if you blow it – tough!'
Young person – FirstKey meeting

'I feel more involved since I have been with the leaving care team. It has made me realise more things than I would have before.'
Young person   FirstKey meeting

8.54 Local authorities are required by Section 24 of the Children Act to advise, assist and befriend each looked after child with a view to promoting his welfare after he ceases to be looked after. They also have a duty to advise and befriend children they have looked after beyond their 16th birthday until they reach 21, but they have only a power – not a duty – to assist them in kind or, exceptionally, in cash.

8.55 The Social Services Inspectorate's recent report, *When Leaving Home is also Leaving Care* [58], summarised the peculiar vulnerability of children looked after by local authorities:

'• More than 75% of care leavers have no academic qualifications of any kind.

• More than 50% of young people leaving care after 16 years are unemployed.

• 17% of young women leaving care are pregnant or already mothers.

• 10% of 16–17 year old claimants of DSS severe hardship payments have been in care.

• 23% of adult prisoners and 38% of young prisoners have been in care.

• 30% of young single homeless people have been in care.'

8.56 The Chief Inspector's letter (CI(97)4) covering the report spoke of *'some very good work undertaken by social workers, carers and through joint work with other agencies. There were many examples of creative and innovative practice, especially with the voluntary sector.'* However, there were also some serious concerns, including some areas where minimum statutory regulations were not met. A whole series of reports in the previous decade highlighted concerns about the inadequacy of the support offered to care leavers at this critical stage of transition.

8.57   Broad[59] found 1,538 young people in leaving care projects in England and Wales. Half were unemployed. The most common form of housing was supported lodgings. *'After care work'*, he concluded, *'is not safe in the hands of the Children Act 1989'*. Biehal and others[60] found that *'Most of the young people we interviewed moved on from their final care placement at the age of only 16 or 17.'*

8.58   Sinclair (submission to the Review) also comments on the lack of support on discharge and the lonely and frightening lives children then lead. We felt a particular concern for young women, especially those with babies. Two 1992 studies (quoted by the NFCA in *Foster Care in Crisis*[15] by Garnett and Biehal, and by Clayden, Stein & Wade) found 1 in 7 young women to be pregnant on leaving care at 16 or 17 and 1 in 4 already having a child. 10% of Craig's[56] sample of homeless young people had become homeless after leaving care either 'in an unplanned, chaotic fashion' or following quick breakdown in independent accommodation. *'The remainder of those who spent time in care during adolescence but who returned to the parental home all left following rows or abuse.'*

8.59   Lee and O'Brien[61] pointed out that *'Connections between the residential care system, young care leavers and prostitution have been highlighted by a number of authors... young people may become engaged in prostitution on leaving care because of financial problems, exacerbated by lack of access to the benefit system and housing, and their detachment from education, training and employment opportunities which is common amongst care leavers'*.

8.60   Leaving care was discussed in the groups of young people from 20 local authorities convened by First*Key*. Those who had left care expressed considerable concerns about their experience. Some of those coming up to the threshold were very anxious about their future.

8.61   Reservations were expressed about being compelled to live independently at 16 or 17 before they felt ready, losing relationships with carers and friends, the hazards presented by unregulated lodgings or flats in hard to let areas, the loss of continuous social work support and – simply but tragically – *'not being able to return to care'*. That last comment illustrates why the care system, with all its inbuilt and acquired failings, still provides many children with better support than is available to them anywhere else – and then deprives them of it at one of the most critical transitional stages in their lives.

8.62   The First*Key* meetings recommended that 'care' should continue to the 18th birthday, check scrupulously the living arrangements then proposed, and enable access to social work and other support afterwards. The Review believes that local authorities should exercise their duties and powers under Section 24 of the Act in the spirit of responsible parents. We commend the many schemes which now endeavour to prepare young people for leaving care. No responsible parent, however, turns a child away at 16 – or even 18 – unsupported financially and emotionally, without hope of succour in distress. We were particularly concerned by the volume of anecdotal information about young people ceasing to be looked after at the age of 16, which suggested that some authorities operated informal policies of encouraging premature 'independence'.

8.63   The Review well understands that some young people are so troubled that the authority may feel that it has no further resource to help them, that young people may appear eager to strike out for themselves, and that there may be difficult decisions about allocating resources according to need and likely outcome. None of these factors absolves authorities from scrupulous consideration of the needs of individuals and attempting to make provision for them. That provision need not be expensive. It is plain from what young people say themselves that what they most lack is someone trustworthy and resourceful to turn to: a continuing role, in particular, for residential and foster carers, independent visitors and for social work. Fry (1992) *After Care: Making the Most of Foster Care* (quoted in Berridge[16]) found that one third of foster carers continued to offer informal assistance to the children who had been discharged from their homes, but that there was little local authority recognition of this.

8.64   The Review is forced to conclude that Section 24 of the Children Act should be amended to extend the duty of local authorities to give assistance to young people they have looked after, including helping foster carers to continue providing support. This appears to be a significant extension: the Inspectorate estimated that 33,450 young people were eligible for leaving care services at 31 March 1995. Nevertheless, additional investment in this highly vulnerable group at this critical stage seems entirely justified. Amendment to the Act should also make clear that provision is the responsibility of the 'looking after' authority.

Chapter 9   ABUSE AND ABUSERS

SYNOPSIS

This chapter discusses the threat posed by persistent sexual abusers and measures that should be taken to deter them. It considers child pornography, child prostitution and bullying.

Abusers

Persistent sexual abusers are a scourge of childhood. Their numbers are difficult to estimate but each one who adopts a lifetime career will amass hundreds of victims. They inflict unspeakable psychological and physical harm. Some of their victims will become abusers. Their success depends on their ability to ingratiate themselves with adults and children. They are largely but not exclusively men. They establish themselves as trusted friends, colleagues or employees. Exposure may be a matter of chance, often after many years of abuse. They seek out situations in which their preferred kind of children are accessible. Children living away from home are vulnerable, some exceptionally so. Some settings are vulnerable to penetration by abusers, as staff or volunteers.

A basic requirement of all settings is that their general safeguards are robust enough to deter persistent abusers. Agencies must be alert to signs of things going wrong, vigilant in stimulating investigation where indicated and effective in taking remedial action. Some institutions and some children require more specific measures to protect them.

The ability of these men to hoodwink people and avoid detection and conviction for their crimes causes grave anxiety. Some may wish to discontinue. Programmes for sex offenders are impressive, but too much should not be expected of treatment. Sexual abuse of children is highly addictive but control, containment and coping can all be enhanced. Treatment offers the prospect of reducing the number of children assaulted. An inter-departmental review of treatment to develop proposals for its co-operation and development is recommended. It is important that it covers adolescent abusers (paragraph 9.8).

Children living away from home are at risk from other hazards. More are at risk from casual or opportunistic abusers. Physical abuse and emotional neglect are continual threats of institutional life. A more general risk is that systems will malfunction and, at worst, *'inflict further harm rather than protect'*.

Those who wish to work with children must acknowledge that people in similar roles have sought and used such roles in order to abuse them. Working with children in any capacity must become a privileged occupation, which requires careful scrutiny of the applicant and continual supervision. Work with children – and residential work in particular – needs a more supportive institutional context and more respect and understanding from the community (paragraph 9.10).

Things appear to have improved, but not enough. More than regulation is needed to cure all the ills caused by abuse of different kinds, the consequences of uncaring regimes and careless people. What is needed is: vigorous rehabilitation of residential care; modernising of foster care; elevation of all boarding schools to the level of the best (paragraph 9.11).

Children abuse each other too. Staff may dismiss abusive sexual behaviour as 'normal' and deprive children of the protection they need. It should be treated seriously for both the victim and the abuser, and child protection procedures and treatment considered for both (paragraph 9.12).

Pornography and Prostitution

Child pornography involves the serious abuse of children. Because of a strong link with paedophiles, its detection is important in preventing further abuse and providing useful information on abusers and their networks. It should be tackled vigorously and the police and Customs and Excise should devote more resources to it. Immigration officers also have a role to play where it is suspected that children are brought into the country for exploitation (paragraph 9.27).

All public departments, agencies and services should work together to protect children even when this is not one of their core functions. They should have effective means of co-operating. The value attached to this work should be reflected in the relevant departmental systems, such as performance appraisals and measurement (paragraph 9.28).

The Review recommends that there should be a ban on the export of child pornography as well as on its import; the Customs Consolidation Act should be amended to cover 'signals' as well as 'articles' so that the Internet is covered (paragraph 9.29).

It recommends that **child prostitution** should be dealt with as a child protection issue (paragraph 9.30).

It calls for a review of the legislation to ensure that there are adequate means of deterring and punishing those who exploit young people in this way (paragraph 9.39).

All agencies should work together to ensure there is a coherent policy for dealing with child prostitution from a child protection perspective. Area Child Protection Committees should take an active interest and social services ensure that there are staff trained in how to deal with it. Those involved in police forces should have knowledge of child protection work, or work closely with those who do (paragraph 9.40).

Bullying

The term bullying is often used to describe activities that are more sinister than this description suggests. It is used to cover physical violence, racial and sexual harassment, sexual exploitation, using threats to obtain money or property, and psychological torture. It is extremely destructive and one of the main problems that worry children. Action is needed to tackle it in all institutional contexts.

There has been an improvement in schools since it has been given greater prominence but it remains an important issue. Initiatives like the Department for Education and Employment's anti-bullying strategy need continual consolidation and reinforcement. Ways of preventing and detecting bullying must stay near the top of the agenda for all residential schools (paragraph 9.42).

Bullying and sexual abuse by foster siblings was encountered. Bullying appeared to be ignored in children's homes. There were other sources of fear and anxiety: a mix of fearsome and vulnerable residents, partly the result of poor placement policies, which amounts to systems abuse. As worrying is the apparent acceptance of this by staff and managers. Staff need leadership and support in establishing and maintaining civilised attitudes and values on these matters. Management should set and monitor standards of acceptable conduct, including the conduct of staff to residents (paragraph 9.44). Organisations providing children's homes should implement effective anti-bullying strategies (paragraph 9.45).

Bullying is endemic in prison establishments. The subject is well researched and understood and the Prison Service has a comprehensive strategy to counteract violence. But tackling such an ingrained problem is a formidable challenge to management. Success is partial and intermittent. The Review urges the Prison Service to take the management action needed to implement anti-bullying strategies consistently in all establishments in which children aged under 18 are detained (paragraph 9.49).

'How nearly can that we most despise and hate approach in out-ward manner to that which we most venerate.'
Sir Walter Scott: Rob Roy.

'When young lips have drunk deep of the bitter waters of Hate, Suspicion and Despair, all the Love in the world will not wholly take away that knowledge.'
Rudyard Kipling: Baa Baa Black Sheep

Abusers   9.1   Persistent sexual abusers are a scourge of childhood. They are habitual criminals whose numbers are difficult to estimate, but each one who adopts the lifetime career of abusing children sexually will amass a library of hundreds of victims. All of these will be damaged, many will be caused unspeakable psychological and physical harm, and some will become practitioners in the abuse wrought upon them.

9.2   People who prey upon children in this way are sexual terrorists whose success depends, paradoxically, on their capacity to ingratiate themselves with adults and children. An outstanding characteristic is their ability to establish themselves in roles in which they are trusted to excess as friend, colleague or employee. Their subsequent activities are concealed by suborning, blackmailing and threatening their victims. Exposure may be a matter of chance; many of those ultimately convicted have practised their horrifying trade for many years. Some are sufficiently skilled in deception to involve parents of the children they have abused in defending them. They are largely, but not exclusively, men. The role of women as persistent abusers now attracts more attention than it did. They may act in concert with a male partner, but also as individuals; in both roles they attract less suspicion than men.

9.3   Such people naturally seek out situations in which their preferred kind of children are accessible. These obviously include settings in which children are living away from home – some of whom, because of their personal circumstances, are exceptionally vulnerable to potential abusers. Certain settings may themselves be vulnerable to penetration by abusers in the guise of staff or volunteers. A basic requirement in all settings is that their general safeguards must be robust enough to deter such people. All bodies must in addition be continuously alert to signs of things going wrong, vigilant in stimulating investigation where this is indicated, and effective in taking remedial action. Some institutions, and some children, require more specific measures to protect them.

9.4   An unpublished Department of Health report into 50 cases of alleged and established abuse of children in residential homes and schools identified the perpetrators as *'frequently in a position of particular responsibility, authority and trust'*, who were likely to have been in post at least 5 years. Two thirds of the abused were boys, and two thirds of the abuse was sexual. It was rarely opportunistic; victims were *'groomed'* and *'counselled'*; the impression was that *'in many cases the abuse had taken place over a long period of time'*. The 44 institutions in which they practised covered the spectrum of children's homes and boarding schools.

9.5   Gallagher [62] commented in one case on *'the nature and extent of the abuse perpetrated by this individual; his ability to infiltrate families and institutions; his manipulation of children, parents and agency workers; his association with other equally ruthless abusers; and his ability to repeatedly avoid justice'*. And a recent Inquiry Report notes *'In this setting [a maintained*

*boarding school for children with emotional and behavioural
difficulties] the vulnerable and less self confident young people were easy prey
for a paedophile who exhibited great skill in gaining their confidence and
grooming them to meet his own sexual needs.'*

9.6   Less sophisticated perpetrators also enjoyed charmed lives. One –
described in an Inquiry Report[63] as *'an aggressive paedophile who preyed
on children placed in his care'* – survived an undisclosed conviction for
wounding, a complaint of harassment, a conviction for being drunk
and disorderly, complaints of physical and sexual abuse, disciplinary
action for physical abuse, and a warning about children visiting staff
houses. Both Frank Beck and Ralph Morris survived several investigations before finally being brought to book. And of the 48 alleged
abusers in the Department of Health study, 3 had previous convictions,
3 had come under suspicion for offences previously, 4 had been
accused of sexual abuse before, 2 had previously been suspended and
reinstated, and 3 had been linked with other establishments under
investigation.

9.7   The ability of these men to hoodwink people and to avoid detection
and conviction for their crimes causes grave anxiety. The Review does
not doubt that some genuinely wish to discontinue the exploitative
and destructive behaviour in which they are engaged. We were
impressed by the programmes of treatment for sex offenders developed by prison, probation, health and social services and by a number
of voluntary organisations. The prison programme has the highest priority for treatment in the Prison Service. It is available for offenders
sentenced to 2 years or more. About half volunteer for the programme;
offenders against children are over-represented. The Probation Service
has also developed convincing programmes, based on group work
methods, for offenders in the community, some of them following
release from prison. We were greatly helped by the Lucy Faithfull
Foundation, not only making a submission but also arranging a visit to
their Wolvercote Clinic which included discussion with offenders in
treatment.

9.8   Too much should not be expected of treatment. Sexual abuse of children is highly addictive and as difficult to break out of as any other
chronic addiction. But control, containment and coping can all be
enhanced. Treatment is important in the eyes of the Review because
it offers the prospect of reducing the number of children who would
otherwise be assaulted. There is now enough experience of the treatment of sex offenders (and of child abusers in particular) to justify an
inter-departmental review of the subject to develop proposals for its
co-operation and development. Several witnesses expressed concern
about the lack of treatment facilities for adolescent abusers, in particular that they may not only have been abused themselves but that they
are also on the threshold of a possible career of child assault. We agree,
and trust that the inter-departmental review would consider this need
also.

9.9   Preferential paedophiles attract most attention in relation to abuse of
children living away from home. The danger they represent should not
be underestimated. Every organisation needs a threshold of entry high
enough to deter them and sufficient vigilance to detect them. It would
be wrong, however, to become so pre-occupied with persistent sex
offenders that the other hazards children encounter are discounted or
neglected. More children are at risk from casual or opportunistic abuse
than from 'professional' abusers. And it would be equally wrong to
reduce the concept of abuse until it meant only sexual abuse. Physical

abuse, and emotional neglect and abuse, are continual threats in institutional life; one can never be sure that they have been eliminated. Most children, however, are at the more general risk that the systems in which they are caught up will malfunction to the extent that in the worst case they will do more harm than good. Human nature and human organisations being what they are, one must be alert to the possibility of the worst happening even where one has confidence in the best.

9.10 As well as providing support and companionship, both adults and other children may present dangers to children away from home. Those who wish to work with children must acknowledge that people in similar roles have abused children in the past and have sought such roles in order to abuse them. Working with children in whatever capacity – salaried staff, foster carer, volunteer, charity trustee – must become a privileged occupation: one which justifiably requires, in the interests of children, careful scrutiny of the applicant and continual supervision of people in whatever position they fill. It should be regarded by the practitioner as an honour, and similarly valued by the rest of the community. Yet the Report to the Department of Health and Social Services (Northern Ireland)[64] pointed to the work environment of residential staff being similar to the social situation of abusive parents: leaving them isolated, unsupported, underpaid and overstressed. Organisations like the Social Care Association, which represents many of the people who work in residential child care in statutory, voluntary and private settings, espouse the highest ethical standards and are dignified advocates of their profession. Work with children – and residential work in particular – needs a more supportive institutional context and more respect and understanding from the community.

9.11 Until that bright day dawns, there will continue to be people grubbing around children for their own purposes because the rest of us (who do not think of ourselves as abusers) do not care enough to change things. At least things are better than they were: ChildLine statistics, for example, show a declining trend in complaints of abuse from children in homes and boarding schools from the beginning of the decade. But they are not good enough. There is still too much abuse on a mundane level: casual or opportunistic; physical, sexual and emotional; in words and in deeds; by uncaring regimes as well as by careless people. Some of the people involved have flawed or immature personalities whose weaknesses are exposed by the demands of the job. Some are socialised into abuse by corrupt environments or by cultures which put the interest of the staff or the institution first and those of the children nowhere. Others are subjected to more stress or more temptation than they can withstand. Others make mistakes. More than regulation is needed to cure all such ills: a vigorous rehabilitation of residential care, the modernising of foster care, the elevation of all boarding schools to the high standards of the best.

9.12 Children abuse each other too. Possibly half the total of abuse reported in institutions is peer abuse. Sexual abuse causes particular anxiety in a number of ways. It can permeate an establishment; one witness to a recent Inquiry said that *'Institutionalised sexual abuse to the point of buggery between pupils at the school would appear to have existed for a number of years'*. Males in early adolescence who sexually abuse children *'may be at exceptionally high risk of continuing to experience paedophilic fantasies and perhaps of continuing to engage in paedophilic behaviour in later life'*[65]. Staff in a residential setting may dismiss abusive sexual behaviour as 'normal' and deprive children of the protection they rightly expect by consciously or unconsciously colluding with what is going on. It should be treated as seriously, for both victim and abuser, as if it had occurred in the open community, and child protection procedures and treatment considered for both.

Child Pornography and Child Prostitution

9.13   We discuss child pornography and child prostitution here because they are forms of abuse to which children living away from home are particularly vulnerable. The most vulnerable tend to be targeted for sexual exploitation, including organised abuse, and these include the poor, the homeless, and those who are in care or living in institutions. It also includes disabled children, particularly those who would find it difficult to report abuse. Children within institutions are vulnerable both to staff within the institution and to those without who target them.

9.14   Child pornography is both abusive in itself and also a weapon used by abusers to help entrap children and then to keep them entrapped. Child prostitution is the exploitation of young girls and boys by adults either as 'customers' or as pimps.

Child Pornography

9.15   Child pornography is not the taking of relatively innocent pictures of children with no clothes on, it is the recording – by photographs or video camera – of a child, or of children being abused by adults, other children or which involves bestiality. It is a visual record of serious criminal offences.

9.16   Even the less extreme examples of pornographic material I saw at New Scotland Yard are records of horrifying abuse. The chapter on 'The Child Pornography Industry: International Trade in Child Sexual Abuse' in Pornography: Women, Violence and Civil Liberties[66] gives a description of what was involved –

"Child pornography ranges from posed photographs of naked and semi-naked children, through more explicit shots of their genitalia thumbed apart to still, film and video recording of oral, vaginal and anal sex. Frequently the children are required to urinate on adults or each other. Almost invariably they are coated with semen when their abuser ejaculates over them. Occasionally they are photographed having sex with an animal."

9.17   As can be imagined from this, the involvement of children in pornography is very damaging. The children have the fear and guilt of knowing that their abuse has been recorded and the worry about who might know about this and whether it will become generally known – for example if photographs appear in magazines. This haunts them well into adulthood. All this comes, of course, on top of the effects of the abuse itself, which may be particularly extreme and sadistic including torture of the most cruel kind.

9.18   There is a strong link with paedophilia. Studies in the USA show a high correlation with active abuse. US Customs statistics show that at least 80% of those who buy pornography are active abusers and at least a proportion of the rest will not have yet been caught. The Chicago police, in 1984, found that in almost all arrests for possession of child pornography they discovered photographs of the abusers having sex with children – taken by themselves.

9.19   Pornography is used in a number of ways. It is used to stimulate the abuser to offend again. It is shown to children to lower their inhibitions – the children involved have always been forced to smile so that it can be claimed, especially to younger children, that they are having fun. With older children it is used to excite them and to show them that what is being done is 'alright'. It is also used to entrap children further – because of fear that others will see what they have done and because of the upset it would cause their parents. And, if they are shown abusing other children, because they too are committing an offence. It is used by 'sex rings' to normalise behaviour or as instruction. It is also used for commercial gain. When produced for this purpose it is at its most extreme. Since it is aimed at an audience it is manipulative and sadistic.

9.20   The child pornography industry is international and highly commercial. In America it is said to be one of the largest 'cottage industries' with a market worth some $2–3 billion per year. It is claimed that producers have filmed one million children in the US alone. A current investigation by French police demonstrates the scale of what can be involved. A fourteen months investigation of a video mail-order company led to 2,500 officers searching 800 homes and to the detention of 345 people and to 235 being charged. Of most relevance for this Review is that many have jobs which bring them into contact with children. They include 31 teachers, 2 holiday centre directors, 2 priests and 6 doctors, one of whom is a paediatrician (The Times: Wednesday June 18 and The Independent: Monday June 23 1997). The trade also crosses boundaries between countries and discoveries of networks in one country have led to the identification of links with paedophiles in others.

9.21   The Internet is also increasingly being used to transmit pornographic images.

9.22   The extent of the market in the UK is clearly considerable. In the first 9 months of 1994 the Metropolitan Police seized 7,200 child pornography tapes, a 50% increase on what was seized during the whole of 1993. *Pornography: Women, Violence and Civil Liberties*[66] gives an example of a British paedophile and pornographer who claimed that thousands of people in his town alone enjoyed his tapes. The Paedophilia Unit of the Organised Crime Group at New Scotland Yard was established originally as the Obscene Publications Branch to deal with adult pornography, but its terms of reference and title were changed to deal with child pornography and paedophilia as a marked increase in offences of possession and distribution became apparent.

9.23   Paedophiles are also known to collect and keep pornographic material and to be quite obsessive about it. It therefore offers both a good way of identifying abusers who may previously have gone unrecognised and provides evidence of this – particularly when it shows them abusing children.

9.24   The main legislation in this area is the Obscene Publications Act 1959, the key concepts of which are whether the material 'depraves' or 'corrupts' the viewer. The Protection of Children Act 1978 was intended to protect children from the taking of indecent photographs. The Criminal Justice Act 1988 made possession of an indecent photograph of a child a criminal offence, but subject only to a fine. The Criminal Justice and Public Order Act 1994 amended the 1978 Act to make offences of the taking, distribution and possession of indecent photographs or 'pseudo-photographs' with a view to distribution and advertising. The maximum penalty is 3 years. It made the offences arrestable, allowed the taking of intimate body samples and allowed detention for 36 hours. The latter means that those in a network cannot warn others – for example to remove incriminating material from their homes. Under the Customs Consolidation Act 1876 it is illegal to import indecent or obscene articles, including child pornography. Section 170 of the Customs and Excise Management Act 1979 set a maximum sentence of 7 years. It is not illegal to export it. Nor is it illegal to import it electronically via the Internet. Conviction for smuggling child pornography is one of the offences for which people are required to register under the Sex Offenders Act 1997.

9.25   Pornography should be tackled vigorously because it is extremely damaging to children. It also provides police with a way of identifying paedophiles and the networks in which they operate. It is, therefore, well worth devoting resources to its discovery. One of the most effective points to identify the transport of such material is when it comes into, or goes out of, the country. HM Customs and Excise therefore has an important role to play. The legitimacy of the passage of soft information between the HM Customs and Excise and other authorities, such as the police or social services departments, should take precedence over civil liberties issues where the safety of children is concerned. Another important area to tackle is the Internet, where it is possible to identify the source and destination of material of this kind.

9.26   There is some recognition of the importance of discovering pornography and pursuing the leads that it provides but the resources that are allocated to this are relatively small. The entrée that pornography provides to paedophile networks and in providing tangible evidence are good grounds for giving much higher priority to this work and for allocating adequate resources to it.

9.27   The police and HM Customs and Excise are urged to dedicate more resources to this and to build up their expertise so that more pornographers are identified and prosecuted and more of their customers are identified and put on centrally held lists of paedophile suspects. A proactive response should include investigation of material on the Internet, since this key area allows the rapid transmission of large quantities of material, speeds up the passage of ideas and acts as a spur to more abuse. Immigration officers also have a role to play where it is suspected that children are being brought into the country for the purposes of exploitation.

9.28   It is vital that all public departments, agencies and services work together to protect children even where this is not one of their core functions and high priority should be given to this. They should have effective means of co-operating through established liaison points and should reflect the priority attached to this in all relevant systems, such as performance appraisals and measurements.

9.29   More specifically, the Review recommends that there should be a ban on the export of child pornography as well as on its import. This will increase the opportunities for the police to use the powers available to them to investigate and convict. In turn this will increase the number of abusers who will be identified when police checks are made when they apply for jobs working with children. It recommends that the Customs Consolidation Act should be amended to cover the importation of 'signals' as well as 'articles' so that the Internet is covered.

Child Prostitution

9.30   Child prostitution is dealt with as a criminal offence – but it is more often the child who is prosecuted rather than the adult who is either controlling their action, and living off their earnings, or who is using their 'services'. The Review believes that these adults should be prosecuted as abusers and that the children involved in prostitution should be dealt with under child protection procedures not as criminals.

9.31   There is no official estimate of the number of children involved in prostitution.

9.32   A controversial leaflet raised awareness of the problem by pointing out that it was not necessary to travel abroad in order to find child prostitutes since there are many 'working' in the UK. Many of those have experience of being in care, some still are, others are 'missing' from care and yet others have left it but have received little support or after-care. Children and young people in care are particularly vulnerable to older people, mainly men, who persuade them that they care for them and love them, but then go on to lure or force them into prostitution and live off their earnings. They often use considerable intimidation and get them dependent on drugs in order to keep them entrapped. The same thing can happen to girls living with their parents but there the girl has first to be estranged from her family. Children who live away from their families are easier to target.

9.33   The law provides little by way of safeguards for young girls who become caught up in prostitution. Instead of being dealt with as children needing care and protection they are cautioned for soliciting or loitering and after two cautions they are deemed to be a 'common prostitute'. The cautions remain on their record for eight years. Boys may be prosecuted for 'importuning' and then carry the label of 'rent boy'.

9.34   This approach is particularly unhelpful since the girls involved are very often the victims of entrapment by pimps. Those who have been sexually abused already are particularly vulnerable. Others may prostitute themselves to earn money for food and lodging if they have run away from home or from care. They are usually dealt with by the vice squads in police forces rather than by the child protection unit. Their treatment is that of young criminals rather than young people in need of care and protection. Even where social services or voluntary bodies such as Barnardos 'Streets and Lanes Project' do offer them help and support, they can be very difficult to help. They are in fear of their boyfriends/pimps who frequently use violence or incarceration to maintain their control. Even if they are moved to another area they may be tracked down and returned by force.

9.35   It is the duty of those responsible for looking after children living away from home to do all that they can to prevent young people drifting into, or being enticed into, prostitution. This can be a difficult task, particularly since pimps may move quickly to target new entrants to children's homes before they have had a chance to settle down. Providing a stable and caring base together with help in addressing problems of low self esteem or poor knowledge of sexual and interpersonal matters and relationships will be of value. But the power imbalance between vulnerable young people and those who prey on them needs to be redressed as a matter of priority if any real progress is to be made.

9.36   Prosecutions for prostitution do not distinguish according to age – a 14 year old is treated the same as a 35 year old. And they are more common than prosecutions of those who control them and live off their earnings or who kerb crawl looking for children to buy sex from. This is no doubt, in part at least, because there have to be two charges or cautions against the prostitute before the pimp can be charged. The maximum sentence for a pimp is 2 years and it is not an offence for which there can be a remand in custody; this leaves the girl open to intimidation as well as further exploitation before the case comes to court.

9.37   Barnardos have described the different perceptions of child prostitution in terms of 3 different triangles, one representing how the girl herself sees it, another how it is currently viewed by society and the law and the third how it should be viewed, as a child protection issue:

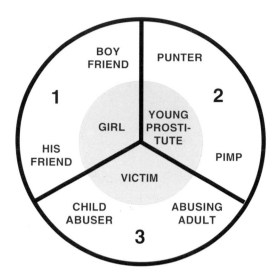

The third is clearly the appropriate view and the Review strongly recommends that it should be adopted by all those working in this area.

9.38   The ADSS Position Statement *Child Victims as Child Prostitutes* (March 1997) states that children and young people aged under 18 should be seen primarily as children in need under the Children Act and *'without exception children under 16 should be considered under the Children Act provision.'* This accords with the guidelines of the Association of Chief Police Officers. We agree that this is the right approach.

9.39   We recommend that there should be a review of the appropriate legislation to ensure that there are adequate means of deterring those who seek to exploit young people in this way and that the penalties are sufficient for this purpose. There should be power to remand in custody those who control young people for the purposes of prostitution and live off their earnings, without first having to criminalise the girls. Those who have sex with under age girls or boys should be treated as sex offenders, prosecuted as such and required to register under the Sex Offenders Act 1997. Their family circumstances should be investigated as their families may also be at risk of abuse.

9.40   All agencies should work together to ensure that there is a coherent policy for dealing with child prostitution from a child protection perspective. Area Child Protection Committees should take an active interest in the problem in their area and social services should ensure that there are staff trained in how to deal with child prostitution. Those dealing with child prostitution in police forces should have knowledge of child protection work, or work closely with those who do. Care will be needed on the part of all the agencies involved in working with the young women since to use force or coercion would confirm their alienation.

Bullying   9.41   Some adult abusers have constructed hierarchies of control, in which children they have seduced and terrorised are in turn employed to recruit and terrorise other children. Institutions characterised by physically brutal regimes have recruited a Praetorian Guard of older boys to keep the rest in order. In other cases, the absence of effective management leaves the strongest children to run the show for themselves.

9.42   Such practices are outside the meaning usually attributed to the word 'bullying'. Bullying, however, is commonly used to describe many activities which are in reality much more sinister than such a generic term suggests. It is used to cover physical violence which might otherwise be the subject of criminal prosecution, racial and sexual harassment, sexual exploitation, using threats to obtain money or property, and psychological torture. It did not surprise the Review that children in independent boarding schools in Oxfordshire put bullying near the top of the subjects that concerned them[27]. What was more interesting was that very few of them experienced bullying; they attached such importance to it because of its destructive effect on the fabric of the society in which they lived (interestingly, prisoners ascribe similar importance to it, presumably for a similar reason). Inspection reports confirm both findings: bullying remains an important issue, even though its incidence is low, and presumably much reduced. This improvement follows the greater prominence given to the subject by schools and parents nationally and the important lead given by the Department for Education and Employment through the programme exemplified by its excellent anti-bullying packs such as *Action against Bullying*[67] and *Bullying: Don't Suffer in Silence*[68]. Advances such as this need continual consolidation and reinforcement. Ways of preventing and detecting bullying must stay near the top of the agenda for all residential schools.

9.43   It seemed strange in this context that so little was said to the Review about bullying in children's homes – except by children and young people expressing past or present anxieties about their personal safety, which extended to the feelings of some of them about their safety in foster care also. Bullying and sexual exploitation by foster siblings were encountered, but children's homes afforded additional dimensions of fear and anxiety. Part of this was due to poor or desperate placement policies producing an unconsidered mix of fearsome and vulnerable residents, amounting in the opinion of the Review to systems abuse.

9.44   Just as worrying is the apparent acceptance of these consequences by staff and managers – as if casual violence, sexual molestation, threats and racial abuse characterised 'normal' adolescent behaviour and were therefore neither more nor less than could be expected in a children's home. Staff need leadership and support in establishing and maintaining civilised attitudes and values on these matters. Management should set and monitor standards of acceptable conduct, which includes the conduct of staff to residents. Demoralised and undervalued staff, unsure of the authority and sanctions they command, may collude with harassment of residents for the sake of a quiet life or practise verbal bullying themselves as a measure of control.

9.45   It should be emphasised that many homes function above the level described, but the Review is satisfied that the subject is sufficiently important for bodies providing children's homes to review their arrangements for dealing with bullying (in the wide sense in which it is used in this Report) and implement effective anti-bullying strategies.

9.46   The nature of the problem in an institution dealing with the most disturbed children was illustrated by the work of Browne and Falshaw 1996 (*Child Abuse Review Volume 5:123–127*). They studied 44 residents at Glenthorne Youth Treatment Centre, two thirds of whom were persistent violent offenders. Half the residents were regular bullies and half (including a majority of the bullies) were regularly bullied. Staff also were at risk of physical assault and sexual harassment.

9.47   Bullying is endemic in prison service establishments. People convicted of offences of violence or disposed towards violent behaviour are confined in numbers at close quarters, creating conditions in which the use or threat of physical force to obtain even marginal advantage becomes commonplace. The subject is well researched and understood. O'Donnell (*Prison Service Journal 109, 15–19*) analysed its components into assault, threats of violence, verbal abuse, cell theft, robbery and social exclusion. Young offenders are particularly vulner-able: of the inmates in the 2 Young Offender Institutions in O'Donnell's study, one third had been assaulted, one quarter threatened and one quarter suffered cell theft.

9.48   The Prison Service has a comprehensive strategy to counteract violence. The whole prison approach involves staff training, environmental controls, acquiring and using intelligence, monitoring inmate behaviour and networking between prisons. Tackling such an ingrained problem is a formidable challenge to local management, and success is partial and intermittent. HM Chief Inspector of Prisons found Lancaster Farms Young Offenders Institution[69] possessing an *'outstandingly positive anti-bullying culture'*, but strongly criticised[70] *'the apparent inability of the Prison Service to provide a reasonably safe living environment for young offenders at Dover'*, where the dormitories were *'the setting for untold bullying and criminal corruption'* and far removed from a safe living environment. Onley, he said[71], houses both young offenders and juveniles *'in conditions which are far from acceptable for either'* and *'has a reputation for violent behaviour between inmates, which it must lose'*; bullying *'was rife throughout the establishment'*. Portland[72], however, *'has treated the introduction of juveniles as a positive and constructive challenge'*.

9.49   The Review urges the Prison Service to take the management action needed to implement anti-bullying strategies consistently in all establishment in which children under the age of 18 are detained.

Chapter 10: CHILDREN'S RIGHTS AND REPRESENTATION

SYNOPSIS

This chapter considers a range of issues related to children's rights and makes some recommendations. These are unpopular in some quarters and myths of child dominance have grown. The provisions of the Children Act have been misinterpreted; it does not say that children must always have their own way. The implementation of the Act in respect of rights has been patchy. Children's involvement in reviews of their progress has not been uniformly successful and the formal complaints procedure has not been much used by children.

The Review is concerned that the arrangements for protecting children from abuse should be effective and consistent across all settings in which they live away from home. There is no justification for different levels of protection against abuse or harm. It supports the recommendation by the British Association of Social Workers that *'the law should establish a set of legal rights and protections applying to all children living away from home.'* The right to use corporal punishment should be removed from those boarding schools which still retain it (paragraph 10.6).

Children have a right not to be returned to a home where they will be abused again. The primary duty is to the child and the balance of risks should always be in the child's favour (paragraph 10.7).

The Review received more information about treatment for abusers than about treatment for abused children. It believes abused children have a right to therapy if they want it and that it should attract high priority from public funds. Local and health authorities should ensure that it is provided. The capacity of staff to assist their treatment should be developed by training (paragraph 10.9).

The Review supports the development of children's rights services. Local authorities should offer a service of this kind to all the children they look after. Children's rights should be included in training for all staff who work in residential settings (paragraph 10.11). Children wishing to use the formal complaints procedure should be entitled to the services of an advocate. This is particularly important for disabled children with communication or mobility difficulties (paragraph 10.12).

Local authorities fall short in providing Independent Visitors as required by the Children Act. All local authorities should provide Independent Visitors (paragraph 10.14). The scheme should be developed to the fullest extent possible. Independent people could also perform such monitoring functions as exit interviews for children leaving care (paragraph 10.15). It is not known how many people are available for this voluntary work and the Review recommends that the Department of Health/Welsh Office supports a project to test the feasibility of providing independent visitors to all children looked after by local authorities who might benefit from them (paragraph 10.16).

The Review considers it important that those who have been in local authority care are represented on bodies which act as advocates and contribute to the development of policy and practice nationally. A new organisation for young people who are or have been in care is needed which should be supported from statutory as well as charitable sources (paragraph 10.17).

Black children encounter institutionalised as well as personally focused racism. Failure to understand and cater for specific health and personal care undermines their self esteem and identifies them as children it is relatively safe to abuse. A positive sense of identity is important. Cultural needs should be met in every setting in which a child is living and experience provided which reinforces cultural identity. A holistic framework based on the Children Act which addresses the needs of ethnic minority children is essential. This needs continual repetition and reinforcement and the claims of black children need continuous advocacy. Providing for them needs an additional dimension to policy, practice and resources. Black disabled children need special attention, as may black girls, who tend to be in a minority (paragraphs 10.19,10.23).

Equivalent effort to that needed to foster a positive sense of identity is needed to combat racism. The Review supports the statement by the Racial Equality Unit that *'Black children and young people have the right to be protected from the harmful impact of institutional and personal racism'*. Bodies with responsibilities for children living away from home should possess effective policies for preventing and confronting all forms of racial harassment and ensure managers enforce them. No adult with responsibilities for children living away from home should 'not notice' it or assume nothing can be done (paragraph 10.25).

Gender issues permeate services for children living away from home. Women staff and girl residents may be sexually harassed by both male staff and residents. This should be regarded as seriously as racial harassment and appropriate sanctions and training applied to perpetrators (paragraph 10.27).

The presence of women can be an effective force in residential services and provide an extra safeguard. The Review recommends an appropriate gender balance in the management of residential services for children, within the overall policy of appointments being made on merit (paragraph 10.28).

The daily reality of sexual feelings in residential settings cannot be ignored. The Review recommends that training materials such as those produced by Kidscape should be used as early as possible to introduce children living away from home to what is 'normal' physical and sexual conduct (paragraph 10.29).

'A central principle of the Children Act..... is that the voice of the child must be heard.'

UK 1st Report on the Rights of the Child 1994.

'Looked-after children are at greater risk than most from negative public attitudes to children, since they are "other people's children".'

The British Association of Social Workers: Submission

'Adopting a children's rights perspective does not mean empowering children to reject order and disregard boundaries, or leave residential workers powerless with no authority or control.'

Christine Barter – Who's to Blame?

10.1   Mention of children's rights provokes a sour response in some quarters, along the lines that the Children Act destroyed parental authority to control and discipline children. There is indeed a set of difficult issues about control and discipline, but they are of long standing and have little to do with the Children Act. Underlying the Act is a strong sense of the value of children, and one of its main purposes is to safeguard and promote their welfare. In the narrower area of rights, however, it specified circumstances in which they were to be consulted about what was proposed for them, and their views were to be taken into account. It is also clear that they have a right not to be physically or sexually abused, and to have factors such as race, culture and religion considered when decisions are made about them.

10.2   These are and remain important. Around them, however, have grown myths of child dominance and omnipotence. A proportion of staff polled for their views by one voluntary body believed that the Children Act 'enabled young people to make decisions that they are ill-equipped to make'. A similar proportion percipiently observed that staff used the Children Act as an excuse for inaction in protecting young people. This view was echoed in a personal submission which deplored *'the growing tendency for the SSD spokesperson to say that the Children Act prevented them from doing the job properly'*. The Children Act does not say that children must always have their own way, or that they must always be believed. Such loose attributions are made by adults grasping for excuses for welshing on their responsibilities to children.

10.3   Indeed, what is so striking in the implementation of the Act is the patchy way in which provisions bearing on rights have been addressed. One of the most fundamental was the participation of children looked after by the local authority in the periodic reviews of their progress. Nothing appears more reasonable to the Review than young people being consulted about major decisions in their lives and their considered views taken seriously into account. Yet in the sixth year since the Act came into force, the former Association of Metropolitan Authorities could say in its submission: *'many children do not like formal review meetings and are unable to express their wishes and feelings adequately. Even when they are able to contribute many children may not feel that their views are given sufficient weight by the professionals who may be present'*. Much importance was also attached to the formal representations and complaints procedure provided under Section 26 of the Act but inspections and other evidence have established that children are unlikely to use this unless they are supported by an advocate.

10.4   The formal settings in which children live away from home remain controlled by adults. The spirit of the legislation is that control should be directed, like the other factors in the situation, to the overall welfare of the child. Responsible adults will need from time to time to exercise that control against the child's immediate wishes for the sake of his or her welfare in the longer term. Wishes ascertained should be considered but may then be discounted in relation to other considerations. SSI standards in *Inspecting for Quality* [73] set out – among other things – the criteria against which performance in implementing children's rights can be assessed.

10.5   The Review's proper concern here is that the arrangements for protecting children from abuse and harm should be effective, and that these should be as consistent as possible across all the settings in which children live away from home. There are obvious differences, derived from statute and regulation, between the restriction of liberty of a 17 year old in a young offender institution and the position of his contemporary in a children's home, but inconsistencies in other respects are more difficult to justify. A child detained under the Mental Health Act, for example, appears to have stronger legal protection than one admitted informally. There is no justification at all for different levels of protection against abuse or harm. This caused me to recommend in 1991 [1] that the Department of Health '*review, with other interested groups, the legislation safeguarding the welfare of children across the full range of residential settings.*' The problem was authoritatively analysed in *One Scandal too Many* (1993). The submission made to the Review by APPROACH recommended that:

> '*The only adequate solution is through a principled legal framework which gives children, wherever they are living, at least equal protection to that enjoyed by adults under the law on assault.*'

10.6   The Review supports the view of the British Association of Social Workers that '*the law should establish a set of legal rights and protections applying to all children living away from home*', and recommends that the Government takes steps to achieve this. My position on these matters is reflected in the report of the Commission on Children and Violence [74] which I chaired for the Gulbenkian Foundation in 1995. '*Reasonable chastisement*' should not constitute a defence to actions for physical assaults on children living away from home. The right to use corporal punishment should be removed from those boarding schools which still retain it. Inspection reports make plain that a number of schools which are able to use this punishment have in fact discontinued it. The Review identified one case where excessive use of the cane was the central form of serious abuse, and the most effective way of discouraging physical violence against children is to make it plain that none is acceptable. Children should also be defended against punitive forms of 'treatment'.

10.7   Children also have a right not to be returned to a home in which they will be abused again. The Review received anecdotal information about children returning for weekends and holidays to families from which they had been removed, and abused again. We were told by some young people that they had been discharged from local authority accommodation to families who abused them again. The Review appreciates (without necessarily approving) the pressure on officials to rehabilitate families as units, but the primary duty is to the child and the balance of risks should always be plainly in the child's favour.

Treatment 10.8 Gough and Murray, in *Research Literature on the Prevention of Child Abuse*[7], report that the effects of abuse include emotional dysfunction, behavioural problems, relationship problems, cognitive distortions and post-traumatic stress. 40% of victims appear symptom free. The worst effects are experienced by children for whom the abuse was frequent, long lasting, penetrative, violent, or conducted by a close relative.

10.9 The Review received more information about treatment for abusers than about treatment for abused children. Provision for the latter, and for those who look after them, seems to depend upon haphazard awareness of need coinciding with the availability of scarce services. Abused children should in the eyes of the Review attract high priority for treatment from public funds – especially children who have been abused while in public care. We believe that they have a right to help. Local and health authorities should ensure that it is provided. Assessment and consent are required, since not all children need, want or would benefit from therapy. The capacity of staff looking after children to assist their treatment should be developed by training.

Children's Rights Services 10.10 One of the most beneficial developments of the last decade has been the arrival and gradual development of children's rights services for young people looked after by local authorities. Children's rights officers are by no means universal (28 in post in 1996), or universally popular. This may be because they inevitably throw grit in the managerial, administrative and professional machines. These engines may work better as a result (that is, more in the interests of the children they are supposed to serve), but harassed people do not always welcome being deflected from other problems to return to those they thought they had cracked. Local authorities need to be committed to life becoming less comfortable for them – in the interests of the children they are looking after – if children's rights officers are to thrive. Another criticism is that they erode still further the role of the field social worker as advocate for the individual child; but the difficulty faced by social workers in 'taking on' their authority on behalf of a child is one of the reasons why children's rights officers are needed.

10.11 The Review offers no observations on whether children's rights officers should be employed by local authorities or provided on a contractual basis by voluntary organisations. The theoretical advantages and disadvantages seem equally balanced, and might be summarised as 'independence' versus 'ownership'. The situation on the ground is perhaps more relevant in deciding who should provide the service. The Review's main concern is that local authorities should offer it to all the children they look after, whether in residential homes or foster care. We also believe that children's rights should be included in training for all staff who work in residential settings.

10.12 A number of voluntary organisations also offer advocacy services for looked after children. The Review believes that children wishing to use the formal complaints procedure should be entitled to the services of an advocate. This is particularly important for disabled children with communication or mobility difficulties.

Independent Visitors 10.13 Local authorities have a duty under paragraph 17(1) of Schedule 2 to the Children Act to provide a child with an independent visitor if he or she is out of contact or in infrequent contact with a parent. I recommended in 1991[1] that independent visitors also be considered for disabled children and other children in residential care. The reality, however, is that local authorities fall short of what is already required, even though a number of voluntary organisations have developed schemes for encouraging and supporting independent visitors.

10.14   Possible explanations are that local authorities may not like what appears to be an incursion upon their own duty to help looked after children. They may not regard it as important in comparison with other statutory duties which fully extend them. They may fear paedophiles descending in the guise of earnest volunteers. They may not know what kind of people they need or how to recruit them. They may not even have absorbed the message. Whatever the reason, there is no justification for failure to discharge this duty 6 years after it came into force. All local authorities should ensure that they are able to provide looked after children with independent visitors in line with Schedule 2 to the Children Act.

10.15   I remain of the view that independent visitor schemes should be developed to the fullest extent possible. There are limitations, of course: if genuine partnership with a parent makes it unnecessary or undesirable, if the care plan does not need it, or if a child is opposed to it. Resources are needed to recruit, induct and supervise the visitors, or to pay a voluntary organisation to do so. Yet the benefits for a child in residential or foster care of a stable and continuous relationship with an adult who is independent of the care organisation and the care staff seem to outweigh both theoretical and practical objections, especially for children who are disabled or placed far from their home authority. Such independent people could also perform the monitoring function of conducting exit interviews for young people leaving care.

10.16   One of the important unknowns is whether sufficient suitable people are available for voluntary work of this kind. Voluntary organisations have so far succeeded in staffing specific projects. Volunteers have been prepared to submit to recruitment criteria at least as stringent as for the paid staff who work with children. The question is whether they are there in sufficient numbers to meet all the needs that might exist for volunteers to staff advocacy and visitor schemes. Further testing of the market is needed. The Review recommends that the Department of Health/Welsh Office supports a project to assess the feasibility of providing independent visitors to all children looked after by local authorities who might benefit from them.

A Collective Voice   10.17   A number of organisations do impressive work in representing the interests of young people in residential and foster care. It is important that those who are or have been in local authority care should be represented by bodies which not only act as advocates but also contribute to the development of policy and practice nationally. Voices From Care does this for young people in Wales, but those in England have been without similar representation since the closure of the National Association of Young People in Care. First*Key* and the National Children's Bureau are completing a study for the Department of Health of the feasibility of establishing a new organisation for young people who are or have been in care. The Review believes that such an organisation should be set up and supported from statutory as well as from charitable sources.

Race   10.18   Submissions to the Review contained few references to the significance of racial issues beyond identifying black children as one of the groups who were particularly liable to abuse and harm when living away from home. Most of the few comments about the vulnerability of black children in the care system were made orally in meetings which black people attended. The Review found this comparative lack of comment surprising. It accordingly commissioned the Race Equality Unit to prepare a paper on safeguards for black children in the care system, which included consultation with black adults and children. What follows draws on this and other material, but the opinions expressed are the Review's.

10.19   Black children and children of mixed parentage have always been over-represented among children in local authority care and in schools for children with emotional and behavioural difficulties. They tend to stay in care longer than white children, a probable indication of weakened family support and, consequently, of personal vulnerability. Barn, Sinclair and Ferdinand[75] found in their study of three local authorities that 1 in 3 Afro-Caribbean children they looked after remained for more than 5 years compared with 1 in 10 of the white children. Black children encounter institutionalised as well as personally focused racism. Failure to understand and cater for specific health and personal care needs may further undermine their self esteem and identify them as disregarded children whom it is relatively safe to abuse.

10.20   A positive sense of identity, of being somebody, of belonging to oneself, is an inner strength which provides the strongest personal defence against harm. Helping children achieve that identity is one of the aims of education, and ought to be an explicit objective of any organisation entrusted with the care of children. This sense of identity is derived from membership of family and other groups with similar values with which early life experience is shared. Detachment from family and culture plainly impairs its development; membership of a distinctive or disadvantaged community may compound the difficulties; in the case of black children, their situation is further aggravated by the pervasive effects of racism.

10.21   The importance of identity was acknowledged in Section 22 of the Children Act, which required local authorities to *'give due consideration... to the child's religious persuasion, racial origin and cultural and linguistic background'* in arriving at decisions about him. Children Act Guidance (Volume 3, 2.40) is as explicit as general guidance can be: *'It may be taken as a guiding principle of good practice that, other things being equal and in the great majority of cases, placement with a family of similar ethnic origin and religion is most likely to meet a child's needs as fully as possible and* **to safeguard his or her welfare most effectively** *(emphasis added).'*

10.22   Cultural needs should be met in every setting in which a child is living. As the Race Equality Unit points out, this is not easily achieved at second hand or at a distance, and casework on the subject provides examples of children stranded between cultures. Culture is best acquired by living it; if it cannot be lived, forms of compensatory experience should be provided. Same race and same religion placements should be sought in fostering, and access provided in residential homes and schools to experiences which reinforce cultural identity, within an overall approach to the total needs of the child as an individual. Same race (or same religion) placement does not over-ride all other considerations. *'Placement decisions (Barn, Sinclair and Ferdinand, op cit) are about finding the best available option to meet all the needs of a child. A holistic framework based on the Children Act and which addresses the needs of minority ethnic children in a comprehensive fashion, while taking account of individual emotional and psychological factors, is essential.'*

10.23   The call for special attention to the cultural needs of ethnic minority children needs continual repetition and reinforcement, or it gets lost amid the everyday clamour of organisational and institutional life. The forces of inertia resume their control, and the organisation reverts to assuming that the needs of minorities are automatically met in serving the interests of the majority. The claims of black children, as of other minorities, need continuous advocacy in this respect. Providing for them requires an additional dimension to policy, practice and – not least – resources: in, for example, a wider range of foster homes, extended support to residential homes and schools, and particular provision for health and personal care. Black disabled children need special attention in order to prevent their being doubly disadvantaged. So may black girls – girls already being in a minority in residential homes and the penal setting.

10.24   Whereas effort is needed on behalf of black children to support the development of personal identity, equivalent efforts are needed to combat the effects of racism. These are so pernicious that sustained and sensitive commitment are needed to overcome them. The Review supports the statement by the Race Equality Unit that '*Black children and young people have the right to be protected from the harmful impact of institutional and personal racism*'. The Unit identifies racial abuse in residential settings by children or staff (including the tolerance by staff of racial abuse by children), racial abuse in substitute families, and racial abuse by others (known – as at school, or by strangers).

10.25   Bodies with responsibilities for children living away from home should possess effective policies for preventing and confronting all forms of racial harassment and ensure that managers enforce them. These policies need to take into account specific features of the setting: very different in foster care, for example, from a young offender institution with a gang-based bullying problem. No adult with responsibilities for children living away from home should 'not notice' racial harassment or take the line that it is one of life's inescapable realities about which nothing can be done.

Gender

10.26   Gender issues permeate services for children living away from home. Physical care and emotional nurturing – subordinated in the hierarchy of importance to objectives such as education or containment – have traditionally been seen as 'women's work'. Women staff were caught in the double bind of less important people doing less important work. In extreme cases, children suffered from regimes so unbalanced that they were emotionally abusive, or from cultures of homosexual abuse by males which depended in part upon excluding women.

10.27   Most of these extreme cases, fortunately, are now part of history. Elsewhere, strains from the past linger stubbornly in the fabric of our institutions. Women staff and girl residents may be sexually harassed by both male staff and residents. Sexual harassment should be regarded as seriously as racial harassment in environments in which children are living away from home, and appropriate sanctions and training applied to perpetrators.

10.28   The Review received strong advice that the presence of women as an effective force in the management of residential services provided an additional safeguard for children, particularly against sexual abuse by members of staff. The Review believes that having women in the senior management of residential services for children is a good thing for other reasons too, providing a broader perspective and a wider range of skills. It accordingly recommends an appropriate gender balance in the management of residential services for children, within the overall policy of appointments being made on merit.

Sexual Behaviour

10.29 More explicit acknowledgement is needed of the daily reality of sexual feeling and of the sometimes highly charged form in which it seeks expression in residential settings, particularly where the majority of residents are adolescent. This is not something that can be ignored or dealt with on the basis that those who are stupid enough to be found out can expect to be punished. Protocols of conduct and control in relation to sex are needed, based on education, and taking account of heterosexual and homosexual feelings. These protocols should be based on the responsibilities of the organisation and its staff towards the children cared for. The diversity of sexual behaviour in society is such that staff as well as children need orientating to what is and is not acceptable in a residential setting. Department of Health Guidance on Permissible Forms of Control in Children's Residential Care[76] noted that *'The problem of sexual attraction between staff and young people in their care is an important one and authorities should also consider including this in their induction programme.'* The effect on children of sexual relationships between staff also needs to be taken into account.

10.30 Children looked after away from home need to understand what is regarded as 'normal' behaviour, particularly in relation to physical and sexual conduct. They also need to know what might be unacceptable in the conduct of others. The Review found material produced by Kidscape and other voluntary organisations helpful in this respect. It recommends that bodies responsible for children living away from home introduce them to such teaching as early as possible and renew it periodically. The review also believes that these children should receive sex education appropriate to their age.

PART IV – COMMON THEMES II: STAFF AND INSTITUTIONS

Chapter 11: THE INSTITUTIONAL CONTEXT

SYNOPSIS

This chapter examines the institutional context in which abuse can occur. It describes some of the ingredients needed for a safe level of care and some of the characteristics of abusive regimes.

It quotes a research-based view that the keys to success are leadership, a clear and achievable job, a philosophy owned by staff, and continuity. The culture of the institution, the role of the head, gender issues and sexual relationships are all important elements. It is suggested that issues relating to sexual behaviour in residential settings need to be confronted more directly by managers and supervisors.

It concludes that the shift in the balance of power between children and adults has not been as great as the legislation intended, or as some believe.

It discusses the relationship between safety and control of children and young people. It outlines the differences and commonality of approaches in guidance for different settings, and suggests that these give rise to four 'levels' in the way the issue is dealt with. Whether or not an approach designed for one setting is appropriate in another gives rise to uncertainty and confusion among carers, particularly in relation to physical restraint.

It recommends that:

> The Department of Health, the Department for Education and Employment and the Home Office consider commissioning a study which surveys issues of control across all settings for which these Departments have a policy responsibility with a view to publishing a handbook of guidance and standards for managers and practitioners (paragraph 11.28).

Culture   11.1   Detailed inquiries into prolonged abuse in institutions have invariably revealed failures in their host organisation which have helped abuse to occur and persist. At the root of these failures is the unwillingness or inability of the organisation to acknowledge or implement its primary task of keeping children safe. This obligation extends with equal force to all children: nice and nasty, criminal and orphan, deserving and undeserving. It is plainly more difficult to fulfil with some than with others. Organisations and institutions working with those 'others' may themselves be rejected by the rest of us, who also play a part thereby in creating the isolation and indifference whereby abuse can thrive in institutional settings.

11.2   The caring task can be so complex that even the most genuinely motivated bodies have difficulty in performing it to the standards set for them. The Welsh Local Government Association (submission) made a succinct statement of what constitutes *'a high level and a safe level of care'* for looked after children:

'a) *a proper needs-led assessment of each child in, or likely to enter, the looked after system*

b) *a choice of accommodation to meet those needs*

c) *access to specialist advice and services*

d) *a high quality of care provided by qualified, trained, supported and secure staff, appointed following a rigorous selection process*

e) *a valid and comprehensive inspection, registration and monitoring process*

f) *the provision of good quality education*

g) *mechanisms to ensure that children can make their voices heard.'*

This prescription for children whom local authorities look after is not easy to deliver to the same high standard throughout. But all bodies discharging parental responsibilities must be able to achieve as much as they promise. Without their commitment and achievement overall, the residential services they rely on are left to drift or to go their own way.

11.3   The culture of the organisation, therefore, is of great general importance to the welfare of the children for whom it is responsible. Its quality does not necessarily determine the quality of all its residential establishments: some homes and schools survive and even prosper in unfavourable environments, while poor provision may occasionally be encountered in very effective organisations. Overall, however, the achieving organisation provides much higher levels of safety and security for children than its failing counterpart.

11.4   It is the culture of the particular residential setting, however, which has the most immediate impact and effect on the children who live there. The worst cultures are graphically described in inquiry reports. The Leicestershire Inquiry 1992 [77] provides a particularly telling account of how Frank Beck established and perpetuated a culture of abuse based on fear and intimidation. This strategy kept management at bay while he suborned colleagues into colluding with and participating in his physical and sexual abuse of children. Another abusive institution from the same period was characterised as 'run for the convenience of the staff'. Management acted out the worst features of a male-dominated clique, and residents were subdued by their fear of staff living on site, who possessed a spurious reputation for expertise in dealing with 'difficult' youngsters. A less extreme example is the care unit attached to a special school, which was described in another inquiry report as subjecting residents to *'a regime which was often uncaring, emotionally abusive and which resulted in physical harm coming to some of those children'.*

11.5   The Final Report of The Support Force[5] reported discussion at a seminar of *'the circumstances in which abuse can occur in residential settings and considered measures which can help to avoid such circumstances arising. It noted the characteristics of institutions which had been found to be abusive; they often had a charismatic leader with apparent expertise; had a good reputation and were seen as being successful; and dealt with a damaged and vulnerable client group with low self-esteem, usually children or young people whom the relevant authority had found hard to place and who were regarded as 'unreliable' witnesses. The context in which abuse occurred usually involved an exclusion or absence of outside contact, such as with the family or field social worker, and a lack of effective scrutiny by external managers. In addition, the accepted pattern of relationships and behaviour within the home often contributed to an environment in which abuse could pass undetected or unreported or be accepted as "normal" behaviour.'*

11.6   Lindsay (submission) speaks of an abusive culture – in terms which apply to children's homes and boarding schools – exhibiting high rates of worrying incidents over a period, high levels of children running away, a restrictive and isolating regime, poor staff morale, a lack of staff whom children trust, children and staff fearful of the consequences of complaining, and abuse taking place under the cloak of therapy. Another distinctive feature of abuse in institutions is the subversion or distortion of formal authority and the acquisition and exercise of illegitimate power by determined abusers. External managers are sidelined, responsible subordinates undermined, collusive colleagues gratified, children frightened into submission, and impressionable outsiders bamboozled by the display of energy and control.

11.7   Corrupt regimes are totally abusive. Children are assaulted physically for sadistic satisfaction or to keep them in order; they are groomed, seduced or frightened into sexual submission; the climate of uncertainty and fear eliminates confidence; the overall effect is destructive of normal emotional development.

Power   *'The primary functions of care and protection were eroded not simply by the behaviour of the skilled lone manipulator, but by the conduciveness of the organisational culture to abuse of power.'*
Colton and Vanstone: Betrayal of Trust

11.8   The gap in power between staff and vulnerable groups of children is used by unscrupulous adults to manipulate every situation in furtherance of their designs. Young children, disabled children, children with learning disabilities and children with emotional and behavioural difficulties are all, for different reasons and in different ways, more dependent than the average on their relationships with caring adults in authority. Abusers exploit this dependence to bring children into the circle of abuse and imprison them there, demonstrating that for those children there is literally no escape.

11.9   The role of the head of the residential home or a school is crucial – for better or for worse. Frank Beck instituted a regime which he controlled by intimidating and corrupting staff as well as children. Others have allowed subordinates licence to indulge their criminal tastes because of their passivity or conniving disregard of their responsibilities. Sinclair (submission) says that children's homes, in particular, run well if they are small; if the head has a clear remit, which is feasible, and has the mandate to do it; if the staff as a group possess a coherent philosophy of care; and if the whole is not undermined by frequent re-organisations. The keys to success are leadership, a clear and achievable job, a philosophy owned by staff, and continuity. The criterion for safeguarding children against abuse is, according to NCH Action for Children (submission), *'Child protection needs to be integrated into the practice of a home and all systems, processes and procedures must be examined from a child protection focus.'*

11.10   Gender issues are important in institutional culture. Institutions in the grip of homosexually or physically abusive men commonly display a 'macho' culture in which female qualities are ridiculed and women staff undermined to the point at which their whistleblowing is not listened to. In other establishments, collusion between male staff and residents in demeaning women may extend to the tolerance of overt sexual harassment of women staff and the creation of an environment which is less safe for children as well as for staff. Herring (submission) speaks of *'the vulnerability of women workers'* and of *'a general neglect of particular issues which may be associated with females giving care and handling the acting-out behaviours and sexuality of adolescents'*. Sexual relationships between staff members may set corrupting examples to children; both male and female members of staff have contracted sexual relationships with children; girl residents – invariably in a minority in mixed establishments – have felt forced into unwanted sexual relationships with other children. Issues relating to sexual behaviour in residential settings need to be more directly confronted by managers and supervisors.

11.11   Power is not invariably displayed by staff against child. Children sometimes assault staff, as well as each other, or themselves, precipitating proper but very difficult questions about control and discipline. The legislation of the last decade has caused a gradual shift in practice in the balance of power between children and adults. Consultation, participation, even complaints are provided for, and encouraged in varying degrees. Some adults allege that children have too much power – including the power of ruining an adult's life by an unfounded allegation of abuse. In reality, the shift has not everywhere been very great, and depends upon the enthusiasm with which the spirit of the legislation – rather than its letter – is put into practice. Kicks against the system, damaging as they may be to individuals, are still the marks of a dispossessed minority reacting against perceived oppression.

The Link Between Control and Safety

11.12   The recent history of concern for the safety of children living away from home bears witness to the interrelationship between their safety and the means of keeping children within reasonable control. It is alarmingly easy for the care and control of vulnerable or difficult children to slip over into abuse. This ease can result in regimes drifting into cultures of abuse. It can be exploited by people intent on abuse.

11.13   The 'Pindown' practices described by Levy and Kahan[6] were a response to the perceived need to control allegedly unruly young people, ill-judged, insular and abusive though they were. Frank Beck's methods involved provoking children into losing their control in order for staff to justify abusive physical intervention. The Review team heard descriptions of special residential schools for children with emotional and behavioural difficulties where the regime appeared to concentrate on discipline and control and the consequent staff culture harboured abusive behaviour.

11.14 The Review team heard directly and graphically from people it met how, in another sense, issues of safety and issues of controlling children were interlinked. When asked about what 'feeling safe' meant to them, young people who had experienced local authority care spontaneously responded in terms of being able to keep possessions safe from being seized by other young people.

11.15 In a largish group one young person spoke of her discomfort at living in a room with a window which was kept locked in order to resist intruders. Voices from the group responded loudly 'break it!'.

11.16 Several young people who had been in care told the Review that on balance it was better for them to live in a place designed for security and control (including closed circuit television and locked bedroom doors) than for them to be living in more homely surroundings. They said it was better to be kept controlled than moved from home to home, because their placement was deemed to have broken down as a result of their uncontrolled behaviour.

11.17 Generally, our contact with young people suggested that they were as keen as their adult carers that they be kept under control. Several recognised that there were times when their behaviour had been intolerable and should have been controlled but in ways which were not abusive and maintained respect for them.

11.18 At the beginning of a meeting about safeguards a group of senior local authority staff referred to the difficulty they had experienced in putting into practice the Department of Health guidance on permissible forms of control.

11.19 During the period the Review was working there was publicity suggesting that staff were powerless to stop young women leaving children's homes to work as prostitutes. Staff wrestle with judgements about how far they can go legally and practically to stop young people leaving so that they neither cause harm or are themselves harmed. Some staff seem to see control as the primary and overriding rationale for the existence of their establishment and are much concerned with how far they can go and still enjoy the support of their employers and the protection of the law. Others recognise their responsibility to keep children safe by exercising control and worry about how far they can take measures before they become oppressive or even dangerous in themselves – a balancing judgement which has to be made every time a decision is made to restrain a child. It is clear that residential care staff and teachers worry about allegations of abuse being levelled at them as a result of their needing to intervene physically to control children.

Control in Different Settings

11.20 Issues of control are not the same in every setting where children are looked after. There will be common ground but there are also clear differences in the feasibility of approaches to control in different settings such as schools, children's homes or foster homes. For example, it would not be sensible to place a child who frequently needed to be physically restrained with a single foster carer. Keeping control in a classroom is not the same as keeping control in a home setting. Techniques for maintaining safety and control in schools for children with severe learning disabilities and challenging behaviour will be different to those used in other settings.

11.21   Guidance has not been directed uniformly at the different settings where children are cared for away from home: residential care, foster care, schools, health units and settings for children with severe learning difficulties and challenging behaviour.

11.22   The primary contemporary guidance for residential care is Volume 4 in the Children Act series written in 1991. Practitioners perceived this guidance as prohibiting measures of discipline without saying what staff could do to control children. The Department of Health responded to this by issuing guidance in 1993[76] which defined the parameters within which staff should make judgements about specific interventions. This brought forth complaints that the guidance did not actually say how to get hold of children to restrain them physically. In 1997, in response to a media campaign which argued that the Children Act took away from staff their power to control children, particularly to prevent them leaving open homes, the Government responded with a Chief Inspector letter (CI (97) 6)[78] which aimed to clarify its interpretation of the law and suggested that staff should lock doors to restrict the mobility of children they were concerned about. There remains no Government guidance on safe techniques for restraining children.

11.23   Despite the requirement in Regulations that foster carers agree not to administer corporal punishment, the guidance issued with the Children Act gave no advice on approaches to behaviour and control in foster care. The assumption is that this would be taken into account in care plans for the child. The Chief Inspector letter (op cit)[78] has the title *The Control of Children in the Public Care: Interpretation of the Children Act 1989* and as such covers foster care. However a substantial section refers to earlier guidance written specifically for residential care and nothing is said expressly for foster carers.

11.24   In 1994, the then Department for Education published a series of circulars collectively entitled *Pupils with Problems*. Circular 8/94, *Pupil Behaviour and Discipline*[79], draws on the Elton Report[80] and is concerned with policies for creating a school ethos which promotes the good order necessary to allow pupils to flourish educationally. Another circular, published jointly with the Department of Health, *The Education of Children with Emotional and Behavioural Difficulties*[33], gives advice on the early identification and assessment of pupils with these difficulties, the use of residential schools, and includes a section on Controls Restrictions and Sanctions which has more to say about intervention than Circular 8/94. This advice is consistent with the Children Act Regulations and Guidance. It also make specific reference to the Department of Health circular on *Permissible Forms of Control in Children's Residential Care*[76] as a source of advice to staff in residential special schools.

11.25   Apart from the Code of Practice to the Mental Health Act 1983, there does not appear to be any Government guidance concerning practices to maintain control of children in health settings. It appeared to the Review that health providers looked to the guidance written for the Children Act when composing local protocols.

11.26   The approach of guidance prepared by the Mental Health Foundation[81] has been shaped by the need to consider specifically how learning disabled children with extremely challenging and self destructive behaviour should be controlled. The point is made that the Department of Health guidance makes no mention of children with severe disabilities and was not intended to address the needs of these children. It suggests that children with extremes of behaviour which threaten their own and others' safety may require extraordinary methods to keep them controlled and safe and that these are legitimate provided they can be defended in law. Grounds for justifying actions must generally be based on the need to act in the interests of the child's welfare.

Different Approaches to the Issue of Control and Discipline

11.27   It is possible from studying the content and gaps in this material to discern approaches to issues of control at different 'levels'.

Ethos   Volume 4 and the Department for Education and Employment guidance are concerned largely with creating conditions to promote good order. Clarity of purpose, clear policies and staff who have a common understanding of what they are doing are common themes.

Intervention   *The Guidance on Permissible Forms of Control* is concerned much more with the direct engagement of staff with children and the judgements they have to make about intervention. This guidance touches on, but does not explore, skills and techniques.

Technique   There is training available on the skills and techniques for intervening physically but no official guidance.

Defensibility   The Mental Health Foundation guidance tackles the issues in terms of defensibility in law.

These four levels for addressing control issues pervade all settings but have varying prominence. Because staff and children move between settings there is a need for consistency wherever possible and, where different approaches are required in order to ensure the safety of children with particular needs, then the reasons for this need to be made clear to all parties. The Review senses that control issues have been fairly well aired in recent years but that there is still considerable uncertainty and confusion. There is an outstanding need for a comprehensive study in the form of a survey which draws together thinking and maps approaches between different settings and at different levels so as to promote clarity of understanding and consistency. Notwithstanding the importance of the twenty-four hour curriculum particular to educational settings, there is sufficient common ground between residential school care units and children's homes in their interest in control to suggest that the Department for Education and Employment and Department of Health explore the possibility of jointly commissioning such a study. There would also be merit in embracing the Home Office in such an exercise to take account of young people in prison establishments and expertise within the Prison Service College. The desired product would be a publication, possibly in the form of a handbook of standards, mapping consistency and difference across all settings where children are looked after away from home, together with supportive literature and guidance consistent with contemporary legislation and the identification of training resources.

11.28   The Review recommends that Department of Health, the Department for Education and Employment and the Home Office consider commissioning a study which surveys issues of control across all settings for which these Departments have a policy responsibility with a view to publishing a comprehensive handbook of guidance and standards for managers and practitioners.

Chapter 12:　**TRAINING**

SYNOPSIS

This chapter takes a broad view of training at various levels and across several care settings. It draws on research findings and addresses the implications of a major study which found no association between the quality of care children received in children's homes and the qualifications of the staff. The chapter suggests that training is likely to be useful if carers work to clear objectives, have a coherent view of what they are trying to achieve and believe in what they are doing. The content of training courses at all levels of qualification must support these requirements, as must the way the institution is managed. We suggest that the training requirements of staff in the care units of residential special schools and staff in children's homes may be so similar as to merit joint consideration by the Department for Education and Employment and the Department of Health.

Recommendations are that:

> The Central Council for Education and Training in Social Work should specify the content of child care training on courses which lead to qualifications by defining the content of a curriculum of learning, in addition to describing the competencies and the standards which must be demonstrated (paragraph 12.22).

> The Department for Education and Employment and Department of Health jointly review and explore the scope for a common approach to developing training opportunities for carers in schools and homes in relation to National Vocational Qualifications and the Diploma in Social Work qualifications (paragraph 12.28).

> The Department of Health and the Department for Education and Employment commission the production of further training materials designed for the in-service training of carers without professional qualifications in schools and homes (paragraph 12.31).

> Local authorities should ensure that training is available for all foster carers and should pay particular attention to the needs of experienced carers (paragraph 12.34).

The chapter also considers the need for training materials dealing with the professional understanding of perpetrators of abuse and recommends that

> the Department of Health and the Home Office jointly explore the potential for developing guidance and training materials designed to heighten awareness of child care professionals about the profiles and methods of perpetrators of child sexual abuse (paragraph 12.37).

Levels of Training

12.1   We have asserted elsewhere that a key determinant of the safety of children living away from home is the general quality of care they receive. This chapter is about how staff are trained to deliver that care.

12.2   Training for social care is a complex field. This Review has not carried out a systematic survey of issues relating to the training of staff engaged in the direct care of children. In the course of our enquiries we have acquired evidence and ideas about training which are pertinent to the safety of children in children's homes, foster care, residential special schools and boarding schools. We do not address training issues for staff in penal and health settings.

12.3   We have identified three broad levels of training: pre-professional in-service training; qualifying training; and post-qualifying training.

12.4   **In-service training** does not in itself lead to a qualification. Its purpose is to equip staff and foster carers to do their jobs better. However in-service training can lead to National Vocational Qualifications (NVQs) if staff can demonstrate competence across a range of occupational standards which make up an award. NVQs are not training courses; they are simply awards. How workers attain competence is secondary to their being able to demonstrate those competencies to the requisite standards. However at the higher NVQ levels (3 and 4) it may be necessary to go on courses in order to acquire the underpinning knowledge required to demonstrate competence. National occupational standards require that underpinning knowledge is specified.

12.5   **Qualifying training** in social work requires participation in a course of training which leads to a Diploma in Social Work. There is a core social work content but the routes (or pathways) and the content of parts of a course can vary in order to accommodate students from different circumstances and with different intended career intentions. In response to the recommendation in *Children in the Public Care* [1] that, as a minimum, heads of children's homes should be professionally qualified in social work, the Department of Health instigated a residential child care training initiative (the RCCI). This initiative supported secondment of personnel to DipSW courses, their practice placements and the curriculum development and maintenance costs of eight special programmes to which the majority of students went. 455 places have been taken up as part of the RCCI, a figure which is more than enough to ensure the objectives of the initiative.

12.6   **Post - Qualifying** social work qualifications in child care specialisms are recognised as extremely important, but although some courses exist, they have yet to become readily available. It was put to the Review that a specialist higher qualification is appropriate for those responsible for running residential settings which care for looked after children because these children have such complex needs as to require higher levels of expertise than is currently catered for within the training and qualification framework.

The Importance and Effectiveness of Training

12.7   It is taken as axiomatic that training is a good thing. Trained staff will be better staff. The quality of care will be improved and the children will be safer.

12.8   However, research into the determinants of the quality of care by Sinclair and Gibbs [82] produced a disturbing result that no statistical association could be found between their measures of the quality of care and the level of qualifying training within the staff group. Good quality care could be associated with heads of home who were clear about what they were setting out to achieve and could motivate the staff group towards these objectives. The only other demonstrable association suggested that quality of care was more easily achieved in smaller homes.

12.9   It seems reasonable to conclude from this that, if we accept intuitively that training must be helpful, it can only be effective in improving the quality of care for children if trained staff are working in settings in which the whole staff group can work coherently towards explicit objectives for the children. The importance of coherence and clarity of purpose as a determinant of good care in children's settings has been known for a long time (see for example *Issues of Control in Residential Child Care*[83]). Recent research by the Dartington Social Research Unit[84] confirms this. Congruence between the statutory expectations of residential child care, the goals of the home and the beliefs of the staff can produce a positive staff culture.

12.10   The research suggests that the management, staff development and training inputs into children's residential care should aim to promote this congruence. If statutory expectations go unheeded or the goals of the home are unclear, the quality of care is likely to be poor. Similarly, if the ideas which individual staff bring to a care setting work against the well intentioned goals of the home or statutory expectations then the quality of care will be undermined. There may, of course, be occasions when individuals need to stand up against the goals of a home when these are malign, but the need to strive for congruence remains. We conclude from this that training which overly emphasises conflict and challenge without firmly establishing a core of accepted knowledge, understanding and practice may not contribute to the provision of good quality care. We also argue that in order to ensure that a core of accepted knowledge and practice is imparted to students in training, expectations of courses need to be defined in terms, not just of competencies, but also in the detail of the input of under-pinning knowledge.

Pre-professional In-service Training for Direct Care of Children

12.11   Children looked after away from their own homes will spend a lot of time cared for by adults who have no professional qualifications for the work that they do. Whether they are living with foster carers, in children's homes or residential special schools, the care of most of these children is far from straightforward. At best they will not be biddable and in some cases their behaviour will be offensive, bewildering and dangerous. The core skills and underpinning knowledge for working directly with such children in care settings are, we believe, distinctive from other child care work but common across settings.

12.12   Although there are local initiatives to provide training for residential and foster carers (supported by materials from the National Foster Care Association and the British Agencies for Adoption and Fostering), there appears to be a need for up-to-date training materials designed to address the direct care of children with complex needs. The training pack *Taking Care Taking Control* designed expressly for staff in children's homes and distributed directly to homes at the beginning of this year appears to have been well received.

12.13   This addresses one aspect of face to face care. There is need for similar materials to be produced which deal with other components of care. We can perhaps define the topics which should be covered by using the Looking After Children framework. This is a practical tool promoted by the Department of Health to help ensure that the developmental needs of looked after children are met and is now in use by almost all local authority Social Services Departments It would make good sense to be guided by these materials in deciding the content of in-service training for carers. If *Taking Care Taking Control* could be said to have addressed behavioural development, then the following topics remain to be addressed: health, education, identity, family and social relationships, social presentation and self care skills. We suggest that this could be the starting point for a curriculum of in-service training to be reflected in training materials applicable to foster care, residential care in homes and in special schools. To this core should be added training in how to ensure the safety of children living away from home and the care of children who have been abused.

Qualifying Training

12.14 In *Children in the Public Care*[1] I made several recommendations that stressed the importance of senior staff, at least, in children's homes being qualified in terms commensurate with their fieldwork and external management colleagues. An expert group reported on the residential child care content of qualifying courses and this was incorporated by the Central Council for Education and Training in Social Work (CCETSW) into guidance to colleges. The Department of Health gained agreement from local authority and training interests to fund the Residential Child Care Initiative to provide qualifying training for senior staff in homes so that all heads of children's homes could gain the DipSW.

12.15 Although arguments have been put forward for an altogether separate qualification for residential care staff (Recommendation 62 of *Choosing with Care*[4]) there has been a prevailing doubt that the sector was of sufficient critical mass to be able to support a dedicated qualifying framework. My reasoning at the time was that the leadership in children's homes should be qualified to a level that was of equal status to, and capable of managing the interface with, fieldworkers and external managers.

12.16 The RCCI has not gone untested with both CCETSW and the Department of Health commissioning evaluative studies. The most recent and substantial study was undertaken by the Evaluation Development and Review Unit of the Tavistock Institute whose final draft report has been sent to the Department of Health. The Review's reading of the evaluation is that whether the initiative has achieved the target of 100% qualified heads of children's homes remains to be seen. The period of the evaluation ended before all students had completed their courses. Figures from the Local Government Management Board suggest that, in 1995, 82.6% of heads were professionally qualified. The evaluation report suggests that structural changes in the sector, with homes closing and others opening, have changed the shape of the workforce in ways which will have influenced the figures. There are still students on courses who are due to return and these should boost the proportion of qualified heads.

12.17 One of the most encouraging findings was that only 13% of students did not return to residential work. However, now that the initiative is coming to an end there is a danger that a haemorrhaging of qualified staff will reverse the gains that have been made. This initiative could only be remedial in the short to medium term. Employers now have to devise workforce and training policies which encourage junior staff with potential to run homes to gain professional qualifications and compensate for those heads of homes who choose to use their experience and qualifications to further their careers. But perhaps of even more immediate importance is that professionally qualified heads of homes are treated in ways that convey a sense of their being valued and that their commitment to residential work is matched by that of their employers.

12.18   The evaluation reported that qualification was felt by the newly qualified heads, other staff in the homes and external managers to have produced noticeable changes. Heads were reported to be more confident and to reflect much more on practice and how to resolve problems, and their return to work secured benefits for the whole staff team.

12.19   The evaluation report contains critical detail and couched alongside its positive comments there is much food for thought. In particular it states that key issues were treated differently between courses and *'even within residential child care modules there was great variation in what was present on the curriculum and how it was presented'*. Children's health and education were poorly addressed. The Review heard from professional commentators and the children themselves about the serious degree of neglect of these areas for children in the public care. The extent of educational failure of these children is such as to jeopardise their safety in the longer term, as are undetected health problems. It is essential that these key developmental aspects of child care are given full recognition on training courses. The evaluation report also cites a tendency on some courses for teaching related to residential care to focus on the negative images such as studies of Inquiry Reports and a relative dearth of positive and realistic inputs about what good residential care can achieve.

12.20   At the same time as reading the Tavistock evaluation and other research directly concerned with the care of children, the Review became aware of the findings from the Marsh and Triseliotis research[85]. This study, based on pre-1995 requirements, drew attention to the enormous variety of theoretical models being taught on DipSW courses. This is bewildering for newly qualified staff entering practice. The authors say *'the situation needs to be improved'*. They argue the need for greater recognition of the fact that specialism is an organising frame of practice. In reality, newly qualified social workers entering work are faced with undertaking specialist jobs. The study supports the need for foundation material at a broadly generic level, with specialism becoming increasingly acknowledged as qualifying training proceeds.

12.21   From the perspective of the Review it also seems that we are dealing with care staff who, when first recruited and unqualified, enter a highly specialised working environment. If they progress through a career in social work the scope of their work will broaden. Indeed, if they become managers they will be taking on skills which are applied well beyond social care.

12.22   The direct care of children is a social work specialism. The qualifying training to support such a specialism requires definition in such a way that qualified staff leave courses equipped with a range of skills, underpinning knowledge and insight which adheres to a recognised standard. Our view, having examined the relevant CCETSW documents on qualifying training course requirements for child care, is that the present approach to specifying expectations should be improved by defining their content further and more tightly by means of a curriculum of learning. We suggest that the dimensions of the Looking After Children materials provide an initial framework. Only in this way can we be sure that essential areas such as the health and education needs of looked after children are covered.

12.23 We were told that training about foster care was not seen as important despite the fact that about 65% of looked after children are cared for in this way. We believe that social workers must have a much better understanding of foster care and so we suggest that this should be included in the child care curriculum.

Post-qualifying Qualifications

12.24 The Review might not have said anything on training at a post-qualifying level had it not been suggested to us that the needs of some children living in care settings away from home were so complex as to require the highest level of expertise. Given that foster carers and residential staff do indeed care for very troubled children, the argument that care services be led by managers and practitioner with higher specialist qualifications carries force. We understand that CCETSW has agreed to the development of national standards for a post-qualifying award in child care. We would encourage these developments but they should not detract from the need to make training for NVQ and DipSW more demonstrably effective in improving the quality of care, and hence the safety, of children living away from home.

12.25 Complex needs of children living away from home include disability and mental health problems. Advanced qualifications in the care of such children will need to take careful account of the interface with the health professions.

Training Needs of Care Staff in Schools

12.26 It was reported to us that there has been significant interest from residential special schools in the training pack *Taking Care Taking Control* even though it was designed specifically for children's homes. Clearly the care of children in classrooms is a specialised matter for the teaching profession. The care of pupils within their living units, on the other hand, looks to have so much in common with the care of children in children's homes that a common approach to training would carry mutual benefits, not least from the economy of producing training materials for a much wider audience.

12.27 It is a requirement for approval as a special residential school that the head of care has an appropriate qualification. The Department for Education and Employment has sought advice periodically from Department of Health as to what qualifications can be recognised as appropriate.

12.28 The Review recommends that the Department of Health and the Department for Education and Employment jointly review and explore the scope for a common approach to developing training opportunities for carers in schools and homes in relation to National Vocational Qualifications and the Diploma in Social Work qualifications.

12.29 Although there is undoubtedly a core of child care practice common to all settings, it may not be helpful to imply that the training requirements for staff looking after children in mainstream boarding schools are the same in every respect as those for staff caring for children with special educational needs. The Review has received information from the Boarding Schools' Association (BSA) about their programme of training and accreditation for staff working in these settings.

12.30 Relatively recently the BSA studied their needs for training in the care of children in mainstream boarding schools. The issues were discussed in the 1994 publication *In Loco Parentis* [86]. At that time there was no accredited training for teachers and other staff with boarding responsibilities. This has now been remedied and the BSA, having decided against the NVQ route, has devised two certificates accredited by the Roehampton Institute, an Institute of the University of London. There is a Certificate for Boarding Staff designed for non-teaching staff and the Certificate of Professional Practice (Boarding Education) designed for teachers with boarding responsibilities.

12.31   The Review has seen some details of the courses available. These have clearly focused very directly on the main welfare issues of the setting. They deal with such topics as appreciating the personal needs of pupils, counselling, and conflict resolution, child protection, loss and change and eating disorders. The Certificate of Professional Practice includes, in addition, material on the organisation, management and ethos of boarding education. The material we have seen is based on a syllabus and learning outcomes. The content is clear and easily understood. We believe that the Department of Health and Department for Education and Employment should commission the production of further training materials designed for the in-service training of carers without professional qualifications in schools and homes.

Training for Foster Carers

12.32   There is evidence from Berridge and Cleaver [87] that foster care placement breakdowns are fewer when carers have had even rudimentary induction training. However, although there has undoubtedly been an increase in the training available for foster carers since the early 1980s, the most up-to-date research reported by Triseliotis and others [88] suggests that training opportunities remain uneven with half the carers in one sample reporting that they had had no training at all.

12.33   The status of training for foster carers is perhaps bound up with the ill defined relationship between foster carers and the authorities who recruit them, place children with them and pay them varying amounts of allowance and reward. Many foster carers will volunteer to undertake training as part of their personal commitment to do their best for the children they care for. But foster care has become an increasingly difficult task and many local authorities expect foster carers to undertake training. The NFCA recommend that training for foster carers should be a requirement. It is possible for foster carers to gain an NVQ at level 3.

12.34   As with residential care, the nature of demands upon foster carers is such that an orientation to continuing learning is an essential component of the job and hence an important contribution to the safety of children in the public care. Being linked into training helps to offset isolation and drift into unacceptable practices. There is an understandable tendency for training to be concentrated on the newer recruits to fostering. Access and take up of training by foster carers appears to attenuate with the length of time a carer has fostered. There is a strong case for local authorities to ensure that training is available to all their foster carers and to examine, in particular, provision designed specifically for foster carers who have been approved for some time.

Training in Child Protection

12.35   The major part of training in support of child protection has been directed at safeguarding and promoting the welfare of the child when abuse is suspected. The sexual abuse of children living away from home occurs in circumstances in which the abuse often goes undetected and is not disclosed, sometimes for many years. For this reason, if abuse of this sort is to be detected in time to help the child victim, reacting to allegations is not enough and proactive approaches to discovery are needed. This requires attention to be directed at the behaviour of the potential perpetrator. Training is necessary to raise awareness of the way perpetrators behave and their methods of abusing children.

12.36   Reports of abuse by such people as Frank Beck, Ralph Morris and Malcolm Thompson and the descriptions of the personalities of child sexual abusers in *The Betrayal of Trust* [89] suggest that they may have characteristics of personality and behaviour, some knowledge of which might improve the ability of senior staff and managers to spot the secondary signs of potential or actual abuse. The Code of Practice for the Employment of Residential Child Care Workers [5] sets out some indicators derived from the work of the Lucy Faithfull Foundation. The Hesley Group of schools have used a check list approach to assess risk.

12.37   The Review is conscious that there have been significant advances in police understanding of the way perpetrators work. While the Department of Health has sponsored much research into intra-familial abuse and its impact on victims, it is the Home Office which sponsors research into the perpetrators of sexual abuse. It seems to the Review that some of this understanding about perpetrators could usefully be made available to social care practitioners and managers. Accordingly it is recommended that the Department of Health and the Home Office jointly explore the potential for developing guidance and training materials designed to heighten the awareness of child care professionals about the profiles and methods of perpetrators of child sexual abuse.

Chapter 13:   **CHOOSING THE RIGHT PEOPLE**

SYNOPSIS

This chapter discusses recruitment and selection procedures.

It concludes that 15 recommendations on recruitment and selection of staff in *Choosing with Care* – the Warner Report – represent good personnel practice to be expected of all employers providing services for children living away from home. It quotes and discusses the recommendations on defining the job, advertising the post, application forms, selection methodology, references and final interviews (paragraphs 13.6–13.13). The chapter's principal recommendation is that :

> All employers should adopt recruitment and selection procedures based on *Choosing with Care* principles; the Department for Education and Employment, the Independent Schools Joint Council, the Boarding School Association, the Prisons Agency and the Department of Health/Welsh Office should take steps to support introduction of these principles in schools, penal institutions and hospitals (paragraphs 13.23).

This is supported with two other recommendations:

> The central Departments should publicise the Support Force's Code of Practice for the Employment of Residential Child Care Workers to all employers providing services for children living away from home (paragraph 13.24);

> Inspection is effective in identifying poor personnel practice and OFSTED and Her Majesty's Inspectorate of Prisons should cover recruitment and selection procedures in their inspections as a matter of routine (paragraph 13.19).

'It is relatively easy for an offender-aware organisation to make....clear in their advertisements, policy statements and staff selection procedures,...that would-be applicants know they are applying for a job with an organisation which has an aware culture. This encourages good applicants and actively discourages offenders.'

The Lucy Faithfull Foundation – submission

'The need to adopt rigorous recruitment and appointment policies is at the forefront of ensuring that staff working in community homes and other child-centred environments are not seeking access to vulnerable children for their purposes.'

Welsh Local Government Association – submission

'Implementing the "Choosing with Care" (Warner Report) recommendations has enhanced recruitment and selection procedures in some authorities thereby increasing confidence in the process.'

SOLACE – submission

'Careful recruitment of staff who will be working with visually impaired children is essential. Strong controls, careful vetting procedures and meticulous recruitment practices must exist for all positions which will involve staff in close contact with visually impaired children.'

Royal National Institute for the Blind – submission

13.1   The legislation regulating private children's homes, independent schools and special schools says little about recruitment and selection of staff. The Children's Homes Regulations require the home to employ enough staff; independent schools run the risk of being removed from the Register if they employ someone who has been barred from working in a school; the Regulations on the approval of schools for children with statements of special educational needs (SEN children) specify that the Head of Care is to be a separate post to that of Head Teacher and must hold a relevant qualification and have suitable experience.

Guidance   13.2   The child care field now has available a plethora of guidance and advice on good practice on this subject. Volume 4 in the Children Act series gives general advice. *Choosing with Care*[4] analyses this subject in depth. The Support Force's Code of Practice for the Employment of Residential Child Care Workers[5] gives more detailed advice, taking forward many of the *Choosing with Care* recommendations.

13.3   General guidance on appointment of staff for independent boarding schools is included in Volume 5 in the Children Act series, which makes it clear that the responsibility for checks on the suitability of staff rests with the school and that inspectors should pay particular attention to this aspect. *The Welfare of Children in Boarding Schools – Practice Guide*[90] lists succinctly and clearly the safeguards and checks which inspectors will be looking for. Local Education Authorities (LEAs) and grant maintained schools are unlikely to be familiar with this body of guidance, but non-maintained special schools, which are inspected under Section 62 of the Children Act, may know about it. However for schools in general the Department for Education and Employment has produced no equivalent to *Choosing with Care* or the Code of Employment Practice. Its circulars on use of police checks[91] and misconduct of teachers[92] refer in general terms to recruitment and selection procedures. The Independent Schools Joint Council (ISJC) has produced general advice for independent schools.

13.4   The rules governing recruitment and selection of staff to Young Offender Institutions (YOIs) and prisons are the same as for the Prison Service generally. Some prison governors responsible for YOIs insist on prospective staff following a training course designed in conjunction with the Trust for the Study of Adolescence on the characteristics of young people.

13.5   Following *The Allitt Inquiry*[40] the Department of Health issued general guidance[41 and 42] to health authorities on selection of staff with particular reference to following proper procedures even when the person was already working in the hospital or had just completed his training there.

Choosing with Care Principles

13.6   The Review heard from children and others that on the whole children living in children's homes now have less fear of abuse by staff and are more afraid of other children. The efforts made by the Department of Health, local authorities and people managing children's homes to improve personnel practice appear to have been beneficial. Chapters 3 and 4 of *Choosing with Care* discuss recruitment and selection. While some of that material is specific to children's homes, much describes good personnel practice to be expected from any employer providing services used by people who are vulnerable by virtue of their age, disability or condition. The principles informing 15 recommendations in these chapters on defining the job, advertising the post, application forms, selection methodology, references and final interviews are quoted and discussed in the following paragraphs.

13.7   **Defining the Job and the Postholder** (recommendations 2 and 3)

'Employers should only recruit staff after preparing a job description clearly related to the home's current statement of purpose and objectives; and a person specification for each post to be filled setting out clearly the competences (i.e skills and personal attributes) and experience required to discharge satisfactorily the responsibilities of the job description.'
(No. 2)

'Employers should use as a basis for job descriptions and person specifications an agreed up-to-date and publicly available statement of purpose and objectives for each home that makes clear the type and characteristics of the children in the home and the objectives of the care and treatment programmes it is providing.'
(No. 3)

The principle underpinning both of these recommendations is that employers should develop job descriptions and person specifications which are specific to the institutions and do not rely on standard material.

13.8   **Advertising** (recommendation 4).

'Employers should ensure that all vacancies are advertised – usually externally – and are open to competition; and that all heads of home posts should be advertised externally and nationally.'
(No. 4)

One factor associated with abuse is a closed institution and it is important that employers take steps to recruit from outside, wherever possible.

13.9   **Use of Commercial Agencies** (recommendation 7)

'Employers who wish to use agencies should satisfy themselves that they represent good value for money and do not have an adverse effect on the resources available for the care of children; and should require any agencies used to adopt selection and appointment procedures as rigorous as those for directly employed staff set out in this Report.'
(No. 7)

Agency staff are expected to provide comparable standards of care to that provided by permanent staff and this principle should underpin their use. Agency work could provide cover and opportunity for potential sex abusers, especially preferential paedophiles. Almost all employers in any of the settings covered by the Review have to use agency staff from time to time. The agreement or contract with the agency must be clear about the importance of safeguarding children and that the agency's procedures are tight enough to prevent potential sex offenders and other undesirable people being accepted on to its books. The agreement or contract could specify that agencies must always take up a reference from the person's last permanent employer. Both parties need to have a clear understanding about responsibility for background checks on individuals. NHS trusts expect this to be done by the agency because there would not be time for the hospital to do this.

13.10   **Application Forms** (recommendations 8 and 9)

'Employers should require applicants for posts in all children's homes to complete application forms specifically designed for these posts and that collect information relevant to the posts, as defined in the job descriptions and person specifications.'
(No. 8)

'Employers should send applicants job descriptions, person specifications and full information about the home where they have applied for a post.'
(No. 9)

These two recommendations follow from those dealing with defining the job and postholder. Job applicants need to have all the relevant information about the particular post and the institution when they fill in the application form. It is important to make sure applicants supply proof that they are who they purport to be – eg by supplying the original copy of a birth certificate. They should also be asked about any criminal convictions *and* whether they have ever been charged with a criminal offence and the outcome.

13.11   **Selection Methodology** (recommendations 10, 11, 13 and 16)

'Employers should use written exercises in the selection process (including shortlisting) to test the ability of candidates to think clearly and to express themselves.'
(No. 10)

*'Employers should use preliminary interviews as a standard part of establishing a fuller picture of the character and attitudes of shortlisted candidates for **all** posts in children's homes.'*
(No. 16)

'Employers should require all shortlisted candidates to visit the home and meet staff and children in advance of the interview. Information about interaction on visits between candidates and staff and children should be made available to those involved in deciding the appointment of candidates by a person involved in the appointment process.'
(No. 11)

'Employers should use appropriate aptitude tests as part of the normal selection process for shortlisted candidates for heads of homes and other senior management posts in residential homes.'
(No. 13)

The principle underlying this group of recommendations is that an appointment made on the basis of just one interview by a large panel is more likely to result in a wrong appointment. *Choosing with Care* quotes from evidence from the Institute of Personnel Management (IPM) that *'the interview is not a good predictor of future job performance. Research findings … suggested that the interview has a validity coefficient of 0.14 (i.e only 14 in 100 appointments based on interviews will meet employers' expectations on job performance). The IPM commented that this is somewhat worse than making decisions on the toss of a coin.'* Employers in all sectors now commonly use a range of measures to assess an applicant's competence. The Lucy Faithfull Foundation told the Review that group exercises in particular would help an employer identify the person who was a bad team player – a characteristic which was one of the predictors for a sex offender. In any case, good care for children depends on team work, so it is essential to establish whether or not an applicant has this skill. Some people have reservations about the recommendation on visits. The Support Force's Code of Practice [5] says *'Knowledge of the targeting practices of some sex offenders leads to the view that only short-listed candidates should visit and these should have passed a preliminary interview prior to visiting the home.'* Visits are an essential part of the selection process. But they do offer preferential paedophiles, who are in the words of the Lucy Faithfull Foundation, *'extremely good con men'* opportunities to start targeting children. It is sensible to follow the Support Force's advice.

13.12 **References** (recommendations 17, 18 and 19)

'Employers should require candidates when applying to provide a full employment history, including periods of unemployment, with dates (to the nearest month) and the names and addresses of previous employers. Candidates should be free to provide the name of a referee in addition to an employer if they wish.'
(No. 17)

'Employers should always approach an applicant's present employer; should tell applicants that they reserve the right to approach any previous employer (or line manager) about a shortlisted candidate's character and performance before interview; should seek written references on the basis that referees have the job description and person specification and are encouraged to comment frankly on shortlisted candidates' strengths and weaknesses in relation to those two documents; and where necessary should explore any aspects of references by telephone with a current or past employer.'
(No.18)

'Employers should keep a record of conversations with referees and pass the result to those responsible for making appointments; and they should retain records of disciplinary offences or concerns that enable them to be passed on to a potential employer when requested in connection with a job which involves working with children.'
(No. 19)

References, especially from the current employer, provide key information about the job applicant and employers need to ensure that their procedures enable this to be supplied. Several organisations told the Review about the difficulties of dealing with references now that open references are increasingly the norm. This practice may make the process more taxing, but previous employers in particular have a moral duty to pass on all relevant information to the potential employer. We support *Choosing With Care*'s analysis of this problem:

'There will be anxieties in the many local authorities where there is an "open file" policy, whereby applicants are able to gain access to references.... This makes it important that references should not say something which the candidate has not already been told by line management.... There is a clear legal liability for references. The person giving the reference should ensure that it contains no material misstatement or omission relevant to the suitability of the applicant for the post. A person.... can be held liable if the statement is defamatory. A statement is defamatory if it is false and lowers the person in the eyes of right thinking members of society. This should not discourage referees from revealing relevant information.... We do not consider that this legal context should prevent an employer from providing honest, frank or timely references.'

The Support Force's Code of Practice says that *'it is good practice for references to be shared by the referee with the candidate. However, as far as the recruiting department is concerned they are provided on a* **confidential basis***, unless it has been made explicit to referees in advance that the contents.... may be discussed. Care therefore has to be taken during interviews not to reveal the contents of references, even if issues contained within them have to be checked out.'*

Employers should not feel inhibited from discussing the content of the written reference with the referee and recording what was said. Some local authorities do this when approving foster parents. It is as important in the case of staff being considered for a post in an institution.

13.13 **Final Interviews** (recommendations 21 and 22)

'Employers should ensure that final interview panels consist of no more than three people balanced by gender and race as far as possible and appropriate; and should include an independent person as well as the line manager and person senior to the line manager – one of whom should be authorised to make the appointment.'
(No. 21)

'Employers should ensure that final interview panels should have available to them and use all the information about candidates from earlier parts of the selection process; and that panels are free to explore areas of doubt and concern in order to discharge their overriding responsibility to make safe and competent appointments in children's homes.'
(No. 22)

The principle underpinning these recommendations is that smaller interviewing panels are more effective.

13.14 The Department of Health wrote to Directors of Social Services on 7 December 1992 to say that the Secretary of State wished them to implement the recommendations on recruitment, selection and appointment in *Choosing with Care*. Directors, as requested, have submitted progress reports at stated intervals. These show that most authorities report significant progress in implementation, although the Department has not yet taken steps through inspection or other means to validate the information provided. However, the Review is pleased to note that the Chief Inspector in CI (97)10[93] asked Directors to review their practices in relation to recruitment of staff and placement of children and report the results to him. The Social Services Inspectorate is to analyse these reports and use them to plan a major inspection of this issue.

Monitoring   13.15   *Inspecting for Quality*[73] includes standards on recruitment and selection. Many local authorities use these standards for their inspections of children's homes, so that recruitment and selection can be covered twice a year in the case of voluntary and registered children's homes. Inspection reports from the Social Services Inspectorate and those produced by local authority inspection units show how the inspection process helps to pick up careless approaches to recruitment and selection and can be used to make providers and proprietors improve their practice. *'In two cases appropriate checks had been made. For the third appointment, a residential social worker, references had been received and requests made for checks with the Department of Health Consultancy List and police records. Replies to these checks had not been received. The staff rota indicated that this person would be working unsupervised for two periods each week.'* (Inspection report on voluntary children's home.) One inspection report on a registered children's home lists among the points for attention that *'All staff must be recruited using clear and thorough recruitment, selection and vetting procedures designed to protect children and achieve appropriate competences and balance in the staff group. Written recruitment procedures must be developed to include guidance on advertising posts and method of selection.'* This is rarely covered in reports on local authority community homes probably because managers of homes are unlikely to be involved in this process, though they do cover staffing issues such as supervision and appraisal.

13.16   The sample of inspection reports on boarding schools seen by the Review do not invariably cover recruitment and selection but, where it is the subject of comment, inspectors identify poor practice in relation to references and making criminal record checks. One report concludes by recommending *'The school must amend its recruitment procedures to ensure written references are, where possible, available before interview.'* Another report comments *'Although all appropriate checks are undertaken for staff it was noted that in several instances requests for this information were not made until after the employees took up their post and in other instances replies were not received before employees took up their posts. This practice is unacceptable.... It is **strongly** recommended that all checks on staff are completed before an individual takes up a post in a school.'*

13.17   HMI do not routinely examine recruitment and selection procedures for independent schools during inspections, though the inspector looks to see if the school has checked whether staff are subject to a Secretary of State's Direction barring or restricting employment. *The Framework for the Inspection of Schools*[94] within which OFSTED's registered inspectors inspect maintained boarding schools and LEA and grant maintained and non-maintained residential schools approved for SEN children does not specifically refer to recruitment and selection. Inspectors *'must evaluate and report on: the adequacy of staffing.... Judgements should be based on the extent to which the number, qualifications and experience of teachers and other classroom staff match the demands of the curriculum.'* Guidance on using the framework for the inspection of special schools does not have a discrete section on recruitment and selection of staff and the section on child protection makes no reference to policies or procedures to prevent abuse by staff. HMI at OFSTED told the Review that the approval process for special schools would not cover this as a matter of routine.

13.18   In the case of reports on Young Offender Institutions and prisons, Her Majesty's Inspectorate covers certain staffing issues but, in reports seen by the Review, this did not include recruitment and selection except to comment on recruitment being devolved from Headquarters, which had increased the workload.

13.19 The Review is particularly impressed with the way in which the local authority Inspection units have picked up poor personnel practice in recruitment and selection by managers in registered children's homes and schools. This helps to improve practice and is a good preventative measure. OFSTED and Her Majesty's Inspectorate of Prisons should cover this during their inspections.

13.20 Social care organisations said that application of the *Choosing with Care* recommendations prevented the appointment of unsuitable people to work with children, but it took more time and more resources. Some were concerned about authorities where the lead rested with personnel departments, who might lack knowledge about child care. The Association of Directors of Social Services (ADSS) wrote *'Our evidence suggests that members of ADSS have made strenuous and successful efforts to reinforce and sharpen the rigour of selection and appointment procedures.'* The Local Government Management Board said *'On the question of employment practice we have been aware of a continuing interest around the country for help and assistance with good practice.... It does seem clear, however, that much more can and should be done....We were also concerned to note the number of agencies who seemed only now to be examining their recruitment practice.... Our experience suggests that a properly focused national campaign to promote best practice, possibly involving regional workshops might do much to improve recruitment practice.'* The Review hopes that the proposed inspection being planned by the Social Services Inspectorate will produce examples of existing good practice which can be reinforced and promulgated to other agencies.

13.21 The Review heard less from the schools sector on this issue. One preparatory school visited by the Review said that their recruitment and selection process involved several stages and more than one interview.

13.22 Children living away from home are entitled to the same degree of protection whatever setting they are in. Some of these children – children with learning difficulties, children with emotional and behavioural difficulties – are more vulnerable than others and schools catering for them need to be particularly vigilant over the recruitment and selection of staff. The Review has also found that some types of school have fewer inbuilt safeguards than others – i.e less frequent inspection and no statutory oversight from social services.

13.23 People who wish to exploit children, particularly career abusers, will seek out weak points in any system, wherever they occur. Therefore the Review recommends that all institutions where children are living away from home should adopt recruitment and selection procedures based on the principles which underpin the 15 *Choosing with Care* recommendations analysed above. The Department for Education and Employment should take steps to support the introduction of these procedures in the maintained sector and discuss with the Independent Schools Joint Council and the Boarding School Association ways of doing so in respect of independent boarding schools in membership of any of its associations. The Prisons Agency should examine its recruitment policy in the light of this recommendation. The Department of Health/Welsh Office should take the appropriate steps to ensure that hospitals adopt these principles when recruiting and selecting staff to care for children in paediatric units and any other units where children are likely to spend time as in-patients.

13.24 The Support Force's Code of Employment Practice for Residential Child Care Workers provides excellent advice on this and other issues. It would help employers in different settings develop good personnel practice and should be widely publicised by the central Departments of State.

Chapter 14:   SOURCES OF BACKGROUND INFORMATION

SYNOPSIS

This chapter explores the use of information about individuals derived from criminal record checks, the Department for Education and Employment's List 99 of people barred or restricted from teaching or working in schools and the Department of Health Consultancy Index of people considered unsuitable to work with children. It comments on the Disqualifications Regulations.

Its analysis of criminal record checks, List 99 and the Consultancy Index concludes that all 3 sources help prevent undesirable people obtaining work with children, but their administration can be improved. The delays in processing criminal record checks are unacceptable and must be addressed by the Home Secretary when he brings into operation the provisions in the Police Act 1997. The new system should also allow enquirers to request checks against List 99 and the Consultancy Index at the same time (paragraphs 14.11–12).

List 99 operates on a higher standard of proof than the Consultancy Index. Cases not put on after referral are not passed on to the Index. It recommends that both Departments examine their procedures to ensure that information about such people can be considered for inclusion on the Index (paragraph 14.20).

The Consultancy Index is well used, though very few checks are positive. The Review recommends that the Department of Health and local authorities monitor its use more closely (paragraph 14.26). The number of names referred by employers is quite small and it recommends that more should be done to publicise its existence (paragraph 14.31).

The recommendation elsewhere for the Department of Health to develop a Code of Practice for Foster Carers should cover use of and referral to the Consultancy Index. The proposed review of the Index is welcomed. It should consider the role of the Secretary of State and whether he should decide that a person represented a risk to children, who should not work with children and pass the information together with his opinion to a third party (paragraphs 14.29–30).

The local authority inspection process covers use of List 99 and the Consultancy Index and requests for criminal record checks in the recruitment and selection of staff. Employers in the children's home and schools sectors are under a duty to notify names. In the case of children's homes this could be strengthened by making it an offence not to notify someone dismissed on grounds of misconduct or who resigned in suspicious circumstances (paragraph 14.35).

The Disqualifications Regulations are intended to prevent people who have been disqualified from one activity regulated by the Children Act from undertaking any other activity covered by the legislation, unless the local authority decides to lift the disqualification. There is little information available about their effectiveness, nor about how rigorously local authorities check their own records when approving foster carers, intending providers of children's homes and appointing staff. The Review recommends that the Department of Health/Welsh Office review the effectiveness of the Disqualification Regulations and associated guidance (paragraph 14.39).

> *'PECS (The Pre-Employment Consultancy Service) cannot give you a foolproof guarantee of someone's suitability. It can only provide information about those people whose activities have come to light – people who have been convicted or formally reported to PECS.'*
> DHSS Northern Ireland: Making the Right Choice

14.1   There are three national sources of information – criminal records, the Department for Education and Employment's List 99 and the Department of Health's Consultancy Index – which prospective employers are expected to consult during the recruitment and selection process in order to check whether a job applicant is already known to be or thought to be unsuitable to work with children. Regulatory bodies are also expected to consult these sources as part of the registration and inspection processes. These sources operate in different ways and in the case of the two lists maintained by Government Departments different standards of proof are applied for putting names on them.

14.2   The legislation governing the conduct of children's homes, the registration of independent schools, and approval of schools to take children with statements of special educational needs does not require employers or regulatory bodies to check on the background of proprietors, managers or staff. The regulation of schools goes some way towards this: it is an offence for a school to employ someone who has been barred or restricted from working as a teacher or in any other capacity in a school by the Secretary of State for Education, so the employer has to check that the person is not barred or restricted. Regulation 19 of the Children's Homes Regulations place a duty on the responsible authority running the home to notify the Secretary of State of *'any conduct on the part of a member of staff of the home which is or may be such, in the opinion of the responsible authority, that he is not, or as the case may be would not be, a suitable person to be employed in work involving children.'* This Regulation does not apply to schools also registered as children's homes.

14.3   The position is different for foster parents. The Regulations governing their approval specify that a local authority or voluntary organisation *'are not to give approval unless [among other things] it has obtained information about criminal convictions.'* (Regulation 3(4) and Schedule 1 of the Foster Placement Regulations 1991.) Following the recent conviction of Roger Saint, a foster carer and adoptive parent, for indecent assault on young boys in his care, the Government intends to introduce Regulations which will prohibit the approval of foster carers and adoptive parents who are known abusers.

Criminal Records   14.4   Records of convictions since 1985 are on a national database. Information on cautions, bindovers and charges not proceeded with are held by local police forces. There are two categories of criminal record check – simple and enhanced. The latter involves local searches for information as well as a check against the national database. Checks on people having substantial unsupervised access to children are in the enhanced category.

14.5   Local authorities, voluntary organisations in membership of the Voluntary Organisations Consultancy Service (VOCS), the Department for Education and Employment and the Department of Health can already request criminal record checks on prospective employees in social services, schools, voluntary and community children's homes and foster parents, but the police have until recently refused to carry out checks on providers and staff in private children's homes. The Home Office and the Association of Chief Police Officers have now agreed that the police will carry out checks on staff working in registered children's homes and also on residential care staff working in the voluntary and private sectors with children aged under 18. This may mean that checks can also be made on staff working in small private children's homes, even though these are not currently registrable.

14.6   The Department for Education and Employment requests checks on behalf of independent and grant maintained schools. VOCS carries out checks for organisations in membership and voluntary children's homes registered with the Secretary of State. Their membership list closed in 1994, so that coverage of the voluntary sector is by no means comprehensive. Local authorities request checks on staff and volunteers working in community homes and maintained schools and on prospective foster parents. The Review was told about confusion as to which organisation is responsible for requesting checks in the case of agency staff, which may result in no checks being made.

14.7   Some 600,000 checks are requested each year (*On the Record*)[95]. The number of positive checks is small – 4% to 4.5% of the total – and some do not relate to sex or violent offences. VOCS processed nearly 9,000 checks in 1995/96 of which nearly 400 came back positive and the Department for Education and Employment nearly 16,000 checks in the same year of which just over 700 came back positive. The Home Office's 1996/97 survey of police forces in England and Wales shows that 6% of checks requested by local authorities, health authorities and independent schools were positive.

14.8   That proportion of positive checks represents nearly 27,000 people, some of whom would present a risk to children. The Home Office[96] estimate that in 1993 there were 110,000 men aged over 20 (out of a total population of 18.5 million) with a conviction for a sexual offence against a child. The Review has to conclude that some convicted sex offenders still try to obtain work with children. The checks are therefore worthwhile. But this has to be seen in context. Most sex offenders abuse children for many years before they are caught, so have no criminal record. A negative result tells an employer or regulator little about a prospective employee's or service provider's propensity to abuse children. Checks will not deter the *non-convicted* preferential paedophile. Such people are known to be manipulative and devious and will have no reason to fear a criminal record check.

Delays   14.9   The main complaint about the current system is delays, mentioned to the Review by many people in their submissions and at meetings. VOCS's Annual Report for 1995/96 shows an enormous variation in the time taken to process the checks it requested. These ranged from an average of 5 days in one police force to 65 days in another, with 24 police forces taking between 10 and 20 days, 12 over 20 days and only 6 less than 10 days. Information from the Home Office survey shows that by 1996/97 many police forces had improved the time taken to process checks, but there are still variations between forces. Some delays may be explained by the fact that the process involves local searches as well as checking the national database. This takes longer when there have been frequent changes of address. But this does not explain the variation between police forces. There can be no justification for one police force to take an average of nearly 3 months to complete a check, when the majority manage to do this in much less than a month.

14.10 Delays are disturbing because they place prospective employers under pressure to take somebody on pending the outcome of the check. Any employer who did this in the police force area, where it took an average of 65 days to complete the check, would allow a preferential paedophile more than enough time to target and groom.

14.11 The Review was told that some local authorities forbid providers of private children's homes to allow someone to start work pending the outcome of the check, even when the provider guarantees that the person will not have unsupervised access to children. This approach complies with the recommendations in *Choosing with Care*[4] and the advice in the Support Force's Code of Practice[5] and, in principle, is the proper way to operate. But it was not surprising to hear that, when people offered posts have to wait months before knowing they can start work, this particular employer found that they went elsewhere. The Review finds it astonishing that in the late twentieth century when credit agencies, for example, can and do use computer technology to provide an almost instant response to a request to check a person's credit worthiness, it takes days, weeks or even months for police forces to check someone's criminal background. It is dismaying to see that the comments about delays made in 1992 in *Choosing with Care* still ring bells in 1997. The Review hopes that, when the Home Secretary's new powers to issue criminal record certificates come into force, the administration of this ensures that requests for checks are usually turned round within a matter of days.

Criminal Records Agency

14.12 Part V of the Police Act 1997 provides powers for the Home Secretary to issue criminal record certificates. The previous Government proposed to set up a Criminal Records Agency to do this on his behalf. The Government is still considering how to administer this. This is a matter for the Home Secretary, but the Review hopes that whatever system is chosen for criminal record checks it adopts the principles of comprehensive coverage and minimum delays. The new system should also serve as a one stop shop for enquirers, so that they can ask for a criminal record check, a List 99 check and a Consultancy Index check at the same time. At the moment a request to the Department for Education and Employment for a List 99 check includes a Consultancy Index check and a request to the Department of Health for a Consultancy Index check includes List 99.

List 99

14.13 This operates under provisions in the Education Reform Act 1988 and Regulations made under it which give the Secretary of State power to make Directions barring or restricting the conditions of employment of unsuitable people – teachers and other workers – from employment by Local Education Authorities, grant maintained schools, non-maintained schools and proprietors of independent schools. The Secretary of State makes the decision and the person making the referral is not required to recommend a particular course of action. The Secretary of State has power to make a Direction on grounds of misconduct, whether or not the misconduct is evidenced by conviction of a criminal offence. The standard of proof for putting a name on the list is set above the balance of probabilities but slightly below that of beyond reasonable doubt. Once a Direction is made the employer may be required *'to suspend or terminate a person's employment, or prohibit a person's employment in relevant employment, or impose specific conditions on a person's employment.'* List 99 is sent to Local Education Authorities and the associations representing independent schools each April and updated at least twice during the year.

14.14   Since 1995 there have been two criteria for putting names on the list:

automatic inclusion in the case of someone convicted of rape, buggery, incest, unlawful sexual intercourse, indecent assault, gross indecency or taking or distributing indecent photographs;

at the Secretary of State's discretion when satisfied beyond reasonable doubt about the alleged misconduct of the person and that he represents a risk to children. To meet the beyond reasonable doubt threshold there would have to be, for example, an admission of guilt or independent corroboration of the allegations.

14.15   The Department's guidance does not define misconduct or specify in detail what might constitute misconduct likely to justify barring someone from teaching or working in a school. Examples given include: violent behaviour towards children and young people; sexual or otherwise inappropriate relationship with pupil, regardless of whether pupil is over legal age of consent; sexual offence against someone over 16; any offence involving serious violence; drug trafficking; any conviction involving a sentence of 12 months or more; repeated misconduct or multiple convictions.

14.16   The main sources for names are the police and employers. The police send the Department for Education and Employment information about convictions of a teacher, youth worker or ancillary worker in a school. The Misconduct Regulations require employers to report to the Department *'where a person is dismissed from relevant employment on grounds of misconduct, or where someone resigns in circumstances where he or she would have been dismissed or considered for dismissal on those grounds'*. Figures supplied by the Department show that the number of referrals now runs at over 100 each year and has increased significantly since the early 1990s. The Department told the Review that employers were reasonably conscientious about reporting names. In the case of independent schools HMI check on the barring or restriction status of staff, which allows them to consider how well schools are complying with this requirement.

14.17   The effect of a Direction is to prevent a teacher from practising his profession and an ancillary worker from working with children in a school. The Direction has the force of law and bites on employers as well as the person barred or restricted. Employers who knowingly employ someone outside the terms of any Direction could be charged with an offence and, therefore, they have to check whether or not someone is the subject of a Direction. The easiest way to do this is to consult List 99 during the recruitment process. If it comes to light that an independent school is employing a barred person, the school may be struck off the Register of Independent Schools.

14.18   There are around 2,000 names on List 99 – about 80% in the automatic category and 20% in the discretionary one. (There are about 500,000 teachers working in any 12 month period plus ancillary workers including care staff in schools.) People reported to the Department and not made the subject of a Secretary of State Direction are not referred to the Department of Health for inclusion on the Consultancy Index. The person is told that the question of barring or restriction has been considered and no action is being taken.

14.19   The Department for Education and Employment process some 40,000 checks per year and aim to respond to a request within 24 hours. A List 99 check requested from the Department includes a check against the Department of Health's Consultancy Index. Local Education

Authorities hold copies of List 99, so will not automatically check the Index in the case of people being considered for posts in LEA maintained residential special or boarding schools. The Review was told that independent schools were conscientious about checking List 99 when taking on new staff. The annual returns submitted to the Registrar by these schools include names of staff who have left and new staff. The Registrar refers all the names for List 99 checks.

14.20 The strengths of this system are: it has a legislative basis; it is easy to find out whether or not someone has been barred or restricted; the turn round is quick. But using the standard of proof of just below beyond reasonable doubt means that any person about whom an employer can only supply evidence which cannot be independently corroborated will not be barred or restricted. It is worrying that the Department for Education and Employment does not consider referring or suggesting to the school that it refers information about these cases to the Department of Health to decide whether or not they meet the criteria for inclusion on the Consultancy Index. The Review is convinced that this sort of person would be likely on the balance of probabilities standard of proof to present a risk to children, and he or she is likely to try to obtain work in other types of children's service. We recommend that the two Departments examine their procedures so as to ensure that someone who, after consideration by the Department for Education and Employment is not made subject to a barring or restricting Direction, is considered for the Consultancy Index.

Consultancy Index 14.21 This has no statutory basis. In 1961, the Home Office – then responsible for maintaining the Index – when challenged about its existence said that, as the Secretary of State had a general responsibility for children in care, if employers consulted him about applicants for posts in a child care service he considered it desirable to draw to their attention any information in his possession which suggested an applicant might be unsuitable to work with children. It operates on the basis that inclusion on the Index does not automatically prohibit the person from working with children. The decision whether to employ someone rests with the potential employer. The main criterion for inclusion is that the *employer* referring a name considers the person unsuitable to work with children. The evidence to support this might be: the person has been dismissed after formal disciplinary proceedings; has admitted unacceptable conduct; there has been an adverse decision by an Industrial Tribunal. Employers have to give the Department of Health a positive assurance that they will provide a reference with a full explanation of the circumstances leading to their referral, even if a subsequent check against the Index is sought years after the person left their employment.

14.22 There are around 750 names referred by employers on the Index. In addition the Department maintains a list of names – currently 4,800 – referred by the police of child care workers or ex-child care workers who have received convictions and police cautions. Anyone asking whether a name is on the Index will also have it checked against the names referred by the police and against List 99. Access to the Index is not restricted to particular types of organisation, so it provides a route for checking someone's background for agencies not able to access criminal record checks. Not all police forces send caution/conviction information to the Department and some of those that do send details about relatively trivial offences – eg shoplifting – as well as the more serious.

14.23   The Index is well used. There are about 7,000 requests for checks against the Index made each month. The number of positive checks per month runs at about 6 or 7. The Department of Health does not routinely monitor the organisations requesting checks, so cannot say whether all relevant organisations – eg all local authorities – use the Index. The Review's study of some inspection reports of community and registered children's homes suggests that checking against the Index is now part of routine personnel practice when appointing staff. It is important that this is included in the inspection standards and covered on every inspection.

14.24   The Department receives around 10–12 referrals from employers per month with the majority being put on the Index. It takes less than 4 weeks for a name to be put on the Index provided the employer supplies complete information about the individual. The individual is notified at the same time as his name is put on the Index, even though the letter gives him the opportunity to object to this. The Department maintains the Index in this way because the duty to ensure that children are protected from harm is paramount.

14.25   The value of the Index is wholly dependent on employers and local authorities as regulators passing on information about an employee, or service provider or foster carer who is considered on the balance of probabilities to present a risk to children. There is not much evidence that employers or regulators routinely consider the question of referral when disciplining and/or dismissing staff. It is listed in *Inspecting for Quality*[73] as a measure of performance. Many local authority inspection units use these standards, so this should be checked during inspections of children's homes. Schools can ask for names to be put on the Index, but this is not well known. Of more concern to the Review is the fact that local authorities do not routinely refer foster parents who have been removed from their lists.

14.26   At the request of the Review the Department checked its records to test whether the range of authorities referring names was what might be expected or not. They found that one or two quite large authorities very rarely made referrals, though it seemed reasonable to postulate that there would have been cases which should have been referred. The Review suggests that the Department of Health and local authorities should take steps to monitor this more closely.

14.27   The number of requests for checks would suggest that the existence of the Index is well known and the Review would expect this to be reflected both in the number of names on the Index referred by employers and in the rate of referrals. It is therefore surprising to discover that employer referrals number only 750 and the referral rate is quite low. While it is understandable that some employers will be relieved when a troublesome employee leaves or they manage to dismiss him and will thankfully close the file, it does children no service for the employer to fail to take all possible steps to prevent that person getting another job working with children. In the case of foster parents the Review cannot understand why consideration of referral is not standard practice.

14.28   The main strength of the Index is that it enables organisations providing or regulating children's services to refer people who on the balance of probabilities standard of proof present a risk to children. It is the only system available for dealing with soft information cases, which is valuable. The Department told the Review that it is to re-examine the operation of the Index. We agree that this is necessary and hope that one of the guiding principles for its future operation will preserve the balance of probabilities standard of proof. The Review is convinced that using this standard helps to ensure that people with a propensity to abuse or harm children are identified at an earlier stage in their careers and thus children in general are better protected.

14.29 A more difficult issue for the re-examination is the role of the Secretary of State and his Department and how the information in the Index is used. At the moment the Department's role is confined to giving the enquirer the name of the previous employer who referred the case. It is left to the enquirer to approach the referring agency and to decide in the light of the information provided whether to employ someone, who in very rare cases is found to be on the Index. Operating in this way can create practical problems where it is learnt that the referring agency or company no longer exists or where the relevant personnel records have been destroyed, although this might be overcome by requiring referring employers or authorities to provide a full reference at the time of referral. It is also thought that discovering that the person is on the Index is enough to make the enquirer decide not to offer the job.

14.30 It would be open to the Secretary of State to adopt a more interventionist approach and pass on the information supplied by the referring employer to the enquirer, together with his opinion that the person is considered on the balance of probabilities standard of proof to present a risk to children. The Review does not take a position on this, but considers that the proposed review must address the issue.

14.31 The Review recommends that more is done to publicise the Index, so that all employers working with children in any setting use it to check names against it and refer appropriate people. Guidance on the Index is currently contained in annexes to circulars on criminal records issued jointly by the Department, the Home Office, Department for Education and Employment and the Welsh Office and is difficult to track down.

14.32 The Review is pleased that Scotland is to have a similar list to the Consultancy Index. This means that, as Northern Ireland now has its Pre-employment Consultancy Service, the whole of the United Kingdom is covered. The Review suggests that the Department of Health, the Northern Ireland Office and the Scottish Office arrange to share these sources of information with a view to making a check against one Index cover all three.

14.33 These sources of background information on people are by no means perfect, but there are ways in which each can be made to work better. Criminal record checks can be processed more quickly. Cases referred to the Secretary of State for Education and not barred or restricted can at least be referred on to the Department of Health. The Consultancy Index can be made better known.

14.34 The Review thinks that the arrangements for monitoring that independent schools and providers of children's homes use these sources to check the backgrounds of prospective staff are reasonably satisfactory, as they are covered during the inspection process. The position is far less satisfactory in the case of foster parents. We recommend in Chapter 3 that the Department of Health develops a Code of Practice for Foster Carers and the question of checking foster parents should be considered as part of that.

14.35 It is difficult to establish whether employers and regulators are rigorous in referring names to the Department for Education and Employment or the Department of Health. In the case of schools employers are under a duty to notify names and the same applies to children's homes. This could be strengthened in the case of children's homes by making it an offence not to notify someone who was dismissed on grounds of misconduct or resigned in suspicious circumstances. In the case of foster parents this should be looked at as part of the work on developing a Code of Practice.

Disqualification Regulations

14.36 These Regulations made under the Children Act (the Disqualification for Caring for Children Regulations 1991 S.I 1991 no. 2094) are necessarily complex and therefore difficult to follow. They have the effect of disqualifying from private fostering, childminding or providing day care services people whose children have been the subject of a care order, or who have been convicted of any offence involving children or involving violence against children or others, or have been involved in a voluntary or registered children's home which has been deregistered. The disqualification is not absolute as the local authority has power, once the person has disclosed his disqualification, to lift it. In the case of registered children's homes the law is more complicated but the effect is the same: namely someone who has been disqualified from being a private foster parent cannot be granted registration to run a children's home unless he has disclosed the fact and the local authority decides to lift the disqualification. The guidance on lifting disqualification in Volume 8 in the Children Act series makes it clear that local authorities are expected to use this power only in the most exceptional circumstances: *'It is the clear intention....that disqualified people should be prohibited from undertaking **any** (emphasis added) of the activities listed....above, but there may be **rare** occasions where a local authority would feel justified in lifting the disqualification.'*

14.37 The Regulations do not apply to local authority foster parents or community homes. Volume 8 in the Children Act series says:

'While the Regulations do not apply to local authorities' own provision, children who are living in a community home or with a local authority foster parent....should similarly be protected from those who might wish to harm them or are otherwise unfit to care for them. Local authorities will wish to have regard to The Disqualification Regulations *and these notes of guidance when considering the appointment of staff and any person's suitability for the work.'*

14.38 This guidance is not immediately identifiable as the title of Volume 8 is *Private Fostering and Miscellaneous*. It is however clear that the legislation is designed to ensure that a person, who has been the subject of proceedings in respect of his own children or other activity regulated by the Children Act, should not be able to undertake any other activity regulated under the Act unless the local authority decides to lift the disqualification. This implies that local authorities should check their own records when dealing with, for example, registration of a children's home or the appointment of staff to a community home.

14.39 The material read by the Review does not make clear whether local authorities' procedures include anything about checking records within the authority, when checking on their own staff or foster carers or when registering children's homes. Nor were we able to establish whether the Disqualification Regulations were effective or whether the power to lift a disqualification had been used. *Inspecting for Quality* [73] says nothing about local authorities checking their own records. *Working Together*[3] also advises (paragraph 6.54) that *'Care should be taken with case records which contain information about adults suspected but not convicted of offences against children and a **list of such people should not be used.'** (emphasis added)* It is important that local authorities as employers and regulators have procedures which ensure that their own records are checked. The Department should also review the effectiveness of the legislation on disqualifications and its associated guidance. The Review notes that *Working Together* is being reviewed and hopes that this will include consideration of use of information about adults suspected but not convicted of abuse.

Chapter 15:   DEALING WITH UNSUITABLE PEOPLE

SYNOPSIS

This chapter discusses the place of soft information, disciplinary procedures, professional registration and whistleblowing in helping to protect children from harm.

Soft information is a difficult issue. The Review recommends an examination of legislation – the Data Protection Act, law on defamation, employment protection legislation and judicial review – to establish whether a protocol could be developed to legitimise exchange of information between parties with a proper interest in protecting children. It also recommends consideration of the need for legislation to provide some immunity from prosecution for individuals who pass on information they believe to be true to a third party (paragraph 15.7).

Disciplinary procedures properly applied help to safeguard children. The advice on this in the Support Force's Code of Practice represents good personnel practice which is commended to employers in all the settings covered by the Review. The Review notes the Association of Directors of Social Services' view that some Directors are reluctant to dismiss unsatisfactory staff because these decisions may be overturned on appeal to elected members, who may have little knowledge about child care.

Its main recommendation is that local authorities should ensure that appeals from staff dismissed on grounds of misconduct or unsatisfactory standard of child care practice include members with some knowledge of child care and the authority's corporate parent responsibility to safeguard and promote the welfare of children in the public care (paragraph 15.14).

Other suggestions are that employers include in the contract of employment a condition that disciplinary proceedings will be completed even if an employee resigns during the process (paragraph 15.16), and regulatory bodies make arrangements to look at staff turnover and the reasons for departure as part of the inspection process (paragraph 15.17).

The Review supports the establishment of a General Social Services Council, and recommends that both this Council and the proposed General Teaching Council possess robust disciplinary processes for protecting children (paragraph 15.24).

The Review notes that thirty years on from Court Lees **whistleblowing** is still an anxious experience. All staff have responsibilities for reporting suspicions of abuse, and management responsibilities for listening to them.

Members of staff are the adults most likely to suspect that children are being abused physically, emotionally or sexually but fear is a real deterrent. Those who raise concerns still risk their careers and for every individual who is victimised, many more are deterred. Some they have cause to complain about are the heads of the institutions in which they work or are active in political or union circles.

The Review recommends that all organisations which accommodate children instruct staff that they have a duty to their employer and a professional obligation to raise legitimate concerns about the conduct of colleagues or managers. There should be a guarantee that this duty can be discharged in ways which ensure a thorough investigation without prejudice to their own position and prospects (paragraph 15.36).

In addition it says that:

> Cultural change must be led from the top;
>
> Boards of management should adopt and promulgate policies of openness and promptness in dealing with complaints, and designate a board member with special responsibility;
>
> Executive management should investigate and report on all complaints about staff that affect children;
>
> A senior official should be nominated to institute investigations where the complainant feels unable to act through line management;
>
> Codes of conduct should include a duty to report behaviour by staff, managers, volunteers or others which may harm children;
>
> Such reports should normally be made to a member of line management, or to a nominated officer outside it, or to a nominated member of the board of management;
>
> The code should offer confidentiality for the initial reports and protect a complainant in good faith against any subsequent disadvantage (paragraph 15.37).

'Free communication with all the world is their motto and Rowland Hill [founder of the penny post] is the god they worship. Only they have been forced to guard themselves against too great an accession of paper and ink.'

Anthony Trollope: Can You Forgive Her?

'Do you think if anyone was to ask her very nicely not to sing it might stop her? I mean we could let her come and just stand there. Yes, Mrs Hailestone, she does look *like a singer, I'll give her that. That's the annoying part.'*

Joyce Grenfell: Committee

'The outstanding problem adversely affecting the establishment and maintenance of an appropriate workforce is the lack of a coherent and structured approach to unsuitable staff.'

Association of Director of Social Services – submission

'The safety and well being of the children may have suggested a need to remove the person from his caring position, but in the absence of a disciplinary offence efforts to resolve the situation were quite long winded and included the use of sickness procedures.'

London Borough – submission

'Neither the common law nor statute provide adequate safeguards for whistleblowers.'

David Lewis: Whistleblowers and Job Security

15.1 As already noted elsewhere, persistent abusers manage to abuse children over many years before being convicted. More needs to be done to ensure that potential abusers are dealt with at an early stage in their careers.

Soft Information

15.2 This is the most difficult aspect. 'Soft information' is anything not corroborated from an independent source or something which may appear to have no relevance to risks to children. A Director of Education in a Welsh local authority told the Review that proper scrutiny of a job applicant's employment history could identify someone who was a career abuser, because there appeared to be no other reasonable explanation for the changes. Some children have told a trusted adult that their social worker was 'creepy', but could not be more articulate than that. The National Criminal Intelligence Service told the Review that around half the criminal intelligence on career abusers is soft information rather than convictions or cautions. Many of the cases read by the Review show that children can be abused by career abusers in particular for many years before they are caught.

15.3 Two of the national sources of information make no use of soft information. An enhanced criminal record check allows the police at their discretion to disclose information about charges brought but not proceeded with, but that is factual information. List 99 operates on hard information only. Even the Consultancy Index asks referring employers for information about dismissals, resignation and decisions by an Industrial Tribunal. Use of local sources is problematic. The Association of Chief Police Officers suggested (submission) *'Consideration for appropriate legislation to ensure proper assessment is made of those cases which fall short of criminal prosecutions but raise grave concerns as to the suitability of that individual continuing in the child care arena. The legislation should permit all available factual information to be disclosed to the appropriate agency for their use.'*

15.4   Two recent reports comment on this issue. *An Abuse of Trust*[97] says *'The Investigation was concerned....with those persons who for a variety of reasons are not prosecuted but about whom sufficient information is known to suggest that they may present a risk to children.... Concerns for the civil liberties of individuals and respect for the principle of confidentiality in dealing with staff or clients may discourage a number of organisations or professionals from passing on information which has implications for the protection of children.'* That report went on to suggest *'Action to protect children cannot reflect the 'proof beyond reasonable doubt' standard of the judicial system but must be based on the 'balance of probabilities' principle which directs the consideration of child protection agencies. This principle, viewed within the context of an ordinary civil duty of care, should inform the decisions of all organisations in communicating information in circumstances where there is a doubt and should override considerations of the rights of an individual in matters affecting the possible safety and well-being of children.'* The Public Inquiry into the Shootings at Dunblane Primary School[8] noted that *'As matters stand there is no system for co-ordinating information between different areas of the country about persons regarded as potentially unsuitable for work with children and young people.'*

15.5   The Review has already commented on employers' fears about the current open reference climate. Some are also anxious about providing a full reference in cases where there have been unresolved disputes over the facts. They also fear losing a case on appeal to an Industrial Tribunal. Employers and local authorities should accept that aggrieved individuals will use the law to its limit and not be put off, when they have judged from their observations that a person should not work with children, by the risk that a decision by the courts or Industrial Tribunals might go against them.

15.6   Agencies are often reluctant to pass on soft information because of fears of litigation, whereas the protection of children demands free passage of information between agencies. There appear to be particular difficulties with regard to soft information held by police forces, though it is encouraging that 23 out of 43 police forces have now developed joint protocols with social services to underpin exchange of information. This does need to be accompanied by a willingness to share all information with colleagues, even though something may seem trivial to the agency which holds it.

15.7   The Review is not wholly convinced that employers, regulators and central government departments are striking the right balance between fairness to the individual employee or service provider and their various duties to protect children. The Data Protection Act, employment protection legislation, the laws on defamation and the threat of judicial review seem to combine to hinder exchange of soft information. It is not clear whether the legislative framework actually prevents this. Government should institute an examination of this area to see whether a protocol could be developed to legitimise the exchange of soft information between parties all of which have a proper interest in the protection of children. This might require the sort of legislation suggested by the Association of Chief Police Officers which could provide some immunity from prosecution to agencies and individuals who passed on information they believed to be true in good faith to someone who needed the information in order to discharge his responsibility to protect children.

Disciplinary Procedures

15.8   Comprehensive disciplinary procedures and rules, rigorously applied, safeguard children living away from home in two ways: staff on appointment know the circumstances which are likely to trigger disciplinary action; staff who abuse, fail to protect or neglect children can be disciplined for this and ultimately dismissed. All employers will have written disciplinary procedures, but some will not have written rules. There are also codes of ethics for social workers, child care workers and teachers, but none of these currently have any statutory force.

15.9   *Choosing with Care*[4] said little about disciplinary procedures. Chapter 6 says that it is essential for the good management of a home for staff to be treated fairly – and be seen to be treated fairly – in the event of a complaint. Chapter 8 analyses the suspension issue, noting particularly that 'officially' employers see this as a neutral act whereas staff see it as 'punishment without trial' and suggesting the criteria to apply when deciding whether to suspend. Two recommendations flow from this analysis: recommendation 77 that *'staff should only be suspended from duty where a preliminary inquiry and careful assessment by the line manager, taking into account the interests of the children and other staff, suggests that a complaint could lead to dismissal or prosecution....'*; and recommendation 78 that *'staff should be informed on appointment of the policy and procedures on discipline and suspension from duty; should be able to receive assistance from professional associations or trades unions in any investigations of their conduct or disciplinary proceedings'*. The Department of Health told the Review that nearly all local authorities had reported that they had implemented both Recommendations, but there was no information about the situation in the private sector or voluntary children's homes.

15.10   The Support Force's Code of Practice[5] includes sections on suspension (7.10) and disciplinary procedures (7.11) together with a model disciplinary procedure in Appendix S. On suspension it says that 'managers need to consider whether any of these criteria (i.e those listed in *Choosing with Care*) are met before rushing to immediate suspension'. The section on disciplinary procedures sets the issue in the context of the ACAS *Code of Practice on Disciplinary Practice and Procedures in Employment*, advises employers to keep a record of all disciplinary offences so that these can be passed on to a potential employer and lists *'the concerns likely to lead to a finding of gross misconduct and therefore dismissal'*.

15.11   The Department for Education and Employment's circular *Protecting Children from Abuse: The Role of the Education Service*[98], (sent to the maintained sector for action and to independent schools for information), gives general guidance on suspension and the timing for instituting disciplinary procedures. The Independent Schools Joint Council (ISJC) supplies schools in membership of its associations with a checklist of the main legal requirements, including employment legislation, with which schools will have to or are strongly urged to comply.

15.12   The Review has elsewhere recommended that the Department for Education and Employment, the ISJC, the Prisons Agency and the Department of Health take steps to draw the attention of employers running schools, penal institutions and hospitals to the Support Force's Code of Practice. We consider that the material on disciplinary proceedings represents good personnel practice. We particularly commend the advice on keeping comprehensive records about such proceedings as these help to provide a sound evidence base for any future references.

15.13   It is difficult to establish whether employers use disciplinary procedures effectively and appropriately. The Review heard from the Association of Directors of Social Services that, in the case of children's homes, there was still a culture of allowing an unsuitable member of staff to leave rather than invoke the disciplinary process. Furthermore Directors of Social Services were often wary of dismissing a member of staff because the decision was likely to be overturned by elected members on appeal. It was suggested to the Review that this happened because the members involved in hearing the appeal had little knowledge of the ethical and functional context of child care, so that they failed to give proper weight to the need to protect children and were more concerned to be seen to treat the appellant fairly.

15.14   The fact that elected members hearing appeals from staff working with children may have little knowledge about child care makes it more difficult for the local authority properly to discharge its corporate parent responsibility. As the corporate parent the local authority has the duty to protect the child. The Review recommends that local authorities ensure that such appeals include members with good knowledge and understanding of child care and the duty to safeguard and promote the welfare of children in the public care.

15.15   *Choosing with Care* commented (paragraph 8.40) that the survey commissioned from Price Waterhouse (conducted between March and July 1992) found local authorities used suspension more frequently than final warnings or dismissal. The Review has read reports of inquiries and reviews conducted under the provisions in Part 8 of *Working Together*[3] into abuse in children's homes and schools which suggest that employers are reluctant to go through the disciplinary process. In one community home for children with learning difficulties some staff were allowed to leave and, when the local authority did institute disciplinary proceedings in respect of 5 staff, none were dismissed. In one independent school where a teacher was convicted of sexual abuse, two other staff whose behaviour had been investigated by the police were allowed to resign rather than be disciplined.

15.16   It is dismaying to find that employers are still allowing staff being investigated or disciplined to resign, thereby avoiding the consequences of their behaviour. Employers who take this easy way out are making it easier for preferential paedophiles in particular to continue their careers. Barnardos has a policy which prohibits a member of staff from resigning while subject to disciplinary proceedings. All contracts of employment should include a condition which provides for the completion of disciplinary proceedings after an employee has resigned.

15.17   Local authority personnel departments will have information about employees who leave and the reasons for this in respect of their own employees. It is important that all registration authorities have better information about staff turnover and the reasons why staff leave. The Registrar of Independent Schools' annual return from independent schools includes the names of staff who have left and these are checked against List 99. This enables him at least to gather intelligence about some staff movements. *Inspecting for Quality*[73] adopted by many authorities does not include this among its standards. The Review recommends that in the case of children's homes the inspection process includes a question about staff who have left since the last inspection and the reasons for their departure. It is also desirable for this to be included as part of the welfare inspections of schools.

Professional Registration

15.18 For an occupation to be recognised as a profession involves more than developing a distinctive body of knowledge. It is also to become part of a moral community, in which high standards of professional conduct are an integral part of overall professional competence. Membership of an established profession carries with it an expectation that its possessor will uphold in all professional activities the code of ethics to which the profession subscribes. The regulatory and disciplinary processes of the professions operate to prevent, identify, investigate and punish unethical conduct. They can if necessary terminate membership of the profession and remove thereby the ability to practise.

15.19 Professional identity is made up of a complex of shared factors such as lengthy training, advanced knowledge and skills, ethical commitment and corporate morale. Their effects combine to make those who acquire them less vulnerable than members of unregulated occupations to conscious, opportunistic abuse of children. Nevertheless, professionals are also human beings, and their training and discipline may not always control their personal weaknesses. Furthermore, no profession which affords easy and unsupervised access to children is safe from the attentions of active paedophiles, for whom membership of a profession such as medicine or nursing provides the equivalent of invulnerable armour.

15.20 The disciplinary processes of medicine and nursing therefore provide an important supplement to the protection afforded by the criminal law and by disciplinary action by an employer. A professional body can consider complaints against a member on matters that go beyond the concern of the courts or the employer. Neither the criminal law nor the employer can ensure that an unfitted professional does not return to practice at the expiration of the sanctions they impose. Only the self-regulating professions possess the ultimate sanction of withdrawing the right to practise; but they do so on serious and clearly established grounds, within procedures which observe the rights of the person accused, since they too must operate within the law of the land.

15.21 None of the other occupations with which the Review is concerned is subject to such strong internal control. It might perhaps be argued in the case of teachers that List 99 delivers as much in practice as alternative systems could. The arrival of a General Teaching Council, however, offers the prospect of a disciplinary structure which goes beyond the limitations and the rigidity of List 99.

15.22 I was a member of the Action Group which in January 1993 submitted a proposal to the Secretary of State that a General Social Services Council should be established for all social services staff. The first stage of registration of staff was to include 'all social work and social care staff working in residential child care' as well as all field social workers and team managers – in effect, all the social services staff in statutory, voluntary and private sectors who had substantial and unsupervised access to children. The proposal is of general importance to this Review, since its objective of raising overall standards of competence in the workforce is fundamental to the welfare of children. Of particular interest to the Review, however, is a suggested disciplinary system which includes the ultimate sanction of disbarring unsatisfactory or dangerous practitioners.

15.23 Such a system, operating up to the boundary of what the law presently permits, would provide the principal means of preventing people who have abused children from working with children again.

Criminal or disciplinary proceedings are largely unsuccessful in effecting this. Indeed, managers and employers have all too often appeared to wish to avoid action against delinquent employees because of the associated damage to their own reputations and the institutions they represent.

15.24 I continue to support the establishment of a General Social Services Council. I recommend that the disciplinary processes of the General Teaching Council and the General Social Services Council should include identifying and excluding from practice people who abuse children.

Whistleblowing

15.25 The lengthy anonymous letter to *The Guardian* on 2 March 1967 which sparked the inquiry into the Court Lees Approved School[99] concluded *'I regret my name and address are not for publication. My fears over the loss of my house if I were identified with this letter are very real ones.'* Thirty years later, similar tangible anxieties – and some of the real consequences – are still experienced by almost anyone who wishes to 'blow the whistle' on harmful or even criminal practice towards children in institutional settings.

15.26 This section reviews the responsibilities of staff for reporting suspicions of abuse, and of management for listening to them. Numerous reports of inquiries into abuse in residential settings since Court Lees refer to other staff suspecting or knowing what was going on, but not reporting it, or not being listened to, or being frustrated by management's unwillingness to act. Staff who did break ranks were not infrequently left feeling that their careers had suffered because of it. For every individual who was victimised, many others will have been deterred from following their example.

15.27 Fear is a very real deterrent to exposing wrong-doing. The abuser is often in a position of actual or presumed power or influence: in 21 of 48 alleged or proven cases of abuse in residential settings reviewed in an unpublished report, the abuser was the principal, proprietor, head or deputy of the establishment. Other alleged or actual abusers have been active in local union or political circles. Some were bullies who inspired physical or moral fear in colleagues and managers. In at least one case staff were reluctant to press complaints lest they appeared to oppose the equal opportunities policies of their authority. Where staff have pressed complaints they risked ridicule in some cases, ostracism, and worse. Managerial indifference and incompetence (where managers were not themselves the abusers) are constant features of the inquiry reports.

15.28 Volume 4 of the Children Act Guidance acknowledged that *'There is a need for advice to junior staff to encourage them, when necessary, to share with the SSD their concerns about senior staff. This is very difficult for them to do and they need to be reassured that it is the right thing to do. Procedures which ensure this should be set out in written guidance to staff and dealt with in training and supervision.'* The Code of Conduct for Local Government Employees promulgated by the Local Authority Associations and the Local Government Management Board said, in general terms, that *'Employees will be expected, through agreed procedures and without fear of recrimination, to bring to the attention of the appropriate level of management any deficiency in the provision of service. Employees must report to the appropriate manager any impropriety or breach of procedure'*. Choosing with Care[4], reviewing the position in residential care, noted the difficulty expressed by staff *'in making known their views about professional issues in homes ......we have had our attention drawn to several cases where a member of staff has felt that they had to resign before they could express their concerns about their experiences.'*

15.29   *Choosing with Care* recommended that *'Employers should accept that staff in residential homes for children should be able to raise significant concerns outside their normal line management when they consider the line manager has been unresponsive or is the subject of concern; they should enable staff to make use of complaints procedures established by legislation.'* This recommendation was one of those the Department of Health asked local authorities to implement by April 1994 in a circular issued under Section 7 of the Local Authority Social Services Act 1970[100]. Reports on progress were requested from local authorities; by July 1995, 97% of the responding authorities claimed to have implemented it in full. This is difficult to reconcile with the finding by Public Concern at Work in its report *Abuse in Care*[101] that at least 6 social services departments had established whistleblowing procedures for their staff, in that one would have expected the figure to be much greater. In any case, however, the action taken hitherto is required only of local authorities, which accommodate a fraction of the children living away from home.

15.30   The Support Force's Code of Practice for the Employment of Residential Child Care Workers[5] spelled out that *'The responsibility for blowing the whistle rests with any person, whatever their rank, who has evidence of unacceptable practice'.* It gives clear guidance to members of staff who wish to raise issues of bad practice, and to managers about the immediate action they should take. What it could not do is guarantee immunity to legitimate complainants against subsequent acts of vengeance. Only employers can guarantee that.

15.31   A later (unpublished) Report by the Support Force, *Dealing with Abuse in Children's Residential Care*, returns to the theme. *'There must be clear advice to all staff on how to 'share their concerns' about colleagues, including senior staff. It must be made clear to staff that they are under an obligation to share such concerns and that to do otherwise is a neglect of their professional duty.'* .... *'Managers have a responsibility to listen to staff who wish to express concerns in a supportive and encouraging manner.'*

15.32   The Committee on Standards in Public Life (Nolan) identified whistleblowing as a general issue in maintaining high standards of conduct in publicly-funded services. Its comment, in relation to financial propriety in Non-Departmental Public Bodies and the NHS, *'that staff concerns come to light despite rather than because of the system'* accurately reflects the situation that has existed about abuse in residential settings. The Committee's First Report[102] continues: *'The Audit Commission found a third of the NHS staff they interviewed would take no action in the face of impropriety because of fears of losing their jobs if they "rock the boat".'* ...... As Public Concern at Work point out, *'although the employee is well placed to sound the alarm, he or she has most to lose by raising the matter.'* The Committee recommended that each Non-Departmental Public Body and NHS body *'should nominate an official or board member entrusted with the duty of investigating staff concerns about propriety raised confidentially. Staff should be able to make complaints without going through the normal management structure, and should be guaranteed anonymity. If they remain unsatisfied, staff should also have a clear route for raising concerns about issues of propriety with the sponsor department.'*

15.33   The Nolan Committee's Second Report, on Local Public Spending Bodies[103], has as one of two general recommendations that they should institute *'codes of practice on whistleblowing, appropriate to their circumstances, which would enable concerns to be raised confidentially inside and, if necessary, outside the organisation.'* The Committee returns to the charge in its Third Report, on Local Government[104]. Noting that the Local Government Management Board has produced its own recommendations, the Committee emphasises that *'Every local authority should institute a procedure for whistleblowing, which would enable concerns to be raised confidentially inside and, if necessary, outside the organisation.'* The Committee sees the Standards Committee which it expects local authorities to establish as providing an internal destination for such complaints.

15.34 Shifts are needed in three cultures:

- that of directors, trustees and councillors, who for reasons of money, prestige or politics find good reason for keeping quiet about problems in the organisations for which they are responsible,

- that of salaried managers for whom the failures of subordinates may be represented as an indictment of their own performance,

- that of the staff themselves who – from a sense of worker or professional solidarity – are reluctant to rock the boat they are all in together.

The obstacles to change are massive and will not be overcome by promises and procedures. The role of unions is important also: where staff belong to the same union, the whistleblower may be incriminating other members, with both sides demanding the protection and help of their union. It may be desirable for unions to adopt a public interest stance somewhat broader than the interests of their members. Even legal protection is insufficient: *'In the care field the fact that someone has successfully brought a claim for unfair dismissal against a former employer is unlikely to commend him or her to a future employer'* (Abuse in Care[101]). Nevertheless, the individual employee's position would be substantially strengthened by legislation such as the Private Member's Bill on Public Interest Disclosure, which was introduced – but fell – in the last Parliament.

15.35

> *'There should be set up, within all public, private or voluntary bodies which have responsibilities for the care of others, procedures whereby those who work within the organisations will be effectively encouraged and helped to raise issues of concern and conscience so that abuse of those in care, and damage to the organisations themselves, may be prevented or revealed.'*
>
> (Sir Ralph Gibson, Chairman of Public Concern at Work.)

15.36 All organisations which accommodate children should instruct staff that they have both a duty to their employer and a professional obligation to raise legitimate concerns about the conduct of colleagues or managers, and guarantee that this can be discharged in ways which ensure thorough investigation without prejudice to their own position and prospects.

15.37 In addition:

- Cultural change must be led and supported from the top.

- Boards of management should adopt and promulgate policies of openness and promptness in dealing with complaints which affect the safety of children, and designate a board member with special responsibility at board level.

- Executive management should be instructed to investigate and report on all complaints about staff conduct which is likely to affect children.

- A senior official (the Monitoring Officer, for example, in local authorities) should be nominated to institute investigations where the complainant feels unable to act through line management.

- A duty should be included in codes of conduct for staff to report behaviour by staff, managers, volunteers or other people which may cause or result in harm to the children accommodated.

- Such reports should normally be made to a member of line management, or to a nominated officer outside line management, or to a nominated member of the board of management.

- The code should offer confidentiality for initial reports and protect a complainant in good faith against any subsequent disadvantage.

These measures would substantially improve the protection of children in all residential settings. Members of staff are the adults most likely to suspect that children are being abused physically, emotionally or sexually.

Chapter 16: THE ROLE OF LOCAL GOVERNMENT, SOCIAL WORK AND DEPARTMENTS OF STATE

SYNOPSIS

This chapter considers the role of local authorities, social work and Departments of State.

In relation to **local authorities**, the Review stresses the importance of implementing the *Choosing with Care* recommendations on personnel policies. It regards this as the highest priority for all new social services authorities in England and Wales (paragraph 16.4). While it supports equal opportunities policies, it points out that, applied rigidly, these inhibit frank refereeing and the searching interviewing that should precede recruitment of care staff (paragraph 16.5).

It recommends that social services authorities should ensure that measures for safeguarding looked after children are given due priority by the council as a whole and that they review the operation and monitoring of the relevant statutory requirements and central guidance (paragraph 16.7). They should also satisfy themselves that their managerial, professional and reporting systems are adequate for discharging their accountability for these children (paragraph 16.10).

The 'purchaser/provider' split is discussed. Sharing services with other authorities and buying services from other providers is now unavoidable for most social services departments. The motive should be to achieve better outcomes for children not to save money, though better outcomes may be achievable at lower cost. Authorities should still provide some services for looked after children and separation of function should not lead to further confusion or fracturing of accountability (paragraph 16.13).

The **role of the field social worker** and its importance are examined. It is argued that it is in the interest of the child to have one official committed to furthering his or her interests as a whole and that it is effective working practice for one official to plan and oversee the total programme of care. The Review recommends that the Local Government Association should undertake, together with the British Association of Social Workers, a study of the role of the field social worker in relation to looked after children (paragraph 16.19).

The responsibilities of **Departments of State** and their relationship with local government are analysed. The Department of Health's response to casework and other matters requires use of the Secretary of State's powers to be considered positively but not indiscriminately. It recommends that the Department of Health/Welsh Office clarify the criteria for using such powers, and make a small group of administrative and professional staff responsible for applying them (paragraph 16.22).

It recommends that the **Social Services Inspectorate** continues to undertake inspections to monitor arrangements for safeguarding the welfare of children living away from home and that the Department of Health should keep the resourcing of the Inspectorate under review (paragraph 16.24). It recommends that the Welsh Office reassess the resourcing and staffing of the Social Services Inspectorate for Wales (paragraph 16.25).

The Review supports the Welsh Local Government Association's suggestion for a Strategic Plan in **Wales** for services for children in need (paragraph 16.26).

The main recommendations are that:

> All Departments of State with responsibilities for children should adopt the aim of promoting and safeguarding the welfare of children, direct their operations to serving that aim, and evaluate the success of their operations in achieving it (paragraph 16.28).

> A ministerial group should be established to safeguard and promote children's welfare. It should secure a consistent government response to this report and other existing reports such as that of the National Commission on the Prevention of Child Abuse (paragraph 16.29).

Local Government

'The responsibility for ensuring the provision of a properly accountable and robust department lies with the Council of the time and its Senior Officers.'

White – Report into the Management of Child Care in the London Borough of Islington, 1995

16.1 Substantial responsibilities for the care and education of children are placed by statute upon local authorities. They are accountable to the Secretary of State for important areas of performance. They account for their stewardship to an electorate, and report factually to council taxpayers. Many authorities have developed additional means of informing users of services and other interest groups of the ways in which they discharge their responsibilities.

16.2 Their duties are so vast and complex that individual failings are almost inevitable. Failures of organisation and systems are less understandable or excusable. Local authorities do not always, or at every level, apply and monitor essential guidance as they should. Reports of inquiries and inspections continually refer to failures in basic processes. *Corporate Parents* [105], the report of inspections of residential care in 11 authorities between November 1992 and March 1993, found that 2 authorities were not routinely using the Department of Health Consultancy Index and 4 had not yet re-written procedures to take account of the Children Act Guidance or *Working Together* [3]. Authorities needed to comply 'as a matter of urgency' with the regulation which required elected members or external managers to visit and report on homes. The Children's Sub-Committee of Gwynedd reported in 1994 that only 4 out of 40 reports of elected members' visits had been submitted and there was no record of others having occurred. *Choosing with Care* [4] emphasised that *'Members and governors have the final responsibility for the performance of children's homes.'*

16.3 The National Summary Report of the Inspection of Local Authority Fostering 1995–96 (based on 6 local authorities) [20] commented that *'The extent to which authorities fail to comply with regulatory requirements was of particular concern. No authority had a system for monitoring the arrangements for statutory reviews as required by the Review of Children's Cases Regulations 1992.' 'Only one authority set a formal expectation that each child in foster care would have a separately documented care plan. Failure to provide an accessible care plan is a breach of Schedule 1, 2, 3 and 4 of the Arrangement for Placement of Children (General) Regulations 1991.' 'Inspectors considered that case recording practice was often poor. ... Some of these deficits in case recording constituted breaches of the Arrangements for Placement of Children (General) Regulations 1991.'*

16.4 Personnel policies may affect children's services adversely. The importance of the *Choosing with Care* recommendations on recruitment has been emphasised in Chapter 13, but *Emerging Themes* [106], the report by the Social Services Inspectorate in Wales on local authority responses to the Report of the Examination Team in North Wales, pointed out that compliance with these recommendations was not yet completed. The Review regards implementing these recommendations as of the highest priority for all new social services authorities in England or Wales, and a litmus test of their fitness to look after children. The Ty Mawr Inquiry [107] reported in 1992 on events in the past, but its comments about staff recruitment retain their sharpness: *'We were deeply disturbed to establish that recruitment of care staff sometimes occurred simply on a visit to the job centre. Appointments were made by the County Council members. We regard this as unsatisfactory.'*

16.5   White[108] is not the only critic of the effect of seemingly inflexible policies for equal opportunities, but his report is the clearest example of the damage to children that followed their implementation. The Review supports equal opportunities policies, but rigidly interpreted they inhibit frank refereeing and the searching interviewing that should precede recruitment of all care staff. Reference is made elsewhere (paragraph 15.13) to unwillingness in disciplinary proceedings to recognise the special requirements of residential work with children.

16.6   These failings may have led to harm in only a small proportion of the total number of children looked after, but a public authority is expected to do all it can to safeguard all the children it is responsible for and the public itself should be satisfied with nothing less. The responsibility for children looked after is that of the authority as a whole, and needs to be reflected in the considerations of the council as a whole, in the political priorities of the council and in the managerial and administrative priorities of the chief executive and all other chief officers.

16.7   Social services authorities should therefore

- ensure that measures for safeguarding children who are looked after by them are considered and given due priority by the council as a whole; and

- review the operation and monitoring in their authorities of statutory requirements and central guidance for safeguarding children who are looked after.

16.8   The Review was encouraged, however, by the positive attitudes of the Local Government Association and the Welsh Local Government Association to their roles in formulating policies, promulgating central guidance, co-ordinating the activities of their members, and promoting consistently high standards of practice.

16.9   The effects of local government reorganisation have brought issues of accountability into greater prominence. The 117 social services authorities in England and Wales in 1991 have increased to 154, and in 1998 will total 172. This is accompanied by a continuing reduction in the number of children they look after, and in the number of residential units they manage directly. More authorities have fewer children overall, dispersed among a greater number of providers. This is a scenario in which services may become fragmented, responsibility diffused and accountability evaporate. One commentator attributed losses of scale, strategic planning and user views to the effects of the local government reorganisation in Wales. The Social Services Inspectorate in Wales offers a more moderate view, but nevertheless notes that 5 authorities now have no residential facilities and there is less specialised provision or specialist support.

16.10   Bad outcomes need not follow if the local authority looking after a child ensures that it is always able to exact accountability from service providers, and to discharge its own accountability for all acts and omissions concerning the child. The demanding nature of this accountability arises from the concept of parental responsibility contained in the Children Act and the general obligations a local authority has in spending and obtaining value for public money. Managing and co ordinating activity to meet the needs of children as individuals across a number of providers over a period of time requires sophisticated professional and managerial systems. For the authority to be properly informed of what is being done to and for children in its name requires a system of reporting all the way through to elected members. Social services authorities should satisfy themselves that their managerial, professional and reporting systems are adequate to discharging their accountability for the children they look after.

16.11   Issues raised with the Review in this context were the effects of separating purchasers from providers within local authorities, and the increased dependence – arising from the fragmentation of providers and diffusion of specialist services – on shared or purchased services. Sharing services with other authorities, and buying services from other providers, are now unavoidable for most social services departments. Such technical matters tend to be neutral in their effects. The decisive issues are the motivation for entering consortia or contracts for service, and the application to managing them properly. If the motive is to achieve better outcomes for children, and management is consistently directed to that end, the result will be good. If the motive is to save money, the result will be disastrous for the children – and poor value for money. Better outcomes may of course be achievable at lower cost, but the focus for elected members and managers should always be the welfare of the child.

16.12   Contracts, for example, may in a minority of cases be worthless pieces of paper unless they are conscientiously monitored by the commissioning authority. Many providers operate automatically to their own high standards – indeed, to standards higher than the parent authority might itself achieve. Some may fail with individual children, or become neglectful or abusive. Procedures for monitoring the fulfilment of contracts are not yet so developed that they can be uniformly relied on as a principal means of discharging accountability. The observance of regulations continues to provide this bedrock.

16.13   Ideologically based arguments about whether services should be bought in or provided by the authority have little validity in the eyes of the Review. Who provides a service should be determined by the needs of children. These are analysed and aggregated for the purpose of the Children's Services Plan, which proceeds to set out the range and nature of the services available or needed. Some general considerations suggest to the Review that local authorities should continue to provide some services for looked after children. These are:

- doing something practical for children is part of parental responsibility – few parents delegate all such tasks to others;

- providing services keeps elected members and managers in touch with the reality of children's needs and circumstances, and strengthens accountability;

- a wider range of services promotes choice – a major safeguard for children;

- experience of managing services provides benchmarks of performance and monitoring for contracts.

16.14   The history of joint arrangements between local authorities in providing children's services is not uniformly happy. They succeed if all parties demonstrate commitment and display a responsible sense of ownership, irrespective of the size of their investment. Arrangements such as the West Midlands Child Care Consortium, which includes a wide range of stakeholders in child care, seem particularly suited to developing common policies, provision and standards across a whole region.

16.15 The 'purchaser/provider split' in community care has been followed by local authorities in their management and provision of children's services. Many have detached arrangements for commissioning services for children from the management of their own services. Proponents of separation perceive a valuable clarification of function and responsibility. Critics regard it as budget-led: in its worst manifestations an inversion of values to the point at which the needs of children are completely subordinated to saving money. It is not clear to the Review whether such an unfortunate outcome is attributable to the method itself, its incompetent application, or a shortage of resources which distorts every value.

Social Work

16.16 It is nevertheless important to the Review that separation of function should not lead to further confusion or fracturing of accountability. This appears to be of particular importance to the role of field social workers in relation to looked after children, and the varied and sometimes conflicting expectations of them. Young people invariably described their need for a continual and trusting relationship with an official of the care authority, who for some is their key worker in a community home. For the many peripatetic children, however, whose moves are frequent and stays are short, 'their' social worker was the only person who could fulfil this role. Some still do this well. Others were criticised by young people for infrequency of contact, for personal remoteness, and for appearing simply to relay the inexplicable decisions of an uninterested bureaucracy. Part of this criticism clearly stemmed from changes in the social workers' responsibilities or in the mode of discharging them. Their potential for close attention to the needs of children and for forming supportive and therapeutic relationships with them appears to have diminished. Nevertheless, *'frequent contact with a social worker who is prepared to listen and advocate for a young person is seen as a protection from neglect and harm'* (FirstKey).

16.17 The Review is unable to attribute this diminution in the role of social work either to the separation of purchase of services from their provision or to its implementation. Both may have had some effect. Another factor mentioned to the Review was a general decay in the understanding of social work responsibilities for looked after children, due in part to gaps opening between case management and 'therapeutic' social work and in part to a downgrading of work with looked after children compared to such 'specialisms' as child protection and fostering and adoption. A third was that the pressures on social work were such that achieving a seemingly satisfactory placement put children on a 'care and maintenance' basis (or on an 'unallocated' list) from which they were removed only when a point of crisis was reached.

16.18 Social services departments must meet the needs of large numbers of children. The arrangements for doing so are inevitably complex, involving numbers of officials and others with differing and partial responsibilities for each child. For such a system to work requires the capacity to perceive and treat each child as an individual. The case for one official to be responsible for watching over the programme of care for each child seems unanswerable. It is plainly in the interests of the child to have one official committed to furthering his or her interests as a whole, to the extent of acting as the child's advocate within the welfare bureaucracy, so that the child is the subject of care rather than the object of unrelated caring processes. It is also in the interests of effective working that there should be one official to plan and oversee the total programme of care. From the authority's point of view, this also provides the clearest possible starting point for establishing accountability for every child it looks after.

16.19   This important role still appears to be expected of field social workers. What has changed is how it is now accommodated, defined and prioritised within the developing role of social work in local government and the separation of some social work functions between commissioning and providing services. The Review therefore believes that the Local Government Association should undertake, with the assistance of the British Association of Social Workers, a study of the role of the field social worker in relation to looked after children.

Departments of State

16.20   The powers and duties of the Secretary of State bring their own responsibilities. Forming national policy, making regulations and issuing guidance, for example, impose burdens of getting them right and making them timely. The Secretary of State accounts to Parliament for the performance by the responsible Departments of their functions relating to children living away from home.

16.21   The Secretary of State also has an important role in exacting accountability from bodies which accommodate such children. The Secretary of State for Health possesses specific powers of inspection, direction and inquiry which are among the principal means of calling local authorities and others to account for the services with which they provide children. It is important that these powers are exercised consistently and whenever the public interest requires. They may be subject, however, to conflicting pressures, especially if the central Department is in any way uncertain of its role. There is a sense that some re-shaping of the relationship between the Department of Health/Welsh Office and the local authorities is occurring. Factors in this are the changing role of local government overall, the consequences of local government reorganisation, the changing need for services and the changing shape of provision. The central departments need a tighter grip nationally without eroding the local accountability of the statutory authorities. The new Local Government Association may develop a more effective facilitating role in this relationship than its predecessors.

16.22   The needs of children living away from home require use of the powers of the Secretary of State to be positively considered in the Department's response to the casework and other matters referred to it. This is far from an endorsement of indiscriminate intervention: the Review encountered situations which – in its opinion – the Department of Health was involved in unnecessarily as well as those in which it might have been more active. What is needed is a consistent response, according to criteria approved by Ministers, based on the needs of the children in the current situation and of all those whose future welfare would be influenced by the outcome. The Review recommends that the Department of Health/Welsh Office clarifies the criteria for using the Secretary of State's powers, and makes a small group of administrative and professional staff responsible for applying them.

16.23   It is important that the response referred to takes in the Department's reaction to the reports of its own Inspectorate. The Review is aware that the Inspectorate undertakes unpublicised follow up work to its inspections, and approves the policy of working with agencies to put right any major problems observed. Nevertheless, both national overview reports and reports on individual authorities disclose situations which – in the light of the Secretary of State's responsibilities –

seem to call for formal Departmental action. It is not clear that this always occurs. Again, the Review is not concerned with minutiae, but with examples of organisational irresponsibility, crass management or professional incompetence.

16.24   The work of the Social Services Inspectorate is dedicated to supporting the responsibilities of the Secretary of State. Its programme of inspection reflects Departmental priorities and is drawn up in consultation with the Local Government Association. The Review has been immeasurably assisted by Inspectorate reports. There is every prospect of children's services retaining their comparative priority within the current resources of the Inspectorate. The Review nevertheless recommends that the Inspectorate continues to monitor arrangements for safeguarding the welfare of children living away from home by inspections which support the functions of the Secretary of State. The Department should keep the resourcing of the Inspectorate under review in relation to the national monitoring needed to support discharge of the Secretary of State's responsibilities.

16.25   The permanent establishment of the Inspectorate in Wales is small in relation to the experience, knowledge and skill required to cover the full range of the personal social services in the detail that may be needed. Moreover, local government reorganisation means that it now links with 22 local authorities instead of 8, and that it must also contribute to the Welsh Office's concern to achieve consistently good standards of service post-reorganisation. The Report of the Examination Team on Child Care Procedures and Practice in North Wales[21] recommended strengthening the staffing of the Inspectorate, and the Secretary of State immediately approved additional posts. The Review is unsure that even this improvement will enable the Inspectorate, in the context of its other tasks, to monitor the safeguards for children living away from home with sufficient thoroughness for the Secretary of State's responsibilities to be fulfilled. It accordingly recommends that the Welsh Office re-assess the resourcing and staffing of the Social Services Inspectorate for Wales.

16.26   The danger of children's services fragmenting in Wales is an argument for a unifying strategy at national level. So too are the advantages of local government reorganisation, which brings members and managers closer to service users, and promotes the integration of education, housing and social services. Successful All Wales strategies in the past offer encouraging precedents. The Welsh Local Government Association urges the need for a Strategic Plan in Wales for services for children in need. The Review commends this to the Welsh Office as the necessary context to promoting and safeguarding the welfare of children living away from home in Wales.

16.27   The Review has also been brought into contact, directly or indirectly, with subjects for which a range of government departments are responsible. Matters affecting the welfare of children living away from home connect with the welfare of other groups of children and ultimately with that of all the nation's children. Submissions to the Review commented on the different perspectives that government departments adopt on matters concerning children, and some recommended the appointment of a Minister for Children to co-ordinate work in this field across government. Several submissions complained of poor co-ordination between government departments of policies affecting children, and of changes in major services being made without considering their effects on other services for children.

16.28   The Review acknowledges that policies and their implementation might be better harmonised between different Departments of State, and was impressed by the discussion of these matters in *Effective Government Structures for Children* [109]. A first step would be for all Departments of State with responsibilities towards children to adopt the aim of promoting and safeguarding the welfare of children, direct their operations to serving that aim, and evaluate the success of their operations in achieving it.

16.29   The Review believes that further steps are needed in government to safeguard and promote children's welfare by assigning the responsibility to a ministerial group. The moral, legal and social issues involved are so varied and important that overview at this level is required. The group would also secure a consistent government response to matters raised by this Review and by the weighty and authoritative reports already extant – such as that of the National Commission on the Prevention of Child Abuse [7].

PART V – COMMON THEMES III: SYSTEMS

Chapter 17 # MAINTAINING STANDARDS

SYNOPSIS

This chapter covers regulations and guidance, management, monitoring and inspection, and enforcement.

It argues that the quantity of current **regulations and guidance** detracts from its effectiveness and sets out views on their nature and coverage. A major recommendation is that the Department of Health /Welsh Office should, in the medium term, review and re-issue the regulations, circulars and guidance associated with the Children Act. This might be done under the aegis of the Children's Strategy Group (paragraph 17.7).

Registration issues are dealt with in the chapters on particular settings.

Both internal and external **management** must be continually vigilant in safeguarding the welfare of the children for whom they are responsible. This cannot be taken for granted. **Monitoring** by management is a necessary activity and proper resources should be devoted to it. Governing bodies or their equivalents should require annual reports on safeguards. External monitoring is also needed and **inspection** is the main source of this locally. Progress in the work of local authority inspection units is discussed and a number of recommendations made. These include action by the Secretary of State where local authority inspection units do not meet the frequency of inspection required (paragraph 17.22) and continued oversight of such units by the Social Services Inspectorate (paragraph 17.26).

The Social Services Inspectorate should study the action taken by local authorities to consider and implement the findings of reports by local authority inspection units (paragraph 17.28).

It suggests that reports on children's homes should have a common structure. The Social Service Inspectorate should promulgate a model. Reports on boarding schools must have a common structure (paragraph 17.30).

Inspection reports on boarding schools should be available to the public (paragraph 17.31).

The Government's intention to form new local inspection units containing both health and social services personnel is discussed. Whether or not this happens, it is recommended that arrangements should be introduced for the inspection of welfare arrangements for all health provision in which children are accommodated (paragraph 17.32).

The need for **enforcement** is discussed and the need for speedy action when necessary (paragraphs 17.34 – 40).

The chapter notes that exchanging relevant information between responsible agencies about institutions appears as fraught and sensitive as it is about suspicious individuals. It recommends that the Government should examine the need to strengthen the privilege of information communicated to registering authorities about the people and places they are responsible for registering (paragraph 17.41). It also recommends that public authorities pursue legal process to the fullest extent possible in the interests of children. Only by testing the boundaries of the law will its capacity for safeguarding children confidently be known. If the law proves inadequate, this provides evidence for improving it (paragraph 17.42).

Regulations and Guidance

'Full many a gem of purest ray serene
The dark unfathom'd caves of ocean bear:
Full many a flower is born to blush unseen,
And waste its sweetness on the desert air.'

Thomas Gray: Elegy written in a Country Churchyard

'It is the vulnerability of the user rather than the particular
service offered which should determine whether a degree of
regulation is necessary.'

Tom Burgner: The Regulation and Inspection of Social Services (1996)

17.1   The regulations and guidance about children being looked after by
local authorities appeared formidable in volume and complexity to
one returning to them after an absence of 6 years. The Department of
Health's investment in comprehensive guidance to the Children Act
was undoubtedly necessary to the successful launch of such major
new legislation. The Children Act Guidance is still referred to with
admiration and respect. The total corpus of regulations, statutory
guidance, departmental circulars and letters, Inspectorate and other
reports, is now so large, however, that responsible managers have
difficulty in comprehending all of it and it is less a tool for
practitioners than a subject for their research.

17.2   Another consequence of bulk and variety is the difficulty of distinguishing what is essential from what is desirable. A third is that they
may actually conceal what is essential. Many factors contribute to
regulations and other requirements being disregarded; ignorance
may be among them. One of the consequences of local government
reorganisation is that staff with specialised knowledge of children's
services are now shared by a larger number of social services
authorities. Where now are the managers and social workers who
are fully conversant with all the requirements of regulations and
statutory guidance? A report on a recent seminar commented *'There*
is a serious problem of information overload for social workers and other
staff, made worse by continuous changes in legislation, policy, procedures,
administrative structures and financial processes' [110].

17.3   Statutory regulation sits at the top of this hierarchy of exhortation,
with statutory guidance just below, and both are disregarded at one's
peril; yet it would be unwise to assume either that they contain all
that is essential or that all that they contain is in the strictest sense
necessary. Letters from administrators and chief inspectors, or reports
from groups such as the Support Force, may contain material of
similar importance. Not only the content of the communication but
also its level in the hierarchy of communication (Regulation, Section 7
guidance, Circular, Chief Inspector letter, Departmental letter) is
relevant to the recipient, who needs all the help he or she can get in
determining the importance and urgency of what is crossing the desk
or coming up on the screen. Presentation is the third relevant factor:
Department of Health/Welsh Office circulars and letters present a
deadpan face to a world which is now accustomed to highlights
and soundbites helping it to decipher the messages received and to
understand their relative importance. If the material is to be used, its
authors must make sure that it is usable.

17.4   Airing these issues in the course of the Review usually provoked
reassurance that the guidance provides a framework for good professional practice and unease at the prospect of my unleashing deregula-
tory zeal upon services which need firm and supportive regulation.
That is far from my intention, since I go on to recommend extending

statutory regulation in certain areas. I should do so with less confidence, however, if this were simply to pile another load of paper on an already unwieldy mass.

17.5   One group told us that Department of Health guidance on the Children Act was *'irrelevant to reality'*. The British Association of Social Workers found that *'the result is a set of very useful handbooks, but this style of presentation does not create a clear "statutory" framework, in the sense of legislation plus directions and guidance issued under statutory authority.'* In Wales, we were told that there was insufficient recognition of the Welsh dimension. References to quality and standards needed to be related to the cultural context.

17.6   My general view of those regulations and guidance for which the Department of Health/Welsh Office is responsible is that

- regulations should cover only that which it is essential to regulate,

- statutory guidance (issued under Section 7 of the Local Authority Social Services Act 1970) should be limited to statements or clarifications of national policy which the Secretary of State considers should be consistently implemented by all authorities,

- guidance on procedures and advice on good practice should be issued under ordinary circular and professional letter,

- guidance should be as simple as possible, clear, and easily accessible, and

- adherence to regulations and statutory guidance should be monitored and enforced.

17.7   I therefore recommend that the Department of Health/Welsh Office should review the regulations, circulars and guidance associated with the Children Act in order to:

- clarify essentials, simplify content and reduce volume,

- allocate the revised material to the categories of regulations and guidance according to strict criteria of weight and importance, and

- make them easier for people to use.

This is a task for the medium term in view both of its size and of the need for consultation. Its nature suggests that it might be undertaken under the aegis of the Children's Strategy Group. It should be repeated at regular, but not frequent, intervals.

17.8   The British Association of Social Workers and the Association of Directors of Social Services both raised in their submissions related and larger points. BASW expressed difficulties because there was *'no properly functioning national system which systematically sifts through this official literature, brings it together with research findings and practice experience, distils from it a national development programme and oversees the implementation of that programme'*. Such activities need not all be undertaken by the same agency provided a system exists to bring them together. The Review has already recommended that the Department of Health develop and implement a national strategy for residential child care, and that the Welsh Office establish a strategy for children in need in Wales. Experience of these developments would decide the desirability and feasibility of the comprehensive approach BASW recommends.

17.9   ADSS looked across the residential settings in which children live and found that *'this complex web of regulatory framework and responsible bodies creates the potential for a range of unsafe situations'*. It urged the

Departments of State to establish a coherent framework of regulation and registration for all residential provision for children. Appendix D sets out the current arrangements for regulating residential schools and children's homes. The differing circumstances in which children live away from home may render what the Association recommends unattainable in its entirety. The Review's recommendation of common legislative protection, however, is a step towards it. The Review has also recommended above a revision of Department of Health regulations and guidance. It has noted elsewhere confusion about the status of establishments run by voluntary organisations (paragraph 4.48) and about the registration of certain schools as children's homes. (paragraph 4.52)

Management

'Poor management is not the cause of any abuse that may have occurred; it does however create fertile ground in which abuse can occur and go undetected.'
Leo Goodman 1997

'This feeling of lack of concern for staff from senior departmental managers has been mentioned in earlier inspections.'
Inspection report 1996

17.10   Management gets a bad press in reports of cases of institutional abuse. This is understandable: management is accountable not only for its own acts and omissions but also for those of its subordinates, and even when blameless itself is tarred by association with what has gone wrong. In some cases, of course, managers and others in positions of authority have themselves assaulted children physically or sexually. In others, both internal and external managers appear to have blinded themselves to what was going on and carried denial to the point of obstructing investigation. The Review came across examples of this, not only in reports of abuse in children's homes (*'the response of senior managers within the Department was unco-ordinated and totally lacking in focus or drive'*), but also in less well known reports of abuse in each of the categories of boarding and residential schools, where the most charitable interpretation of management's reaction is that it was disorientated by panic. ChildLine's submission to the Review declared that *'Regimes of abuse prosper because people turn a blind eye to what is happening, or minimise or rationalise it.'* There are times when for 'people' it would be legitimate to substitute 'managers'.

17.11   Both internal and external managers must be continually vigilant in safeguarding the welfare of the children for whom they are responsible. The role of external management is critical to the prevention of abuse. The Support Force addressed a final comment to external line managers in its report *Staff Supervision in Children's Homes* [5]:

'1   Your support for staff is crucial. Are the supervisors in the home receiving good supervision?

2   Effective supervision will improve the quality of service in the children's homes. That service is delivered through the staff. Supervision will improve their performance. It is a proper function of line management.

3   Supervision is cost-effective. It will help you retain a well motivated staff team.'

The Review believes that these comments apply with force and relevance to all the settings in which children live away from home.

17.12 Inspection reports since the Children Act came into force revealed flaws in the management of some services for looked after children. *Corporate Parents* [105] found '*considerable weaknesses in the external management and monitoring of residential child care services*'. The SSI Inspection of Local Authority Fostering [20] found no routine monitoring of visits to foster carers by managers in the authorities studied. They were consequently unable to tell if statutory visits were made to children in foster homes. In 1 of the 3 authorities where private fostering was inspected [25], '*Neither social workers nor managers seemed to understand it*'. The inspection of small unregistered children's homes [11] revealed that 14 authorities did not know that they were using such accommodation, some of which, '*at the very least, is unsuitable and, in some cases, is placing (children) at risk*'.

17.13 Citing only these examples does not give a fair assessment of social services management, which is faced with running a range of diverse services in a context of high public expectations and straitened resources. This Review, however, is concerned with safeguarding children, and keeping children safe is a fundamental responsibility of social services departments. The Review hopes that the weaknesses identified have been put right. Willingness to put right what was wrong seems to the Review to be a necessary condition for retaining public confidence in local authorities as guardians of children – or in any other institution which accommodates them. The Review is surprised by the reluctance shown by a few schools, for example, to establish basic safeguards.

17.14 The operation of senior management in all settings also affects the welfare of children living away from home, directly and indirectly. Members of local authorities have specific as well as general duties towards the children they look after. Chief executives play a key role in establishing a corporate approach to children's issues across the local authority. Boards of Governors of schools and the trustees of voluntary organisations take unjustifiable risks if they neglect requiring reports from head teachers and chief executives on all matters concerning the welfare of children. The buck stops with them.

Monitoring and Inspection

'Great fleas have little fleas upon their backs to bite 'em,
And little fleas have lesser fleas and so ad infinitum.
And the great fleas themselves, in turn, have greater fleas to go on;
While these again have greater still, and greater still, and so on.'

A De Morgan: The Fleas

17.15 Good management has means of monitoring all the operations of an organisation. The Review restricts its discussion to what is relevant to safeguarding children who live away from home.

17.16 Monitoring by management is a necessary activity and it is proper to devote to it a due proportion of the resources of the organisation. It was not the Review's business to examine the managerial processes of the numerous bodies which provide accommodation for children living away from home. They should afford high priority to monitoring their arrangements for keeping children safe. '*The monitoring of the welfare of children in care is a fundamental part of a social services department's child protection responsibilities*' (Case Review, 1993 [111]). The governing bodies (or proprietor) of schools with duties under Section 87 of the Children Act should require annual reports on the workings of their arrangements for safeguarding children. Similar reports should be required by health and local authorities (Section 85) and by the proprietors of residential care homes, mental nursing homes and nursing homes to which Section 86 applies.

17.17   External monitoring is also necessary. Instructions and advice may be ineffectively implemented or even disregarded. The bodies which issue them and the people responsible for implementing them ought to check regularly that they are put into practice. In this context, the Review particularly welcomes the action taken by the Department of Health under the recent Chief Inspector Letter[93] to monitor local authority procedures for safeguarding children in the public care. The assumption that subordinates automatically follow orders or that even statutory authorities always do what the law requires was laid to rest long ago. At the same time, the resource requirements of external monitoring through inspection need careful consideration, particularly in view of the Review's recommendation that Section 87 of the Children Act should be extended to all residential schools.

17.18   Inspection is the principal means of external monitoring locally. It can never substitute, however, for the routine monitoring which is a fundamental responsibility of management. It supports management with an expert appraisal of services from a viewpoint independent of the vested interests involved in supplying them. The primary function of inspection, however, is serving the public interest by providing an additional safeguard for vulnerable people.

17.19   The Social Services Inspectorate inspects provision for which the Secretary of State has various responsibilities: voluntary children's homes, secure accommodation in community homes, and the Youth Treatment Centre. Local authorities register and inspect private children's homes, inspect the welfare arrangements of independent schools, and inspect their own community homes.

17.20   The performance of local authority inspection units, which have had a formal existence only since 1991, has been monitored by the Social Services Inspectorates in Wales and England. SSI completed in 1995 the large task of inspecting all local authority inspection units in England. These units have a massive workload. They dealt in 1994/5 with 17,000 new, changed or cancelled registrations and appeals, undertook nearly 71,000 inspections, investigated complaints, employed nearly 2,000 staff and cost £41m (of which about one third was recovered in fees). They were responsible for inspecting 16,665 residential care homes, 1,042 children's homes, 802 independent boarding schools and 48,841 units of day care.

17.21   Progress in their performance has been marked since 1991, but it is not surprising that some inconsistencies still remain between the approach and performance of the authorities. Units must obtain the services of staff and of lay people who are able to operate confidently across a wide range of client need and service provision. Professional staff should be qualified and experienced in their particular discipline. Both they and lay colleagues need training in inspectorial methods. These matters are particularly important in the aftermath of the creation of new and smaller authorities, since the SSI work uncovered the difficulty of small units in covering the full range of work.

17.22   The most serious criticisms of units from the Review's perspective was that 60% did not meet the frequency of inspection required, and that one of the areas of difficulty was the inspection of children's homes. The Review is baffled that some public authorities should as matter of policy inspect less often than required. The Secretary of State should take action to bring such authorities into line.

17.23   *Quality Care in Children's Homes in Wales*[112] confirmed the contribution local authority inspection units made to improvements in quality.

The Independent Reviews of Social Services Inspection Units in Wales 1994–95[113] reported that '*All units carried out the basic registration and inspection activities required of them.*' There was an 'overwhelmingly positive response' from heads of homes. Even before local government reorganisation, however, Welsh units were on average only half the size of those in England. Arrangements for joint use are coming into force between some authorities.

17.24 The Children Act exposed the boarding provision of independent schools to inspection by these units. There was some early awkwardness in the meeting – occasionally, the collision – of differing philosophies, but actual problems were fewer than anticipated. Experience of working together, and the clarifying and amended guidance introduced by the circular *Further Guidance on Inspection of Boarding Schools*[29] have produced a relationship which benefits children and is valued by the majority of the schools involved.

17.25 The Review was provided with over 150 recent reports by local authority inspection units on registered children's homes, local authority community homes, and the arrangements in independent schools for promoting and safeguarding the welfare of pupils. These reports provide valuable information at particular points of time about the state of the settings in which children live and the degree of safety they provide. They also confirm the judgments of the central Inspectorates about the levels of performance achieved.

17.26 The promulgation by the central Inspectorates of standards for services and criteria for inspection has provided local authority inspection units with invaluable practical guidance and helped towards more consistent standards nationally. The Social Services Inspectorate should continue its oversight of local authority inspection units on behalf of the Secretary of State in order to achieve consistently high standards of inspection nationally.

17.27 The Review regards local authority inspection units as providing important additional protection for many children living away from home. As much has been achieved as could reasonably have been expected in 1991 of units assuming new areas of work in independent schools and local authority community homes, especially in view of the difficulty of consolidating child care experience and promoting inspectorial work across 117 social services authorities. Some of the recent reports are of high quality. Particularly refreshing – in view of the deep suspicions entertained of the capacity of these units to criticise their own authorities – is the robust tone some employ about poor policies, management and practice in their own authority, as if membership of the family permits freer speech than the more sensitive tone needed for communication with others.

17.28 The best reports display the ability to accommodate detail within an overall assessment of the institution, and to present their findings briefly and in language accessible to lay as well as professional readers. Many have adopted the sensible distinction between 'requirements' for what is indispensable and 'recommendations' of what is desirable, and pursue in subsequent inspections (or earlier in the case of requirements) the action taken to implement them. One of the tests of the value of inspection is what changes it brings about. The Social Services Inspectorate should undertake a sample study of the action taken by the bodies inspected by inspection units – including the local authorities – to consider the findings of inspection reports and to implement their recommendations.

17.29   Weaknesses remain in the content, structure and availability of reports. Inspection must check that regulations are observed, but a process limited to trotting through the regulations from beginning to end may say very little about what this place is like to live in or even how safe it is. The reports of full inspections should set out, according to the evidence and the inspectors' knowledge, what experience this particular institution offers to those who live there. Reports are rarely too short; excessive length is often the product of a preoccupation with detail which impedes perception of the institution as a whole.

17.30   A common structure would be advantageous in reports on children's homes, especially to organisations with homes in more than one local authority area. The Social Services Inspectorate should promulgate a model. A common structure for reports on the boarding provision of schools is necessary to facilitate analysing and aggregating the information they contain. Such a structure was included in *Further Guidance on the Inspection of Boarding Schools* [(29)]. It is not followed by a considerable number of local authority inspection units – some may have overlooked the guidance, others automatically adopted their less appropriate model for children's homes, while others have evolved a structure which they believe improves on that recommended. The Department of Health/Welsh Office should revise and re-issue guidance on the structure of these reports and monitor its application. They should re-emphasise the need for local authorities to adhere strictly to the procedure which requires a covering letter to identify matters which require urgent consideration or action by the Registrar of Independent Schools.

17.31   These reports are made to the Registrar and the school. They are not available more widely. The Review supports the principle that reports of statutory inspections should normally be available to the public. The improvements suggested above would have the practical outcome of making the reports on boarding schools useful to parents in assessing how safe they are for children. It is therefore recommended that reports of inspections under Section 87 of the Children Act be regarded as public documents. Information about reports by local authority inspection units on registered homes (including voluntary homes if the recommendation in Chapter 2 is accepted) and community homes should be included in local authority newsletters and information to taxpayers. Copies of reports should be placed in public libraries.

17.32   The White Paper *Social Services: Achievement and Challenge* [(114)] announced the Government's intention to form new local inspection units containing health and social services personnel. The Review apprehends that this development is primarily motivated by the need to resolve anomalies in the registration and inspection of services for adults. Inspecting services for children is likely as a result of the proposed change to engage an even smaller proportion of unit resources and attention. Safeguarding children should be made an explicit priority for the new organisations, backed by both professionals and managers, and aggressively implemented. It will otherwise be submerged by the vast preponderance of adult institutions and adult attitudes, and by the vested interests of the major purchasers and providers of services for adults. If this change is proceeded with,

•   it should be done quickly – many local authority inspection units (especially in Wales) are adjusting to the changes arising from local government reorganisation, and prolonged turbulence is undesirable;

- the specific needs of inspecting children's services should be recognised, afforded due priority, and adequately resourced;

- the Secretary of State should require the arrangements for safeguarding and promoting the welfare of children to be inspected in all health provision in which children are accommodated.

17.33 If the merger does not take place, the Health Advisory Service and Social Services Inspectorate should be asked to report on the arrangements for safeguarding and promoting the welfare of children in health settings.

Enforcement

'The inseparable imperfection annexed to all human governments, consisted, he said, in not being able to create a sufficient fund of virtue and principle to carry the laws into due and effectual execution.'

Dr Johnson, reported by Boswell

17.34 Government cannot, regrettably, depend upon virtue and principle in securing adherence to the requirements of statute. Monitoring and inspection reveal deficiencies – some of them widespread, some likely to endanger children – in the observance of regulations and statutory guidance by providers of all kinds: public authorities, voluntary organisations and private businesses.

17.35 Part of this arises from obstinate perseverance in courses of harmful behaviour. Other failings derive from ignorance, carelessness, greed, stupidity, arrogance and poverty, all of them the properties of organisations as well as individuals. Many of these can be improved, if not corrected, with proper care and attention.

17.36 Regulations are usually enforced by inspectorates and registering authorities in this positive spirit. Time is usually given (may even be required by statute) to put right what is wrong; inspectorates or collaborative agencies may offer advice and practical support to the work that is necessary. Such policies are to be applauded: services should not be hounded to closure for venial failings; the nature of children's facilities means that operational problems are daily occurrences; the best services will sometimes malfunction. The terminally incompetent or impoverished institution usually dies of natural causes during this process, or voluntarily ends its existence as its clientele dwindles past the point at which it can survive.

17.37 An appeal may be made to a Registered Homes Tribunal against a local authority's decision to remove registration from a home. The Review is satisfied that the interests of proprietors are adequately protected by the constructive approach to enforcement adopted by local authorities, the formal processes leading up to de-registration, and the workings of the appeal mechanism. Indeed, the overall effect of these procedures, if they are simply applied by rote, may be to provide the rare harmful establishment with more protection than its endangered residents. There is no substitute for evaluating each case that causes concern on its merits and acting accordingly. Some authorities appear slow to act when they should respond more quickly. One correspondent complained of the 'recalcitrant attitude' of the registering authority when asked to take action where widespread abuse had been established. Such instances are unlikely to escape notice by the Department of Health; the Review expects the Department to remind registering authorities forcefully of their responsibilities in such circumstances.

17.38   The Registrar of Independent Schools is handicapped in the remedial action he can take when problems about the welfare or safety of pupils are reported. Failure to safeguard health or welfare may constitute grounds for withdrawing registration, but the process for securing this is cumbersome and protracted. The legislation is based historically on the nature of an educational system, in which the rhythms of both decay and amelioration are slower than those which affect the immediate safety of pupils. The process of calling a school to account requires official letters to be followed by inspection before grounds for objection to the school can be identified. If they are, the Secretary of State has a duty to issue a Notice of Complaint, which gives the school at least 6 months to put things right. Any school which is removed from the Register may appeal to the Independent Schools Tribunal. The Department for Education and Employment is able to move faster with schools approved for pupils with statements of special educational needs: *'Where the health, welfare or safety of pupils is at risk, approval may be withdrawn without prior consultation'* [31]. The Review recommends elsewhere (paragraph 4.31) introducing a power to order immediate de-registration and allowing for shorter periods of notice for child protection reasons.

17.39   Circumstances requiring immediate de-registration of children's homes or schools rarely occur. Means of safeguarding individual children by withdrawing them from situations of harm exist and are used. Occasionally, however, the entire population of a malfunctioning institution is at risk, and to leave it open simply exposes further intakes of children to risk of similar harm.

17.40   A few determined or litigious proprietors exploit every gap in registration and every delay in the disciplinary process. Closing one tiny institution and calling its owner to account required the combined efforts nationally of three Departments of State and two Inspectorates, and locally of the police, the social services department, the housing, environmental health and fire services; at unquantifiable and disproportionate cost – most of all to the children who continued to be abused during the early part of the process.

17.41   Exchanging relevant information between responsible agencies about institutions appears to be as fraught and sensitive an issue as exchanging information about suspicious individuals. One institution was finally de-registered 19 years after concern about it was first recorded; it is a perhaps pardonable exaggeration to say that the catalogue of complaints against it by then seemed as long as Leporello's list of his master's conquests. Government should examine the need to strengthen the privilege of information communicated to registering authorities about the people and places they are responsible for registering.

17.42   One of the constraints on public authorities in instituting or defending legal process is the cost to public funds they incur or the criticism they may attract if they are unsuccessful. The Review believes that these are less important considerations than the safety and welfare of the current residents and of all those who will follow them. It recommends public authorities to pursue legal process to the full extent possible in the interests of children. There is a sense at present that children in some homes and schools do not receive the full protection the law might afford because registering authorities are too cautious in proceeding against unsatisfactory proprietors. Only by testing the boundaries of the law will its capacity for safeguarding children be confidently known. If the law proves inadequate, there is then evidence for improving it.

Chapter 18: CHILD PROTECTION

SYNOPSIS

This chapter deals with child protection, complaints procedures and helplines.

Working Together provides a sound basic framework for the child protection element in investigating complaints of abuse in residential settings. The promised revision will take account of experience of subsequent child protection investigations. The problems of vulnerability to accusations and the appropriate responses from employers are considered.

The standards relating to child protection in *Inspecting for Quality* should apply to all settings in which children live away from home (paragraph 18.4).

The Review believes that suspicion, complaints and allegations must be properly and sensitively investigated and that this is particularly important in residential settings (paragraph 18.10). Investigations require careful management and particular experience and expertise. The practice of using police officers and social workers from dedicated groups is commended. In complex cases investigations should be carried out by staff who have specialised in such work and are not employed by the authority under investigation (paragraph 18.11).

It draws attention to the importance of effective systems through which children can complain and makes a number of recommendations for improvement.

Children wishing to use the statutory complaints procedure should be offered the help of an independent adult or children's rights officer (paragraph 18.14).

Local authorities should ensure that independent sector providers have effective formal complaints procedures and should enable children to use their own procedures (paragraph 18.15).

There should be a faster and less formal procedure for airing grievances. Local and departmental managers should establish a culture in which minor problems can be sorted out on the spot (paragraph 18.16).

Local authorities should satisfy themselves that adequate formal complaints procedures exist in all the residential schools for which they are responsible. Disabled children and others with special educational needs are likely to need help in making use of formal systems (paragraph 18.17).

Telephone helplines and counselling are also important for children living away from home. They should be accessible to children and receive financial support from statutory and charitable sources (paragraph 18.21).

Child Protection

18.1   *Working Together* [3] is the authoritative *'guide to arrangements for inter-agency co-operation for the protection of children from abuse'.* It is currently being revised by the Department of Health. The Department for Education and Employment issued an important Circular [98] *Protecting Children from Abuse: The Role of the Education Service. Working Together*, while it devotes a short section to children living away from home, sets out policies and processes for protecting all children, and the Circular follows this by not distinguishing between children in day and boarding schools.

18.2   The role of the Area Child Protection Committee (ACPC) in co-ordinating and reporting on local arrangements is fundamental to the protection of children. *Working Together* reinforces the primacy of the Committee's arrangements for protecting children living away from home. *'Whether the child is placed with a foster parent or living in a residential home or a school, the agencies' actions must take place within the agreed child protection procedures'. 'There must be clear written procedures on how suspected abuse is dealt with, for children and staff to consult and available for external scrutiny.'*

18.3   *Working Together* provides a sound basic framework for the child protection element in investigating complaints of abuse in residential settings. *'Where abuse by a member of staff is suspected, the action to be taken would be the same as with any other suspected abuse'*; if a social services worker is suspected, the investigation *'should, as far as possible, include an independent element'* and be carried out by a senior officer not in the suspected person's line of management. In inspecting schools, social services departments should ensure that their child protection procedures comply with *Working Together* and ACPC procedures. *Working Together* is clear that abuse by other children should be treated seriously and *'always subject to a referral to child protection agencies'.... 'in many cases, policies of minimal intervention are not as effective as focused forms of therapeutic intervention which may be under orders of the civil or criminal courts'.*

18.4   The experience of the Review confirms, from the mass of material it has examined, the prescience and continuing relevance of *Working Together's* guidance. Understandable difficulties occur in putting it into practice because this calls for the continual exercise of judgement in complex circumstances. More worrying is the culpable obduracy of the occasional school which has not yet absorbed these lessons in spite of strong exhortations from the Department for Education and Employment. The Review considers that the standards, outcomes, home practices and management action relating to child protection, which are set out on pages 18–22 of *Inspecting for Quality* [73] should be applied in all settings in which children live away from home.

18.5   The promised revision of *Working Together* will obviously take account of the substantial experience of child protection investigations which has accrued since its publication. As Wendy Rose said [115] , *'We have underestimated in residential settings*

–   *the prevalence of abuse*

–   *the extent of denial and collusion in some settings*

–   *obstacles to disclosure, acceptance by responsible adults, and successful prosecution*

–   *the nature and extent of paedophilia.'*

18.6   Investigations into allegations of abuse in foster care or residential settings differ significantly from investigations into allegations against parents or others in the child's own home. Social workers find themselves examining the actions of people regarded as co-workers or professional colleagues. If they are members of the same department, its management may wittingly or unwittingly obstruct the investigation because it is reluctant to have failures or weaknesses exposed or is unable to acknowledge the possibility of harmful misconduct by its employees. NCH Action for Children said in its submission: *'where the investigating authority is the same as the abusing authority it has been demonstrated that objectivity may become compromised'.*

18.7 Some investigations into residential establishments are almost unbelievably complex because of the number of places and people involved. But many investigations into single homes or schools are also difficult and protracted. The Castle Hill Report Practice Guide[116] is a textbook example of how to conduct such an investigation. Another investigation into a boarding school took 3 years from its commencement to the conviction of the proprietor and others for offences against boys. The Review received a number of submissions which expressed anxiety about the nature and duration of investigations: in which members of staff were suspended and left unsupported for long periods, the entire staff came under a cloud, the functioning of the home or school was seriously impaired, and current and former residents were disturbed. Heavy handed investigations, it is said, are not in the interests of children: *'If people are to do this difficult work at the level necessary to help children, they must know that in a crisis they can rely on being treated with respect and justice'* (Association of Workers for Children with Educational Difficulties: submission). Social workers are said to treat allegations as true before they have been investigated; the police come in looking for convictions.

18.8 One feeling shared by the subjects of all investigations, simple or complex, is that there is little official recognition of their effect on those who are innocently involved. No one says 'sorry', or helps with the re-building; there is no sense of being finally cleared. Residential social workers and teachers express a particular sense of vulnerability to unfounded accusations. One staff association speaks of a climate of fear which obstructs performance of the primary caring task. Foster carers are even more vulnerable. Their own children may be regarded as at risk, the whole of their family life may be disrupted, and may involve children who were previously placed with them. Disturbed children may mistake or misunderstand the meaning or intention of an action more easily than mature adults. Some allegations may be malicious: the girl at the centre of Josephine Tey's novel *The Franchise Affair* is the archetype of the manipulative 15 year old entrapping innocent adults. It would be counter-productive, however, to categorise all such allegations as malicious: those who abuse children have the greatest interest in discounting their complaints. People working in residential care and teaching must live with a degree of vulnerability (lower, it must be said, than the vulnerability of most of the children). What they deserve is an employer who does not panic and act precipitately when trouble comes, but accompanies investigation with support for troubled individuals and institutions, and remains committed to staff who have faithfully discharged the employer's policies.

18.9 Some part – perhaps some large part – of these problems stems from the requirements of the criminal law. The difficulty of obtaining convictions for offences against children leads to evidence being exhaustively pursued. The mills of the law grind exceedingly small, and exceedingly slow. Some police services now have much experience of complex inquiries and have developed methods of work which are as skilled and sensitive as is practicable within the system of criminal justice. Social services authorities are not infrequently commended for their part in complex investigations into institutional abuse.

18.10   There is general agreement that suspicion, complaints and allegations must be properly investigated. The Review believes that this is particularly important in residential settings, where so much may be at stake for the institution that the drawbridge goes up at the first signal of danger and children, parents, staff, governors and trustees man the walls to pour the contemporary equivalent of molten lead on the officious intruders. ChildLine (submission) expressed two particular concerns: *'Regimes of abuse prosper because people turn a blind eye to what is happening, or minimise or rationalise it'*, and *'Again and again, apparently responsible adults appear to consider it much more serious for a fellow adult to face the ignominy of being found responsible for sexual misconduct, than for a child (or many children) to be assaulted.'*

18.11   Child protection investigations in residential settings require careful management and particular experience and expertise. The Review commends the practice of drawing participants from a dedicated group of police officers and social workers. Complex investigations should wherever practicable be undertaken by staff who have specialised in such work and are not employed by the authority or organisation under investigation.

Complaints Procedures

18.12   Ways of raising matters that worry or affront them are particularly important for children who do not have a parent on the spot to confide in or to act on their behalf. They have in the eyes of the Review an essential preventative function. Their general effect is to identify anything that is going wrong within the totality of the system of care or education. Putting something right about assessment, selection, review, consultation or placement at an early stage can only improve the effectiveness of the overall process and reduce the risk of subsequent harm. Remedying a potential abuse at an early stage has a specifically preventive effect in protecting a child, and possibly other children. Moreover, aggregating and analysing information from complaints is useful in making services more sensitive to the needs of the children who use them.

18.13   Successive reports by the Social Services Inspectorate demonstrate steadily growing confidence and competence on the part of local authorities in implementing representations and complaints procedures.

18.14   Unsurprisingly, perhaps, only a tiny proportion of complaints emanate from children. A formal procedure is not the most appealing way for children to air grievances. Children in foster care appear less informed about complaints procedures than their contemporaries in residential care. The complicated appearance of the statutory system means that most children would need the help of an informed adult if they are to use it successfully. Nevertheless, it has worked well in cases concerning children when the child has been supported by a children's rights officer or independent adult. Children using the statutory procedure should always be offered such support.

18.15   Providers of service in the independent sector have developed different methods for children to make formal complaints. Local authority purchasers should satisfy themselves about the effectiveness of these methods, and should also enable the children they place to use their own complaints procedures. This is in keeping with the fundamental proposition from the second report of the Nolan Committee: *'Where a citizen receives a service which is paid for wholly or in part by the taxpayer, then the government or local authority must retain appropriate responsibility for safeguarding the interests of both user and taxpayer regardless of the status of the service provider.'*

18.16   Children need ways of airing and resolving grievances which are faster and less formal than statutory procedures. Local and departmental managers should establish a culture in which minor problems can be sorted out on the spot by the people concerned. A major frustration for older children who are looked after is the difficulty of talking to the person who is authorised to make the decision they are concerned about. Departmental policies and procedures constructed to cope with the worst eventuality are experienced in the majority of cases as oppressive and unreasonable. Negotiation is needed to identify issues on which sufficient flexibility is possible for key worker or head of home to make the decision.

18.17   Many boarding schools have ways for children to raise matters that worry them without labelling the process as a complaints procedure. Local inspection units are asked by LAC(95)1 [29] to verify that schools have procedures conforming to the guidance in Volume 5 in the Children Act series. All residential schools should possess such systems to complement their formal procedures. Local authorities should satisfy themselves that adequate formal procedures for dealing with complaints exist in all the residential schools for which they are responsible. Disabled children and others with special educational needs are likely to require independent help in making use of formal systems; the model of the independent representative service developed in secure units by A Voice for the Child in Care and now extended to children's homes is commended.

Helplines   18.18   Telephone counselling has developed into a major source of help for children. The anonymity it offers enables them to use it on their own terms, without their problems being immediately taken over by adults who carry the burden of statutory duties. It also offers the prospect of an immediate response by skilled people. Its popularity is demonstrated by use: ChildLine counselled 600,000 children in its first 10 years, 90,000 in the last full year, and answers 3,000 calls a day.

18.19   ChildLine and the NSPCC helpline have from their earliest days recognised the special needs of children living away from home, and committed specific services to children looked after by local authorities and children in boarding schools.

18.20   The value of these services is now generally acknowledged, and they are widely – and properly – publicised. Regulations require children's homes to make a telephone available for private use by residents. The display of Helpline numbers and private access to a telephone for children living away from home are now benchmarks of good practice in both residential care and education.

18.21   Telephone counselling provides an important service for children living away from home as an alternative or preliminary to the more formal help or intervention of statutory agencies. It should continue to receive financial support from statutory and charitable sources.

Chapter 19:   INQUIRIES

SYNOPSIS

This chapter discusses the importance of inquiries in establishing what went wrong so that steps can be taken to ensure it does not happen again. Most are carried out by the bodies concerned but statutory powers provide both a spur to local action and a longstop. The important ingredients are independence, adequate resourcing and that the report is published (paragraph 19.3).

The Review recommends that:

> The Secretary of State should possess powers of inquiry into all residential schools under Section 81 of the Children Act (paragraph 19.5).

> Departments of State should respond to the recommendations of reports they have commissioned (paragraph 19.6).

Inquiries
'Vested interests are hardly ever on the side of the exposure of wrongs, but far more concerned with damage limitation for public reputations.'
Ann Craft.

19.1   Holding inquiries into things that have gone wrong builds up a bank of information about strengths and weaknesses which is invaluable in reinforcing safeguards for children away from home. Some inquiries into individual tragedies – from the Monckton Report[117] onwards – have gone further, and proved turning-points for generations of children. The impulse to find out what went wrong and to take steps to ensure that it never happens again is as laudable as it is powerful.

19.2   Section 81 of the Children Act gives the Secretary of State powers to order inquiries into *'the functions of the social services committee of a local authority, in so far as those functions related to children...., the functions of a voluntary organisation, in so far as those functions related to children, a registered children's home or voluntary home; a residential care home, nursing home or mental nursing home, so far as it provides accommodation for children; a home provided by the Secretary of State under Section 82'*. These statutory powers are rarely invoked, and have usually been reserved for matters of grave national, public and political concern. Their existence, however, provides the Secretary of State with powerful leverage in ensuring that local and other responsible authorities account to the public for their stewardship on matters to do with the care of children. Bodies which might have resisted such an examination have preferred setting up their own inquiries when the alternative of an inquiry under statutory powers, with its considerable costs, has been put to them. A culture has now developed of authorities establishing their own inquiries into situations that have gone badly wrong, drawing upon the guidance of the Department of Health/Welsh Office and the substantial body of experience that is now available.

19.3   The essential elements of this process are that the person or group conducting the inquiry should be independent of the commissioning authority, that the inquiry should be adequately and appropriately resourced, and that the report of the inquiry should be published. The statutory powers continue to provide a longstop if the conduct or outcome of the inquiry is unsatisfactory, or the commissioning body unreasonably disregards its findings.

19.4   It is right that the relevant Department of State should continue to monitor all inquiries relating to the care of children and receive and consider their reports. A few are not effective. The recommendations of even the best must be tested for priority and practicability before they are implemented. The authority of the Secretary of State may also be required to resist inappropriate calls for inquiries when management reviews or investigations by Area Child Protection Committees under Part 8 of *Working Together*[3] would suffice. Calls for a public inquiry into every misadventure are understandable, but other levels or kinds of action may be a better response to what has happened than the sledgehammer of statutory powers. They would certainly be much quicker and cheaper. Formal inquiries are costly and divert resources from other needs. Rules of proportionality and parsimony should apply to inquiries as elsewhere. But the essential requirement is that things that go wrong must be properly investigated.

19.5   The Review was informed of past events in schools run by independent bodies which would – in its opinion – have been the subject of formal inquiry if they had occurred in the public sector. Inquiry reports on some similar situations in maintained schools were submitted to the Review. It is entirely proper that occurrences causing serious concern in services provided by statutory authorities should be carefully scrutinised. The Review believes that there is a strong public interest in the protection of children which also justifies the formal examination of serious failings in the independent sector. Section 80 of the Act already gives the Secretary of State powers of inspection of independent schools and access to records. Section 81 appears to allow inquiry into a school run by a voluntary organisation or registered as a children's home. The Review recommends that the Secretary of State should possess powers of inquiry into all residential schools.

19.6   This Review is one of many similar exercises that might be brigaded under the general heading of inquiries. It has encountered uncertainty in the field about the status of the recommendations of the reports of earlier inquiries: in particular, about whether the Department of Health approves them and expects them to be given effect. It would be unreasonable to expect a Department of State to comment on all the recommendations of every report that is issued, but right to expect it to respond to the recommendations of reports it has itself commissioned.

Chapter 20: # CRIMINAL JUSTICE

SYNOPSIS

This chapter examines the role of the criminal justice system in safeguarding children. It concludes that it is ineffective in deterring offenders and in securing convictions of those who are guilty. Its failings are most marked in relation to those who are most vulnerable – the very young and the disabled. The process itself is damaging to children. Action is needed to make it more effective: the reliability of systems of notification of sex offenders depends heavily on guilty people being convicted.

Its main recommendations are that:

> The Pigot recommendations should be implemented in the next parliamentary session (paragraph 20.19).

> There should be a wide ranging review of the arrangements for prosecuting alleged sex offenders against children in order to improve their effectiveness and afford greater protection to children in general (paragraph 20.27). It should also consider the arrangements in magistrates courts and civil proceedings (paragraph 20.28).

It makes a number of suggestions aimed at increasing the proportion of cases which go to trial:

> The memorandum of guidance for interviewing children should be reviewed (paragraph 20.20).

> There should be flexibility in allowing evidence in a form suited to the age of the child and they should be helped to communicate if necessary (paragraph 20.21).

> The Severance of cases should only be allowed if requested by the prosecution (paragraph 20.22).

It describes a proposal for modifying the balance of probability and suggests that the Home Office investigate it further (paragraph 20.24).

Information should be kept, monitored and published on charges and their outcomes in relation to offences against children (paragraph 20.30).

It suggests action which could be taken to make the process less damaging for the children involved. These include the greater use of video recordings and television links (paragraph 20.32); the use of judges and barristers who specialise in work with children (paragraph 20.33); preparation for the child via the child witness pack and programmes such as the NSPCC's Witness Support Project (paragraph 20.33): minimising the time it takes cases to come to court and making careful arrangements for child witnesses (paragraph 20.36).

It urges the Crown Prosecution Service to issue the Code of Practice on pre-trial Therapy as soon as possible (paragraph 20.35).

*'As matters currently stand, child sex offenders have little
reason to fear detection and even less reason to fear conviction.'*
Bernard Gallagher: Complex Cases of Child Sexual Abuse

*'Children cannot be adequately safeguarded from abuse without
reform of the court system. As it currently operates, it is unequal,
discriminatory towards child witnesses, and achieves an
extremely poor level of convictions.'*
ChildLine– submission

20.1   A fundamental element in safeguarding children – whether they live at home or not – is the criminal justice system. It should be both an effective deterrent to potential offenders and an effective way of dealing with those who offend. At present our system does neither. It fails to protect children and the process of prosecution adds harm to that already inflicted by the abusers. It leaves some children effectively 'sitting ducks' – particularly the young and the disabled. Criminal justice is important to the Review on two counts. Firstly, the children with whom the Review is concerned are more vulnerable to abuse by other people than children living with their parents. Secondly, the protective system for communicating information about people who seek work with children depends heavily upon convictions for criminal offences. If offenders are not convicted, the system cannot be effective.

20.2   The recommendations in this report are intended to improve the safeguards for children who do not have the day to day protection of their parents. It is hoped they will be fully and rigorously implemented. Some of them, it is hoped, will lead to the earlier identification of abusers. However, efforts to protect children against those determined to abuse them will prove ineffectual for large numbers of children unless the criminal justice system is rendered more effective and less damaging.

20.3   *Childhood Matters* [7] said that the number of successful prosecutions has been steadily declining since 1989 although more cases have been notified to the police. Some said this was in order to avoid the trauma of a court appearance and some that it was because the Crown Prosecution Service were reluctant to put cases forward because of the difficulty in securing a conviction.

**Numbers of
Prosecutions**

20.4   In the opening address to the North Wales Tribunal of Inquiry, Gerard Elias QC said that the police had interviewed two and a half thousand people, leading to the investigation of 500 complaints of physical or sexual abuse and that *'arising out of this major inquiry, 8 individuals were prosecuted. On the face of it, this appears to be a surprisingly small number.'* 6 were convicted.

20.5   Home Office statistics confirm the decline in the number of successful prosecutions for sexual offences against children. Recorded offences of unlawful sexual intercourse with a girl under 13 went down from 299 in 1985 to 178 in 1995 and convictions dropped from 110 to 81. The conviction rate increased slightly from 37% to 45%. In 1985 an additional 19% received a caution, in 1995 this figure increased to 23%. Most marked, however, is the trend in relation to offences of gross indecency with children under 14. In 1985 there were 633 offences notified to the police and 266 convictions – a 42% conviction rate. A further 7% received a caution. In 1995 the number of offences recorded had doubled to 1,287 but there were only 155 convictions, a rate of just 12%. The figure for cautions was also lower, at a little over 2%.

20.6   The total number of cases involving children under 16 is not known for the period until 1995, since until then the age was not recorded separately for a number of offences, including rape and physical violence. It will now be possible to monitor the trends for rape of children under 16.

20.7   The Home Office believes that a significant proportion of those convicted of offences like rape and indecent assault have committed offences against a child. They estimate that half of those convicted of rape are convicted of the rape of a child aged under 16. For the offence of indecent assault on a male the proportion is two thirds and for indecent assault on a female three quarters. (In the years preceding changes in legislation in 1995, the relevant proportions may be different.)

20.8   In the light of this, one can make some inferences from the conviction rate of these offenders. Criminal Statistics for England and Wales: 1995 show the trends in relation to indecent assault on a female and rape. In 1985 there were 11,410 offences of indecent assault on a female and 2,138 convictions, a conviction rate of 19%. In 1995 the figures were 16,876 and 2,365 respectively, a conviction rate of 14%. For rape the 1985 figures were 1,842 and 430, a rate of 23%. In 1995 they were 4,986 and 569, a rate of only 11%.

20.9   Developments arising from the Sexual Offenders Act 1997 will raise the stakes even further for offenders – as would community notification of convicted sex offenders in their area. It is feared that fewer will admit their guilt at an early stage and more cases will be contested in court. It will be important to research the effects of the Act and to keep the area under scrutiny.

20.10   Many paedophiles go undetected for a very long time and abuse large numbers of children in the course of their 'careers'. They take great care to limit the chance that they will be caught by manipulating both their victims and those who might otherwise protect them. They target those whom they think they can persuade or intimidate, who would be least likely to be believed if they complained, or who would not be regarded as a credible witness in a court of law. This category includes children with learning difficulties and those with sensory or communication problems which make the giving of compelling evidence very difficult. It also includes very young children. One in three children who report sexual abuse are under 8 yet a recent survey of police authorities for the Channel 4 Dispatches programme *Death of Childhood* found that prosecutions are 'extremely rare' in this age group. Of the four authorities that gave figures, South Wales said that 5% reached court. In Somerset and Devon and Cornwall less than 2% had done so. Essex said that no case had gone to court over a three month period. It is not acceptable that criminal justice should fail the weakest in society in this way.

Standard of Proof   20.11   Reference is made elsewhere (paragraph 9.6) to the charmed lives some of the most serious abusers lead. They survive investigation and even prosecution for years before finally being brought to book. Frank Beck was found not guilty of assault occasioning actual bodily harm but in a later trial was sentenced to life imprisonment. Ralph Morris was investigated 3 times before finally being convicted of offences for which he received 12 years' imprisonment.

20.12   In their overview report[118] on the children of Frederick and Rosemary West, The Bridge said *'the detailed descriptions given by some of the children about their lives to date makes painful reading and, in fact, is quite appalling .... but there was ultimately insufficient evidence to achieve guilty verdicts in criminal proceedings.'* And *'the outcome was similar to so many child protection cases where children find the ordeal of giving evidence beyond them, or they have been subjected to intimidation or been discredited as witnesses, and explains for the most part why so few cases either reach court or result in guilty verdicts.'*

20.13   A number of factors account for this: the private nature of the offence, the lack of corroborating evidence, the age of the child and his or her ability to explain what has happened. The adversarial nature of the criminal justice system treats accuser and accused as equal – clearly not the case where the former is a child.

20.14   The evidence of the child is crucial, yet too often it is decided that he or she would not make a credible witness or would be too damaged by the trial process to make it in the public interest to put him/her through the ordeal. Both issues need to be addressed.

20.15   Most importantly, action is needed to change the procedures for prosecutions relating to the abuse of children in order to strengthen the prospects of securing convictions against those who are guilty. There is ample evidence from the many reports the Review has studied that serious offenders escape justice. One example of concern about this is the Northern Ireland Report *An Abuse of Trust*[97] which said *'Concern remains, however, about significant numbers of persons who are considered by professionals to have perpetrated abuse but who will continue to elude conviction due to the nature of evidence required by the criminal justice system.'*

20.16   It is an essential part of our judicial system that the scales are weighted in the favour of the defendant and that some who are in fact guilty will go free. The nature of child sex abuse and the problems attached to applying processes designed for adults is such that it becomes extremely difficult to secure a conviction. Because it is so difficult and since the process in itself is a damaging one for the children, there is a tendency not to bring cases to court at all. The Crown Prosecution Service, when deciding whether a case should go to court, makes a judgement as to whether the case is more likely than not to result in a conviction. To a non-lawyer this would roughly translate as there being a greater than 50% probability of conviction. There are of course other factors involved, such as the public interest criterion, and the likely decision of magistrates and judges on the strength of the case. A conviction rate of only 12% for the offence of gross indecency with a child, however, lets far too many who are guilty go untried and unpunished. A system which was more effective would not only provide redress for the abused children but protect other children by taking the offender out of circulation temporarily and by preventing his or her future employment with children. It would also provide a deterrent to other potential offenders.

Pigot Recommendations

20.17   Part of the problem is the weight placed upon the evidence the child can give. The report of the Advisory Group on Video Evidence – the Pigot Report[119]– said *'It is worth emphasising that in other parts of the world where the quality of justice is not inferior to our own, listening to what very small children have to say and providing suitable means for children to describe their experiences outside the public arena of the court-room is not regarded as unusual, unreasonable or a threat to the principle that the prosecution must discharge the burden of proof.'* The report concluded that *'The difficulties which exist in bringing those who commit offences against children to justice and the damage which the courts often inflict upon many children both constitute a grave and hitherto intractable social problem.'* If fully implemented these would go a long way to address the problem.

20.18 Many of the Report's recommendations have been enacted in law. These include the use of pre-trial video evidence for the child's evidence; that the defendant cannot personally cross-examine the child and that all children should be presumed to be competent witnesses. However, it appears that practice lags behind the law and that much remains to be done to ensure that these helpful provisions are implemented properly and consistently. We urge that action be taken to ensure that this is the case.

20.19 However key recommendations remain unimplemented or only partly implemented. We entirely endorse the Pigot view that *'no child witness to whom our proposals apply should be required to appear in open court during a trial unless he or she wishes to do so.'* We believe that the remaining Pigot recommendations, particularly 3, 4, 7 and 8, should be fully and urgently implemented. The Labour Party Manifesto promised greater protection for victims in trial for rape and other serious sexual offences and for those subject to intimidation, including witnesses. The Review hopes that the Government will see the implementation of the Pigot recommendations as an important element in that and we urge that priority be given to this in the next parliamentary session.

Forms of Evidence

20.20 There has been some amendment to the law to allow younger children to give evidence. The 1991 Criminal Justice Act made it possible for very young children to do so. However, the circumstances in which they can do so are tightly defined and make it very difficult. The Review believes that the arrangements for interviewing children are too restrictive and should be looked at again. In particular the child should be able to have someone present with whom he/she is familiar and who can provide the necessary support. Shorter interviews which are suited to the child's attention span and, if necessary, more interviews should be allowed.

20.21 There also needs to be flexibility in allowing evidence in a form suited to the age and understanding of the child. Some children will need help in understanding the questions put to them and may need to communicate their responses in an unusual way – through drawings for example. Others may need the help of a Human Aid to Communication. Such assistance as is needed for communication should be given. It should not be assumed that because a child is disabled, has a learning disability, or is young, he or she cannot give evidence. Nor that he or she will necessarily be damaged by doing so. Some may be more upset at not being able to play their part in getting their abuser punished.

20.22 There are pitfalls even in cases where more than one child is involved – where it might be thought that the cumulative evidence would have more effect. If children all appear to be telling a very similar story they are accused of colluding, if their stories differ this gives scope for undermining them. If the credibility of one key witness is undermined, others may not even be called. The defence may ask for cases to be 'severed' so that they are heard separately. If the first falls the others may be dropped. This, again, allows those who are guilty to go free. There is a strong case for leaving it to the prosecution to decide whether cases should be taken together or separately.

20.23   Implementation of Pigot and the action advocated here is unlikely in our view to ensure sufficient improvement in securing convictions against the guilty. There is a strong case for going much further and considering whether some of the basic tenets of the law should apply in these cases.

A More Radical Approach

20.24   One suggestion was made to the Review for a specific adjustment to the criminal justice system to make it more effective. Given the low rate of convictions, it was proposed that the Crown Prosecution Service should be required to initiate proceedings in the County Court with the single, main purpose of obtaining a certificate from that court that the case is fit for trial at the Crown Court. Unlike the old committal proceedings, when the magistrates had only to decide whether there was a prima facie case, the County Court judge would hear the evidence and decide, on a balance of probabilities, whether the criminal event occurred in the way described by the victim and witnesses. The immediate effect of that finding would be that the victim would know whether he/she had been believed. On a finding in favour of the Crown Prosecution Service, the County Court judge would decide whether it is in the public interest for the case to be sent for trial. Irrespective of certification for trial, the judge would have the additional power of granting the victim an injunction (if necessary) and could award damages. This seems an attractive suggestion and the Review recommends that the Home Office should investigate it further.

20.25   Other suggestions that have been made include:

- considering whether the test used should be the same as in other criminal cases – beyond reasonable doubt – or modified to something nearer the civil test of a balance of probability, or between that used in the criminal and civil courts;

- using people with specialist knowledge in some cases – for example when a blind, deaf or brain damaged child with considerable communication difficulties is involved;

- reviewing whether adversarial cross questioning is essential, even in recorded interviews, or whether the necessary information could not be obtained in a way better suited to obtaining the truth in a less damaging way;

- and making information on previous offending, and any other cases pending, available to the court when it makes its decision.

20.26   The Review is aware that these raise significant questions about the nature of justice, civil liberties and equal treatment of these offenders in comparison with others. Our contention is that the present arrangements make it almost impossible to provide appropriate legal redress for children who have been abused and actually impossible for significant numbers of the most vulnerable – those who are young or disabled. Many of those with whom this Review is concerned are the most vulnerable both to the initial abuse and to the damaging consequences of what follows. Unlike other children, some will not have loving and supportive parents to help them through the process and its aftermath. We believe that a review of these matters is needed if children are to get the protection they both urgently need and deserve.

20.27   We do not possess the expertise to evaluate these suggestions and recommend specific changes. We urge that this whole area should be the subject of a wide ranging review which considers fundamental changes to the current arrangements for prosecuting alleged sex offenders against children. It should aim to improve their effectiveness, provide a real deterrent to offending and afford more protection to child witnesses and to children collectively. Such a review should include lay people and those representing the interests of children as well as those expert in the legal system.

20.28 It should also consider arrangements in magistrates courts, as recommended by Pigot, so that these are brought into line with changes elsewhere. It will help little if changes are made in crown courts but children are made to confront their abusers in committal hearings. Civil proceedings should also be covered since there are problems where there are concurrent care and criminal proceedings. As Alan Levy QC has said, *'there is an overwhelming need to scrutinise the inter-relationship of the two sets of proceedings, criminal and civil, and perhaps come up with a better way of dealing with both.'*

20.29 In the meantime systems of notification which rely on convictions are ineffective if the criminal justice system cannot convict offenders. The Review therefore considers it vital that use is made of 'soft' information, including charges as well as convictions, in the arrangements for checking the backgrounds of potential employees. This is also discussed in Chapter 15.

20.30 There is a dearth of information in this area. Data should be kept about the numbers of cases where charges are made but not proceeded with, together with the reason for this. The ages of the child or children involved, the nature of the alleged offence(s) and other relevant data – for example whether the child was disabled – should be included. This would enable policy makers in both the criminal justice and the child protection area to see the extent and nature of the problem, to identify any trends and assess the need for action. The information should be published on an annual basis so that others with an interest, notably parents and professionals involved with children, can see what progress is being made.

Changes to the Court Process

20.31 While it remains necessary for children to attend court, there should be changes to the court process so that it is less damaging to them. The Review believes that the treatment of children in court cases amounts to systems abuse of a very harmful kind and that urgent action should be taken to redress this. It believes there are a number of measures which can be taken which would improve the situation while not undermining the cause of justice.

20.32 Some measures have been introduced in recent years to ease the difficulty for children acting as witnesses. It is now possible for their main evidence to be video recorded and used when the case comes to court. They may also be allowed to give evidence and be cross examined by live video link when the court comes to trial or to give evidence in court from behind a screen so that they do not have to face the alleged abuser in court. These concessions are, however, at the discretion of the judge and can be appealed against. The Pigot recommendations would be a big improvement here. It has also been suggested that the use of an intermediary, such as is used in South Africa, to put questions to children on a live TV link would help reduce the scope for confusion when barristers ask too many, or too complicated questions at once.

20.33 The adversarial nature of a trial is very difficult for anyone but especially for abused children. Their evidence can too easily be undermined. They are accused of lying about what happened to them and find this distressing and confusing. Their self confidence and esteem is often even more damaged as a result of court hearings. It is not easy for adults to adjust their normal court room behaviour and method of cross examination if they are unfamiliar with dealing with children. There is a strong case for specialising in this area of work and for judges, defence and prosecution barristers to receive training. The guidance given in the helpful video *A Case For Balance* should be followed as a matter of routine by judges and barristers. The Crown Prosecution Service already make it a requirement that counsel they instruct have seen it.

20.34   The atmosphere should be as informal as possible. The child should be given preparation on what to expect through the child witness pack and through programmes such as the NSPCC's Witness Support Project. This provides a comprehensive service of preparation and support to all children and young people living in Surrey who may be called on to give evidence in criminal proceedings. It provides direct support, assistance and information to enable them to give full and accurate testimony. It also provides an advisory/consultancy role to other professionals working with children involved as witnesses. In 1995–96 75% of the Project's cases involved sexual abuse and 16% physical abuse.

20.35   Cases should be heard as quickly as possible. Delay before a case comes to trial can be very distressing for the child, especially since care has to be taken in the meantime in relation to the type of counselling and therapy he/she can receive without risking a claim that the evidence has been contaminated. It is in the interests of the defendant to delay matters as much as possible in the hope that the child will change his or her mind about giving evidence, or become confused about some aspects of his or her evidence. We understand the Crown Prosecution Service is producing a Code of Practice on pre-trial Therapy. It is important that children get as much help and support as possible and that the prospects of a successful prosecution are not affected. We urge that this be finalised and made available as quickly as possible.

20.36   Care should be taken with detailed arrangements for children's attendance in court. They should not be brought to court until they are needed and should certainly not be expected to wait in the same area as their abuser. Their addresses should not be given in court. They should also be kept informed of the progress and outcome of the trial and assisted, if need be, with any matters arising from it (for example protection and support).

Chapter 21: # RESOURCES

SYNOPSIS

The Review is not authorised, or able, to assess what the spending levels on children's services should be. It received a number of representations about resources and accepts that some of the shortcomings it heard about stemmed from a shortage of money or other resources, such as skilled and experienced staff. But any extra resources should be matched by managerial and professional efforts to improve general performance.

Many of the Review's recommendations do not require additional resources other than time and thought. Some do. These will need to compete with other priorities. The Review argues the needs of children should rank high and indicates which areas, within its remit, it believes have the strongest claim (paragraph 22.4).

21.1   The Review received numerous comments about resources which clustered about 2 themes. Firstly, on the domestic and environmental impoverishment which led to large numbers of children being 'in need' in a prosperous society. Secondly, that services for children in need are seriously under resourced for the task expected of them. The burden of these comments was that spending on disadvantaged children was unfairly constrained at both central and local levels.

21.2   The Review is neither authorised nor able to assess what levels of spending ought to be. It is familiar with demands for more resources as the reflexive response of incompetent management. Nevertheless, it is impressed by the consistency with which representative and other bodies have communicated the difficulties of resourcing their services. The Review accepts that some of the shortcomings it has learned about arise from the scarcity of money and other resources such as skilled and experienced staff. It does not know which shortcomings or how many, or whether these are due to the determination of priorities at central or local level. Since the major part of the money local authorities spend is allocated by the centre, the latter is presumably more responsible.

21.3   Many of the examples the Review encountered of things going wrong arise from organisational and individual errors or worse which might collectively and charitably be described as inefficiency. If organisations and people did what they were supposed to do they would serve children better and avoid the waste of public resources which inefficiency incurs now and – in the case of children – stores up for the future. Sustained managerial and professional efforts are needed to eliminate the gross errors which have marred these services in the past and to improve their general performance.

21.4   Many of the Review's recommendations and exhortations do not require additional material resources. They do need time and thought, to which there is an unavoidable opportunity cost. Others require increased material resources: revitalising residential care, regulating private foster care, improving standards of care in residential education, extending inspection, getting children out of prison, giving care leavers a better start in life. They must take their place among competing priorities for public expenditure. The Review argues that the needs of children should rank high; that among children, those who are in need and live away from home rank higher; and that the strongest case for additional resources is that of children in the public care, disabled children, children with emotional and behavioural difficulties, and children in prison.

REFERENCES

1. Utting Sir William (1991) *Children in the Public Care– A Review of Residential Child Care* (Department of Health)

2. Social Services Inspectorate Wales (1991) *Accommodating Children– A Review of Children's Homes in Wales– Volumes 1 and 2* (Welsh Office)

3. Working Together under the Children Act 1989 (1991) (HMSO)

4. *Choosing with Care– The Report of the Committee of Inquiry into the Selection, Development and Management of Staff in Children's Homes* (1992) (HMSO) (also referred to as Warner)

5. Support Force for Children's Residential Care publications (Department of Health)

   Strategic Planning Framework: Part 1– Analysing Need (1994)

   Out of Authority Placements: Checklist of Information to be obtained (1994)

   Recruitment and Selection Techniques: Database (1994)

   Staff Supervision in Children's Homes (1995)

   Strategic Planning Framework: Part 11– Implementing Change (1995)

   Code of Practice for the Employment of Residential Care Workers (1995)

   Contracting for Children's Residential Care (1995)

   Unit Costing and Financial Management in Children's Residential Care (1995)

   Specialisation in Residential Child Care: Discussion Paper (1995)

   Matching Needs and Services: The Audit and Planning of Provision for Children Looked After by Local Authorities (with Dartington Social Policy Research Unit) (1995)

   Good Care Matters– Ways of enhancing good care practice in residential child care (1995)

   The Use and Development of Databases of Residential Child Care Resources (1995)

   Progress Report to the Secretary of State for Health (1995)

   Final Report to the Secretary of State for Health (1996)

6. Levy A QC, Kahan B (1991) *The Pindown Experience and the Protection of Children* (Staffordshire County Council)

7. *Childhood Matters*: Report of the National Commission of Inquiry into the Prevention of Child Abuse–Volumes 1 and 2 (1996) (The Stationery Office)

8. *The Public Inquiry into the Shootings at Dunblane Primary School 1996* (Cm 3396)

9. Burgner Tom (1996) *The Regulation and Inspection of Social Services* (Department of Health/ Welsh Office)

10. Berridge D, Brodie I (1996) Residential Child Care in England and Wales. *Child Welfare Services* (ed Hill and Aldgate)

11. Social Services Inspectorate (1995) *Small Unregistered Children's Homes* (Department of Health)

12. Social Services Inspectorate/ OFSTED (1995) *The Education of Children who are looked after by Local Authorities* (Department of Health/ OFSTED)

13. *The Health of Children in Wales* (1997) (Welsh Office)

14. *Banged up, Beaten Up, Cutting up* (1995) (Howard League)

15. *Foster Care in Crisis: A Call to professionalise the forgotten service* (1997) (National Foster Care Association)

16. Berridge D (1997) *Foster Care: A Research Review* (HMSO)

17. Pithouse A, Young C, and Butler I (1994) *All Wales Review: Local Authority Fostering Services* (University of Wales College of Cardiff, School of Social and Administrative Studies)

18. Association of Directors of Social Services (1997) *The Foster Care Market: A National Perspective* (ADSS)

19. Waterhouse S (1997) *The Organisation of Fostering Services: A Study of the Arrangements for Delivery of Fostering Services in England* (National Foster Care Association)

20. Social Services Inspectorate (1996) *Inspection of Local Authority Fostering 1995–96 National Summary Report* (Department of Health)

21. *Report of the Examination Team on Child Care Procedures and Practice in North Wales* (1996) (Return to an Address of the Honourable the House of Commons dated 17 June 1996) (HMSO)

22. *Safe Caring* (1994) (National Foster Care Association)

23. Social Services Inspectorate (1995) *Independent Fostering Agencies Study: Report by Geoffrey James* (Department of Health)

24. *Black Children and Private Fostering* (1993) (Race Equality Unit)

25. Social Services Inspectorate (1994) *Signposts: Findings from a national inspection of private fostering* (Department of Health)

26. *The Best of Both Worlds: Parents' Experience of Boarding Schools* (1995) (Independent Schools Information Service)

27. Morgan R (1993) *School Life: Pupils' Views on Boarding* (HMSO)

28. Department of Health (1994) The Children Act 1989: *Use by Local Authorities of Voluntary Organisations and Independent Fostering Agencies* (Local Authority Circular LAC (94) 20)

29. Department of Health (1995) *Inspection of Boarding Schools (Section 87 of the Children Act 1989): Further Guidance* (Local Authority Circular LAC (95) 1)

30. Morris J (1995) *Gone Missing?: A Research and Policy Review of disabled children living away from their families* (Who Cares? Trust)

31. Department for Education and Employment (1994) *The Development of Special Schools* (Circular 3/94)

32. Department for Education and Employment (1994) *Code of Practice on the Identification and Assessment of Special Educational Needs* (HMSO)

33. Department for Education and Employment and the Department of Health (1994) *The Education of Children with Emotional and Behavioural Difficulties* (Circular 9/94, Local Authority Circular LAC (94) 9)

34. Grimshaw R, Berridge D (1994) *Educating Disruptive Children* (National Children's Bureau)

35. *The Health Needs of School Aged Children* (1995) British Paediatric Association

36. *Suicide and Self-Harm: Report of a Review by Her Majesty's Chief Inspector of Prisons for England and Wales of Suicide and Self-Harm in Prison Service Establishments in England and Wales* (Cm 1383 HMSO)

37. Liebling A and Krarup H (1994) *Suicide Attempts in Prison* (Home Office Research Bulletin No. 36 1994)

38. Skett, Braham and Samuel *Drugs and Violence in a Young Offender Institution* (Prison Service Journal 106)

39. Social Services Inspectorate (1996) *Inspection of Facilities for Mothers and Babies in Prison* (Department of Health)

40. *The Allitt Inquiry: Independent Inquiry relating to deaths and injuries on the children's ward at Grantham and Kesteven General Hospital during the period February to April 1991* (1994) (HMSO)

41. Department of Health (1994) *Protection of Children: disclosure to NHS employers of criminal background of those with access to children* (Health Service Guidelines HSG (94) 43)

42. Department of Health (1994) *Occupational Health Services for NHS Staff* (Health Service Guidelines HSG (94) 51)

43. *The Welfare of Children and Young People in Hospital* (1991) (HMSO)

44. Social Services Inspectorate (1995) *Unaccompanied Asylum Seeker Children* (Chief Inspector Letter CI (95) 17

45. Crosse S B, Kaye E, and Ratnofsky A C (1993) *A Report on the Maltreatment of Children with Disabilities* (Washington DC : National Center on Child Abuse and Neglect)

46. Sobsey D, Varnhagen C (1988) *Sexual Abuse and exploitation of people with disabilities: a study of the victims* (unpublished)

47. Westcott H, Clement M (1992) *Experience of Child Abuse in Residential Care and Educational Placements: Results of a Survey* (London: NSPCC)

48. Kennedy M (1990) *The deaf child who is sexually abused – is there a need for a dual specialist?* Child Abuse Review, 4 (2) 3 – 6

49. Westcott H, (1993) *Abuse of Children and Adults with Disabilities* (London: NSPCC)

50. Craft A (1987) *Mental Handicap and Sexuality: Issues and Perspectives* (Kent: Costello Publishers)

51. Middleton L, (1992) *Children First* (Venture Press)

52. Marchant R, Page M (1993) *Bridging the Gap: child protection work with children with multiple disabilities* (NSPCC)

53. Association of Metropolitan Authorities (1994) *Special Child: Special Needs. Services for Children with Disabilities* (Local Government Association)

54. Barter C (1996) *Nowhere to hide* (Centrepoint)

55. *We don't choose to be homeless: The Inquiry into Preventing Youth Homelessness* (1996) (CHAR)

56. Craig TKJ, Hodson S, Woodward S, Richardson S (1996) *Off to a Bad Start* (The Mental Health Foundation)

57. *In Care Contacts: the West Case : The Report of a Review of over 2,000 files of Young Persons in Residential Care* (1996) (The Bridge Consultancy)

58. Social Services Inspectorate (1997) *When Leaving Home is also Leaving Care* (Department of Health CI (97) 4)

59. Broad B (1994) *Leaving Care in the 1990s: The Results of a National Survey* (Royal Philanthropic Society)

60. Biehal and others (1995) *Moving On: Young People and Leaving Care Schemes* (HMSO)

61. Lee M, O'Brien R (1995) *The Game's Up: Redefining Child Prostitution* (The Children's Society)

62. Gallagher B (forthcoming) *The Investigation and Management of Complex Cases of Child Sexual Abuse* (University of Manchester)

63. *A Review of Malcolm Thompson's Employment by Sheffield City Council 1977–1990* (1993) (Sheffield Area Child Protection Committee)

64. *Report of the Committee of Inquiry into Children's Homes and Hostels* (1986) (Belfast, HMSO)

65. Skuse D, Bentovim A etc (forthcoming) *The Influence of Early Experience of Sexual Abuse on the Formation of Sexual Preferences during Adolescence* (Institute of Child Health)

66. Itzin C (ed) (1993) *The Child Pornography Industry : International Trade in Child Sexual Abuse in Pornography: Women, Violence and Civil Liberties* (Oxford University Press)

67. Department for Education and Employment (1992) *Action against Bullying* (Department for Education)

68. Department for Education and Employment (1994) *Bullying: Don't Suffer in Silence* (Department for Education)

69. Prisons Inspectorate (1995) *Inspection of HM Young Offender Institution Lancaster Farns* (Home Office)

70. Prisons Inspectorate (1997) *Inspection of HM Young Offender Institution Dover* (Home Office)

71. Prisons Inspectorate (1997) *Inspection of HM Young Offender Institution Onley* (Home Office)

72. Prisons Inspectorate (1997) *Inspection of HM Young Offender Institution Portland* (Home Office)

73. Social Services Inspectorate (1994) *Inspecting for Quality – Standards for Residential Child Care Services* (HMSO)

74. *Children and Violence* (1995) Calouste Gulbenkian Foundation

75. Barn R, Sinclair R, Ferdinand D (1997) *Acting on Principle – an examination of race and ethnicity in social services provision for children and families* (British Agencies for Adoption and Fostering)

76. Department of Health (1993) *Guidance on Permissible Forms of Control in Children's Residential Care* (Local Authority Circular LAC (93) 13)

77. Kirkwood A QC(1993) *The Leicestershire Inquiry 1992* (Leicestershire County Council)

78. Social Services Inspectorate *The Control of Children in the Public Care: Interpretation of the Children Act 1989* (CI (97) 6)

79. Department for Education and Employment (1994) *Pupil Behaviour and Discipline* (Circular 8/94)

80. *Discipline in Schools: Report of the Committee of Inquiry chaired by Lord Elton* (1989) (HMSO)

81. Lyon C (1994) *Legal Issues arising from the Care and Control of Children with Learning Difficulties who also present Severe Challenging Behaviour: A Guide for Parents and Carers* (The Mental Health Foundation)

82. Sinclair I, Gibbs I (forthcoming) *Quality of Care in Children's Homes* (University of York)

83. Dartington Social Research Unit (1981) *Issues of Control in Children's Residential Care* (HMSO)

84. Dartington Social Research Unit (forthcoming) *Structure and Culture in Children's Homes* (Dartington Social Research Unit)

85. Marsh P, Triseliotis J (1996) *Ready to Practise? Social Workers and Probation Officers: Their Training and First Year in Work* (Avebury)

86. Anderson E (ed) (1994) *In Loco Parentis: Training Issues in Boarding and Residential Environments* (David Fulton Publishers)

87. Berridge D and Cleaver H (1987) *Foster Home Breakdown* (Oxford Blackwell)

88. Triseliotis J, Sellick C, and Short R (1995) *Foster Care: Theory and Practice* (Batsford/ British Agencies for Adoption and Fostering)

89. Colton M, Vanstone M (1996) *Betrayal of Trust* (Free Association Books)

90. Department of Health (1991) *The Children Act 1989: The Welfare of Children in Boarding Schools – A Practice Guide* (HMSO)

91. Department for Education and Employment (1993) *Protection of Children: Disclosure of Criminal Background of Those with Access to Children* (Circular 9/93 (issued jointly with Home Office 47/93, Department of Health LAC (93) 17 and Welsh Office 54/93)

92. Department for Education and Employment (1995) *Misconduct of Teachers and Workers with Children and Young Persons* (Circular 11/95)

93. Social Services Inspectorate (1997) *The Safety of Children and Young People in the Public Care* (Chief Inspector Letter CI (97) 10) (Department of Health)

94. Her Majesty's Chief Inspector of Schools (1995) *Framework for the Inspection of Nursery, Primary, Secondary and Special Schools* (HMSO)

95. *On the Record* (Cm 3308) (HMSO)

96. Marshall P (1997) *The Prevalence of Convictions for Sexual offending* (Home Office Research and Statistics Directorate – Research Findings No. 55)

97. Social Services Inspectorate (1993) *An Abuse of Trust: The Report of the Social Services Inspectorate Investigation into the case of Martin Huston* (Department of Health and Social Services, Northern Ireland)

98. Department for Education and Employment (1995) *Protecting Children from Abuse: The Role of the Education Service* (Circular 10/95)

99. Gibbens E B QC (1967) *Administration of Punishment at Court Lees Approved School– Report of Inquiry* (Cmnd 3367) (HMSO)

100. Department of Health (1993) *Implementation of Warner* (Local Authority Circular LAC (93) 15)

101. *Abuse in Care– A Necessary Reform with Practical Guidelines on Whistleblowing Policies* (1997) (Public Concern at Work)

102. Committee on Standards in Public Life (1995) *First Report* (Cm 2850–1)

103. Committee on Standards in Public Life (1996) *Second Report* (Cm 3270–1)

104. Committee on Standards in Public Life (1997) *Third Report* (Cm 3702–1)

105. Social Services Inspectorate (1993) *Corporate Parents* (Department of Health)

106. Social Services Inspectorate Wales (1997) *Emerging Themes: Local Authority Responses to Recommendations in the Report of the Examination Team on Child Care Procedures and Practice in North Wales* (Welsh Office, unpublished)

107. Williams G QC, McCreadie J (1992) *Ty Mawr Community Home Inquiry* (Gwent County Council)

108. White I A, Hart K (1995) *Report of the Inquiry into the Management of Child Care in the London Borough of Islington* (London Borough of Islington)

109. Hodgkin R, Newell P (1996) *Effective Government Structures for Children: Report of a Gulbenkian Foundation Inquiry* (Calouste Gulbenkian Foundation UK)

110. *Bringing about Changes in Practice – Report of a Seminar* (1996) (Joseph Rowntree Foundation)

111. *Case Review* : Mr & Mrs H (1993) (Sheffield Area Child Protection Committee)

112. Social Services Inspectorate Wales (1995) *Quality Care in Children's Homes in Wales* (Welsh Office)

113. Social Services Inspectorate Wales (1996) *Independent Reviews of Social Services Inspection Units in Wales 1994–95* (Welsh Office)

114. *Social Services: Achievement and Challenge* (1997) (Cm 3588)

115. Rose W (1996) *Next Steps in Child Protection, Policy and Practice* (Sieff Conference)

116. Brannan C, Jones R, Murch J (undated) *Castle Hill Report Practice Guide* (Shropshire County Council)

117. Monckton Sir Walter (1945) *Report on the Circumstances which led to the boarding out of Dennis and Terence O'Neill at Bank Farm, Minsterley, and the steps taken to supervise their welfare* (Home Office, London)

118. The Bridge Child Care Consultancy Service (1995) *Part 8 Case Review – Overview Report in respect of Charmaine and Heather West* (Gloucestershire Area Child Protection Committee)

119. *Report of the Advisory Group on Video Evidence* (The Pigot Report) (1989) (Home Office)

BIBLIOGRAPHY

The following is a selection from the hundreds of documents consulted by the Review which are not referred to in the text of the Report.

Association of Metropolitan Authorities (1993) *Children in our Care* (Local Government Association)

Barter C (1997) *Who's to blame ? Conceptualising Institutional Abuse by Children* (in Vol 133 Early Child Development and Care)

BASW (1995) *Guidance for Social Services on Free Expression of Staff Concerns* (British Association of Social Work)

Bibby P C (ed) (1996) *Organised Abuse* (Arena)

Bullock R, Little M, Milham S (1993)*Residential Care for Children – A Review of the Research* (HMSO)

Cawson P (1997) *Who will guard the Guards? Some questions about the models of inspection for residential settings with relevance to the protection of children from abuse by staff* (Vol 133 Early Child Development and Care)

Cooper P (1993) *Effective Schools for Disaffected Students* (Routledge)

Department of Health (1995) *Child Protection: Messages from Research* (HMSO)

Elliott M, Browne K, Kilcoyne J (1995) *Child Sexual Abuse Prevention What Offenders tell us* (Elsevier Science Ltd)

Kahan B (1994) *Growing up in Groups* (HMSO)

Kelly L, Wingfield R, Burton S, Regan L (1995) *Splintered Lives – Sexual exploitation of children in the context of children's rights and child protection* (Barnado's)

Kurtz Z (1996) *Do Children's and Young People's Rights to Health Care in the UK ensure their best interests* (Chapter 13, in Royal College of Physicians Adolescent Medicine)

Lewis D (1995) *Whistleblowing and Job Security* (The Modern Law Review Ltd)

One Scandal Too Many: The Case for Comprehensive Protection of Children in All Settings (1993) (Calouste Gulbenkian UK Ltd)

Police Research Group (1996) *Preventing School Bullying* (Home Office)

Saradjan J (1996) *Women who sexually abuse children: from research to clinical practice* (Chichester Wiley)

Sinclair R, Grimshaw R (forthcoming) *Planning and Reviewing under the Children Act* (National Children's Bureau)

Smith J QC (1992) *Report of the Scotforth House Inquiry* (Lancashire County Council)

Smith P K , Thompson D (1991) *Practical Approaches to Bullying* (David Fulton Publishers)

The Quality of Care (1992) (Local Government Management Board)

Troubleshooter: Lessons for Policy and Practice on 15 Year Olds in Prison (1997) (Howard League)

Westcott H , Cross M (1996) *This Far and No Further* (Venture Press)

Willow C (1996) *Children's Rights and Participation in Residential Care* (National Children's Bureau)

APPENDIX A: COMMISSIONED WORK

The Review commissioned work from these organisations and individuals. The Review is grateful for all the contributions.

FIRST*KEY*

First*Key* set up and reported on 2 meetings – in London and Leeds – to discuss safeguards with groups of young people who had been or were in the care system. Members of the Review attended both meetings.

LONDON BOROUGH OF CAMDEN

The London Borough arranged for the Review to meet some children being looked after by the authority with their carers. The meeting was hosted by the Review in the offices of the Department of Health.

NATIONAL CHILDREN'S BUREAU

The Bureau visited one children's home and two schools to discuss safeguards with groups of disabled children and submitted the results in the report *Safety First: Some Discussions with disabled children and young people living away from home.*

NATIONAL INSTITUTE FOR SOCIAL WORK

The Institute used its contacts in Western Europe, Scandinavia and North America to produce a paper on safeguards in other countries for the Review and the Scottish Children's Safeguards Review.

RACE EQUALITY UNIT

The Unit researched the literature on the racial dimension to safeguards, held consultation meetings with Black adults and children to discuss the issues and issued a questionnaire to other Black adults and young people. A report summarising the findings was produced.

UNIVERSITY OF DUNDEE

Dr Andrew Kendrick in the Department of Social Work carried out a literature review of safeguards which was jointly funded by the Scottish Children's Safeguards Review and the Review.

DEREK TURNER (retired HMI)

Derek Turner submitted a paper on the history, development and changes over the past 50 years in boarding education and the impact of the Children Act. The paper also drew attention to particular types of school or pupil that appeared to be especially vulnerable.

APPENDIX B: LEGISLATION AND GUIDANCE

This Annex lists the main Acts of Parliament, Regulations and Circulars which bear on the Review's terms of reference.

ACTS OF PARLIAMENT

The Children Act 1989

The Education Act 1996

CHILDREN ACT REGULATIONS

Arrangements for Placements of Children (General) 1991

Children's Homes 1991

Contact with Children 1991

Definition of Independent Visitors (Children) 1991

Foster Placement (Children) 1991

Inspection of Premises, Children and Records (Independent Schools) 1991

Representations Procedure (Children) 1991

Review of Children's Cases 1991

Children (Private Arrangements for Fostering) 1991

Children (Secure Accommodation) 1991

Disqualification for Caring for Children 1991

Placement of Children with Parents Etc 1991

Refuges (Children's Homes and Foster Placements) 1991

EDUCATION ACT REGULATIONS

The Education (Special Schools) 1994

The Education (Special Educational Needs) (Approval of Independent Schools) 1994

The Education (Grant-maintained Special Schools) 1994

The Education (Particulars of Independent Schools) 1982 as amended

CHILDREN ACT REGULATIONS AND GUIDANCE SERIES

Volume 3: *Family Placements* (HMSO 1991)

Volume 4: *Residential Care* (HMSO 1991)

Volume 5: *Independent Schools* (HMSO 1991)

Volume 8: *Private Fostering Miscellaneous* (HMSO 1991)

Working Together: Under the Children Act 1989 (HMSO 1991)

CIRCULARS

Department of Health

LAC (90) 8:   Child Protection

LAC (91) 13:   Sir William Utting's Review of Residential Services for Children

LAC (92) 14:   Inspection of Community Homes

LAC (93) 13:   Guidance on Permissible Forms of Control in Children's Residential Care

LAC (93) 15:   Implementation of Warner

LAC (93) 16:   Provision of Accommodation and Maintenance of Children Looked After

LAC (93) 17:   Protection of Children: Disclosure of Criminal Background of those with access to children (issued jointly with Department for Education and Employment (Circular 9/93), Home Office (HOC 47/93) and Welsh Office (WOC 54/93))

LAC (93) 24:   The Children's Homes Arrangements for Placement etc Regs

LAC (94) 4:   Guidelines on Smoking and Alcohol Consumption in Residential Child Care Establishments

LAC (94) 16:   Inspecting Social Services

LAC (94) 18:   The Children's Homes Amendment Regulations 1994

LAC (94) 20:   Use by Local Authorities of Voluntary Organisations and Independent Fostering Agencies

LAC (94) 22:   Protection of Children: Disclosure of Criminal Background to Voluntary Sector Organisations (issued jointly with Home Office (HOC 42/94) and Welsh Office (WOC 64/94))

LAC (95) 1:   Further Guidance on Inspection of Boarding Schools

LAC (95) 14:   Respite Care: Series of Short Term Placements of Children

LAC (96) 10:   Children's Services Plans

LASSL (95) 4: Consultation about delegation of fostering duties to profit-making organisations and easement of respite care regulations

Chief Inspector Letters

CI (97) 6:   The Control of Children in the Public Care Interpretation of the Children Act 1989.

CI (97) 10:   The Safety of Children and Young People in the Public Care

Welsh Office

36/94:   The Development of Special Schools

35/96:   Care Procedures and Practice in North Wales

Department for Education and Employment

3/94:   The Development of Special Schools

8/94:   Pupil Behaviour and Discipline

10/95:   Protecting Children from Abuse: The Role of the Education Service

11/95:   Misconduct of Teachers and Workers with Children and Young Persons

10/96:   The 1996 School Premises Regulations

Department of Health and Department for Education and Employment Joint Circulars

LAC (94) 9/ Circular 9/94:   The Education of Children with Educational and Behavioural Disorders

LAC (94) 10/ Circular 12/94: The Education of Sick Children

LAC (94) 11/ Circualr 13/94: The Education of Children being looked after by Local Authorities

APPENDIX C: STATISTICS ON CHILDREN, INSTITUTIONS AND STAFF

1. INTRODUCTION

This annex paints a picture of the numbers of children and young people living away from home, where they are, and some of their characteristics, in the context of all children and young people. Information about the numbers of staff in contact with these children and young people in some settings is also given.

SECTION I: CHILDREN

2. POPULATION FIGURES

It is estimated that in England and Wales in 1995 there were nearly 12 million children and young people aged under 18, an increase of around 350,000 (3%) over the 1990 figure. Projections to 2000 suggest a further increase of some 110,000 (1%) in the numbers of children and young people.

There are considerable variations within these overall increases: a 7% increase in the 5 to 9 age group between 1990 and 1995; a 9% decrease in 16 to 17 year olds in the same period but a projected increase of some 7% for this latter age group between 1995 and 2000 (see table 1).

These variations are primarily explained by changes in the live birth rate (see figure 1). The birth rate dropped from over 800,000 in the 1960s to around 570,000 in 1977, increased to 706,000 in 1990, and is forecast to be around 630,000 in the year 2000. The change in the age group 5 to 9 between 1990 and 1995 reflects the change in birth rate between the periods 1981–85 and 1986–90. The change in the numbers of 16 and 17 year olds between 1985 and 1990 reflects the changes in birth rates between 1973–74 and 1978–79.

There are around 106 boys for every 100 girls with no significant differences in this ratio over time or between the different age groups.

Fig 1.   Live births, England and Wales

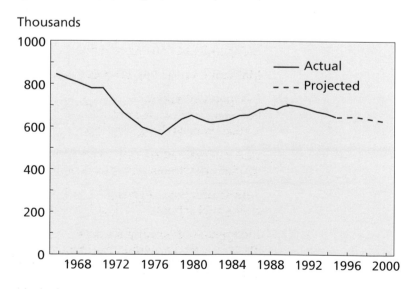

Thousands

Table 1: Population estimates and projections by age group – England

thousands and percentage changes

Age group	Number in 1990	Number in 1995	% change from 1990 to 1995	Number in 2000	% change from 1995 to 2000
0 to 4	3,380	3,388	+0.2	3,357	–0.9
5 to 9	3,194	3,402	+0.4	3,399	–0.1
10 to 15	3,613	3,864	+6.9	4,083	+5.7
16 to 17	1,324	1,208	–8.8	1,284	+6.3
Total 0 to 17	11,511	11,862	+3.0	12,123	+2.

Source: The Office for National Statistics

3. CHILDREN AWAY FROM HOME

Children and young people living away from home are generally defined as people aged under 18 who are away from home for 28 days or more. Not all sources of data are able to supply figures that match this definition. In some cases data relate to shorter periods for particularly vulnerable children – eg in refuges –, in other cases data relate to longer periods where there are legal implications – eg children in hospital for more than three months. Some figures relate to numbers at a point in time and some are estimates of the total number of children and young people who were away from their family at some time during the year.

Out of the 12 million children and young people in England and Wales over 200,000 are away from their families for periods of around four weeks or more in a typical year. These include 110,000 in boarding schools, over 30,000 in hospitals, 50,000 in foster care, and over 10,000 in children's homes.

SECTION II: INSTITUTIONS

4. BOARDING SCHOOLS

Table 2: Numbers of boarding schools and places in England and Wales – 1995

Type of school	Number of schools	Number of boarding places
Independent boarding schools	736	79,500
Maintained boarding schools	39	4,600
Independent special boarding schools approved by Secretary of State	76	3,500
LEA maintained special residential schools	226	13,300
Non-maintained special residential schools	68	3,800
Independent boarding schools also registered as children's homes	41	5,300
Total boarding schools	1,186	110,000

Source : Department for Education and Employment and Welsh Office

The majority of children who live away from their homes for four weeks or more are in boarding or residential schools. Table 2 shows the number of schools and places in each of these six categories: independent boarding schools; maintained boarding schools; independent special boarding schools; LEA and grant maintained special residential schools; non-maintained special boarding schools; independent boarding schools also registered as children's homes.

The majority of these children are in independent or maintained boarding schools, some of which may also contain some boarders aged 18 or 19.

Some of the 370 schools with 20,600 residential places approved to take children with special educational needs may take children as young as 2 and a large proportion take boarders to the age of 19. In more than half of these schools boarding places account for around 90% or more of all places. Very few are single sex schools, and the majority of these cater for boys only.

The 40 or so establishments registered both as schools and as children's homes, have around 5,300 boarding places. Independent boarding schools which provide accommodation for three children or more for more than 295 days a year must be registered with the local authority as a children's home. Schools approved by the Secretary of State for Education and Employment to admit children with statements of special educational needs are exempt from this registration requirement. The data quoted were obtained from the Department for Education and Employment. Department of Health data show a much lower figure.

5. CHILDREN'S HOMES

Table 3: Children's Homes in England at 31 March 1996

Category of home	Number of homes	Total number of places	Children looked after as percent of total number of places[1] [2]
Community homes	836	7,600	78
Voluntary children's homes	64	600	79
Private registered children's homes	202	1,500	50
Registered residential care homes	84	800	8
All homes	1,186	10,500	67

[1] excludes those children receiving respite care   [2] provisional

NB Establishments registered as schools and children's homes are dealt with in section 4.
Source: Department of Health

Table 4: Children and young people in community homes in Wales maintained or controlled by local authorities at 31 March

Year	Age under 1	Aged 1–4	Aged 5–9	Aged 10–15	Aged 16–17	**Total aged 0–17**	Number of community homes
1991	0	5	39	339	105	**488**	56
1992	1	2	19	289	105	**415**	53
1993	1	2	24	238	71	**336**	51
1994	1	1	12	222	62	**298**	46

Source: Welsh Office

Table 3 shows that at 31 March 1996 there were 1,200 registered children's homes in England, including establishments registered both as children's homes and as schools. Over 90% accommodated both male and female children. Two thirds of the children in these homes are looked after by local authorities, as defined by the Children Act 1989.

Information is not available about the ages of all children in children's homes. For the looked after cohort who were placed in maintained and controlled community homes 66% were aged between 10 and 15. This compares with 57% aged 10 to 15 in privately registered children's homes, 52% in assisted community homes and 51% in voluntary homes. In voluntary homes 39% of children were aged 16 or 17. This compares with about one quarter of children aged 16 or 17 in other types of homes.

Small homes catering for three children or fewer are not subject to registration under the Children Act. Local Authorities in England reported using 78 small homes in the year ending 31 March 1996. A study in 1994 found that local authorities had used 118 small homes since October 1992.

There are no registered children's homes in Wales. Table 4 shows that the number of community homes is declining and (like England) most children living in children's homes were aged between 10 and 15.

6. LOCAL AUTHORITY FOSTER CARE

Table 5: Children looked after in foster placements by English local authorities at 31 March of each year

Year	Number of children
1991	34,800
1992	32,700
1993	31,900
1994	31,800
1995	32,600
1996	33,200

Source: Department of Health

Table 6: Foster parents approved by local authorities, Wales

Year	Number on the register	Number of places
1992	1,570	2,420
1993	1,810	2,860
1994	2,100	2,930

Source: Welsh Office

Fig 2.   Children looked after in foster placements at 31 March, England

Thousands of children

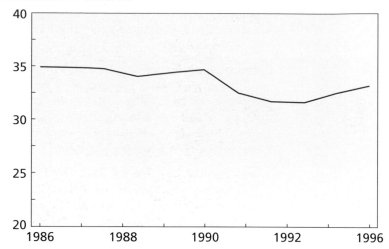

Tables 5 and 6 show the position on fostering. As can be seen in figure 2 the number of children fostered declined over the last ten years, but started to rise again from 1994. Fostering accounts for an increasing proportion of all looked after children. Data collected from local authorities in England do not include the number of foster carers. The data collected from local authorities in Wales suggest that their foster carers now tend to look after one child at a time. In addition there are known to be 3 independent fostering agencies in Wales offering about 50 places.

Not all foster placements are long term. Around one quarter of placement episodes last seven days or less, another quarter last between one week and one month, and a quarter last six months or more.

Children in foster placements tend to be younger than those in children's homes. Around 42% of children in foster placements are aged under 10, compared with only 8% of children in children's homes.

7. HOSPITALS

Table 7: Number of finished consultant episodes in England and Wales in 1994/95 by duration of episode and age at end of episode (rounded to nearest 100)

Age at end of episode	15 to 30 days	31 to 90 days	Over 90 days	Total
0 to 4 years	18,000	8,300	900	27,200
5 to 14 years	4,900	2,300	500	7,700
15 to 18 years	3,600	1,900	700	6,200
Total 0 to 18 years	26,500	12,500	2,100	41,100

Source: Department of Health

Data are not available about the numbers of children treated in hospital as in-patients. The available information relates to finished consultant episodes in England. The numbers of episodes will be slightly higher than the number of children, as a small number of children may have completed more than one episode of in-patient care in the twelve month period.

Fig 3. Number of finished consultant episodes in England and Wales, 1994/95, by duration of episodes and age

Number of finished episodes

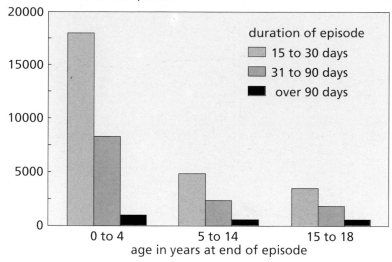

age in years at end of episode

In the year ending 31 March 1995 in England and Wales there were over 41,000 finished hospital episodes lasting 15 days or more for children and young people aged 18 or under (table 7 and figure 3). Two thirds of these related to under fives, whilst 64% lasted between 15 and 30 days.

For those episodes lasting over three months, 79% relating to children aged under 5 were in the speciality of paediatrics, as were 74% of episodes relating to the age group 5 to 14. For the 15 to 18 age group the major specialties were those related to psychiatry (43% child and adolescent psychiatry, 27% mental illness, and 11% learning difficulties). This compares with 8% in the psychiatry group for children aged 5 to 14, and only 2% for the under fives.

8. RESIDENTIAL CARE HOMES AND NURSING HOMES

There are around 1,800 children and young people aged under 18 in residential care homes in England. Around 80% of these children are in homes primarily for people with learning difficulties. Around 300 children aged under 18 are in nursing homes in England, the majority in homes primarily catering for mental illness and people with learning disabilities.

In Wales under 20 children (aged under 16) are in homes catering for psychiatric illness.

9. PRISON SERVICE ESTABLISHMENTS

Table 8: Prisoners aged 17 and under held in Prison Service establishments on 30 June by age

Year	Aged 14[1]	Aged 15	Aged 16	Aged 17	Aged 14–17
1991	10	100	200	1,050	1,340
1992	20	100	230	980	1,330
1993	0	130	290	890	1,300
1994	0	170	420	940	1,530
1995	0	180	450	1,030	1,680

Source: Home Office

[1]Fourteen year olds have not been held in Prison Service establishments since 1 October 1992

Fig 4.   Prisoners aged 17 and under in prison service establishments, 30 June 1995

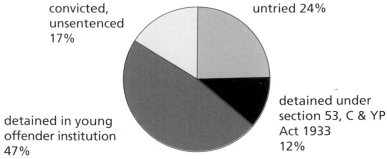

convicted, unsentenced 17%

untried 24%

detained under section 53, C & YP Act 1933 12%

detained in young offender institution 47%

Total = 1,680

Table 9: Population of prisoners aged 17 and under held in Prison Service establishments on 30 June by type of custody

	Untried	Convicted Unsentenced	Detention in a young offender institution	Detained under Section 53 C & YP Act 1933	Total
1991	430	160	660	90	1,340
1992	440	140	680	60	1,330
1993	380	160	640	130	1,300
1994	440	240	680	160	1,530
1995	410	280	790	200	1,680

Source: 'Aspects of Crime Young Offenders' published January 1997, Home Office

Note: Figures in Tables 8 and 9 may not sum to the totals presented due to rounding

These data show that the number of children living away from home in penal settings has increased since 1991, even though 14 year olds are no longer held in such settings.

10. SECURE UNITS

Young people aged between 10 and 18 may be accommodated in secure units because they are likely to cause serious injury to themselves or others if placed in other forms of accommodation. 29 secure units were open during the year ending 31 March 1996.

246 children were accommodated in secure units at 31 March 1996, the majority of whom were boys (79%). Young people aged 14 to 16 accounted for 84% of those accommodated. At this date there were 274 approved places, an occupancy rate of 90%. Compared with 1990 there has been a reduction of 18 (6%) in the number of approved places.

In the 12 months to 31 March 1996 there were 829 admissions, a reduction of over 200 compared with previous years. During the same period there were 814 discharges from secure units, of whom 235 (29%) had been there for under one month.

For those in secure accommodation on 31 March 1996, children aged under 14 comprised 11% of the total. Most of these were admitted under Section 20 of the Children Act 1989 or under care orders in family proceedings.

Conversely, among those aged sixteen or over (28% of the total), most had been admitted either under Section 53 of the Children and Young Persons Act 1933 or had been remanded to local authority accommodation.

In addition the Youth Treatment Centre at Glenthorne treated 67 children during 1996/97.

Private fostering   **11. OTHER CATEGORIES**

Table 10: Private fostering arrangements in Wales approved by the local authority

Year	Number of private foster homes	Number of privately fostered children in these homes
1992	33	37
1993	40	38
1994	27	29

Source: Welsh Office

Information about private fostering in England is not available. Available information for Wales is given above.

Asylum seekers   Unaccompanied children aged under 17 seeking asylum are particularly vulnerable for reasons of language, culture etc. They are likely to be 'looked after' by local authorities. The numbers of such applicants has risen sharply in recent years (Table 11).

Table 11: Number of unaccompanied children aged 17 or under applying for asylum at ports[1] in the United Kingdom

Year	Number of applicants
1992	185
1993	245
1994[2]	357
1995[2]	486

Source: Home Office
[1] Does not include applications in country (59 in 1994, 99 in 1995)
[2] Provisional, and due to the method of recording may understate

Armed forces   **Table 12: Young people in UK regular armed forces, by age last birthday, as at 1 July**

	Age 16	Age 17	Total aged 16 & 17
1990	1,363	8,500	9,863
1995	188	1,937	2,125

Source: Defence Services Analytical Agency

People sleeping rough

It is difficult to obtain information about the numbers and characteristics of people 'sleeping rough'. The information available suggests that the number of children and young people sleeping rough is minimal. The 1991 census enumerated 2,650 persons sleeping rough of whom 35 (1%) were aged under 18.

A monitoring exercise in central London on a night in November 1996 found only 2 young people under 18 out of 270 where information on age was available, (357 people were found 'sleeping rough'). These figures were similar to street counts carried out in previous years.

A survey carried out in 1991 into single homeless people on behalf of the Department of the Environment found that of 501 people in the sample who were sleeping rough and users of day centres or soup runs, 13 were aged under 18 (2.5%).

Other homeless people

A Department of the Environment survey in 1992 looked at people living in hostels or bed and breakfast hotels which provided accommodation for single people without a permanent home. Although age information was not available for all, around 64 (5%) out of the 1,262 people covered were aged under 18.

No data are available about the number of people aged under 18 who live away from home because of their employment, either in residences provided by their employer or otherwise.

SECTION III: STAFF

12. NUMBERS

Table 13: Numbers of staff (full time and part time) in homes run by Local Authority Social Services Departments in England at 30 September 1995

	Homes and hostels mainly for children with learning disabilities		Community homes for children looked after		'Specialist needs' establishments/ resource centres mainly for children	
	Full time	Part time	Full time	Part time	Full time	Part time
Managers and Officers in charge	149	4	664	21	72	3
Deputy officers in charge	186	10	840	96	72	2
Other supervisory staff	335	217	1,567	315	112	18
Care staff	781	1,129	3,960	1,429	442	200
Teaching staff			145	73	15	2
Other support services staff	141	573	557	1,890	84	217
Total staff	1,592	1,933	7,733	3,824	797	442

Source: Department of Health

Table 14: Numbers of teaching staff in boarding schools in England and Wales at January 1996

Type of school	Qualified teachers (wte)
Independent boarding schools	24,100
Maintained boarding schools	2,500
Maintained special residential schools	2,500
Non maintained special residential schools	1,100
Total	30,200

Source: Department for Education and Employment and Welsh Office

Note: The numbers relate to whole time equivalents, not to individuals.

Table 15: Numbers of staff in Young Offenders Institutions

Type of staff	Numbers of staff
Prison officers and governors	3,550
Specialist staff	480
Administrative staff	630
Others	1,460
Total staff	6,120

Source: Home Office

While the data collected by the central Departments are not comprehensive, they suggest that at least 50,000 people work in institutions where children and young people live away from home.

13. STAFFING QUALIFICATIONS

Table 16: Numbers of care staff in specialist needs establishments mainly for children and per cent holding social work qualifications (England)

	1993		1994		1995	
	number	per cent holding social work qualifications	number	per cent holding social work qualifications	number	per cent holding social work qualifications
Officers-in-charge	66	76%	71	94%	75	88%
Deputy officers-in-charge	76	60%	60	58%	74	65%
Other supervisory staff	111	43%	124	67%	130	66%
Child care staff	655	18%	609	17%	642	22%
All care staff	908	27%	864	33%	921	37%

Source: Department of Health

Table 17: Numbers of care staff in community homes and per cent holding social work qualifications (England)

	1993		1994		1995	
	number	per cent holding social work qualifica-tions	number	per cent holding social work qualifica-tions	number	per cent holding social work qualifica-tions
Officers-in-charge	747	76%	703	78%	685	83%
Deputy officers-in-charge	883	45%	995	53%	936	58%
Other supervi-sory staff	1,815	31%	1,807	23%	1,882	25%
Child care staff	5,800	16%	5,731	12%	5,389	18%
All care staff	9,245	27%	9,236	24%	8,892	29%

Source: LGMB Annual Social Service Workforce Analysis

The information on staff qualifications relates to local authority establishments only. The data show the proportion of child care staff who are qualified has increased between 1993 and 1995, but they still represent a minority. The proportions are higher for other supervisory staff, deputy officers in charge and officers in charge.

The Review thanks the Department of Health's Statistics Division – particularly Arthur Sheckley– for preparing this Appendix.

APPENDIX D: CHILDREN'S HOMES AND SCHOOLS – THE REGULATORY FRAMEWORK

This Annex describes how children's homes and schools are registered and inspected. It summarises how the Secretary of State for Education and Employment approves schools to take children with statements of special educational needs. The main legislation is either the Children Act 1989 or the Education Act 1996.

Tables shown landscape on following pages.

TABLE A: CHILDREN'S HOMES

Type	Registered by	Inspected by	Cancellation of Registration	Status of Reports
LA Community Home*	N/A	Twice a year (1 announced and 1 unannounced) by LA***	N/A	Public documents in accordance with Citizen's Charter principles.
Registered Children's Homes	LA**, except for homes for less than 4 children	As for community homes.	Powers in Children Act under which LA has to give notice of proposal to cancel registration and allow home 14 days after notice served to make representations. No power to cancel registration without notice.	Public documents in accordance with Citizen's Charter principles.
Voluntary Children's Homes	SSI on behalf of SofS. No exception for homes with places for less than 4 children.	Twice a year (1 announced and 1 unannounced) by SSI	Powers in Children Act for SofS to give notice of proposal to cancel registration. Home given 14 days after notice served to make representations. If home wishes to make oral representations, SofS has to provide opportunity to appear before someone appointed by him. No power to cancel registration without notice.	Public documents available on request. Not sent to local authorities or other interested parties, except on request.
Residential Care Homes****	LA. No exception for homes with places for less than 4 children.	Twice a year (1 announced and 1 unannounced) by LA.	The Registration Homes Act contains power to cancel registration in emergency by application to court without allowing the owner either to make representations or be party to the court proceedings. Powers also to cancel by giving notice etc with right of appeal to the Registered Homes Tribunal.	Public documents.

* Maintained, controlled and assisted community homes. A maintained community home is provided, managed, equipped and maintained by a local authority, a controlled community home is one where the local authority is responsible for managing a home provided by a voluntary organisation, an assisted community home is one where local authority and voluntary organisation propose that the voluntary organisation is responsible for management as well as the equipment and maintenance.

** Local Authorities' Independent Registration and Inspection Unit

*** Independent Registration and Inspection Unit. LAC (92) 14–issued under S7 of the Local Authority Social Services Act 1970–advised local authorities to subject maintained community homes to the same inspection regime as registered children's homes. LAC (94) 16, also issued under S7, had attached the Inspection Unit Directions 1994 which said that community homes fell within the remit of Independent Registration and Inspection Units. It said that Citizen's Charter principles should apply to the operation of Inspection Units.

**** The Registered Homes Act 1984 provides for registration of a residential care home which 'provides .... residential accommodation with both board and personal care for persons in need of personal care by means of old age, disablement ....or past or present mental disorder.' The Children Act (S63) provides that a residential care home is not a children's home as defined in the Act. A local authority has obligations under the Arrangements for Placement and the Review of Children's Cases Regulations for any children placed by them in residential care homes. The local authority has obligations under the Children Act in the case of disabled children.

TABLE B: BOARDING SCHOOLS – REGISTRATION AND INSPECTION

Type	Registered by	Inspection by Educational Body (OFSTED)	Inspection by Welfare Agency	Cancellation of Registration	Status of Reports
Independent*.	By Registrars **. Provisional registration granted after consideration of application form.*** Final registration granted after registration inspection by HMI and Section 87# inspection by LA****.	Registration inspection by HMI following provisional registration. Inspection by HMI every 5 years thereafter or more frequently if standards thought to be going down or HMI advise closer monitoring.	LA under Section 87 provisions. Triggered by granting of provisional registration. Every 4 years for schools meeting criteria in Appendix 1 to LAC (95)1^ with LA making informal contacts in intervening years. Other schools once a year.	Notice of Complaint Procedure^^ requires Registrar to give school at least 6 months to put matters right, though the Education Act contains power to waive or reduce this period. Right of appeal to Independent Schools Tribunal. No power to cancel in an emergency.	HMI reports are property of Registrar and not public documents. Not sent to school. S87 reports are not public documents, and are sent to Registrar and school^^^. Registrar may send reports to HMI at OFSTED.
Independent Schools also registered as children's homes++.	As above by Registrars and by LA under S63 of the Children Act, and the Children's Homes Regulations 1991, as amended by the Children's Homes—(Miscellaneous Amendments) Regulations 1993+++.	As for independent schools.	LA twice a year– one announced and one unannounced as prescribed in the Children's Homes Regulations 1991.	Subject to Notice of Complaint procedures as school. LA has power to cancel registration as children's home at any time, but no specific provision about emergency cancellation.	As above for HMI reports. LA inspection reports public documents and should also be sent to the Registrar.
Maintained.	N/A	Full OFSTED inspection every 4 years within Framework for the Inspection of Nursery, Primary, Middle, Secondary and Special Schools+.	Not subject to S87.	N/A	Full inspection reports by OFSTED public documents.

* See also Table C re independent schools approved for placement by Local Education Authorities of pupils with statements of special educational needs.

** The Secretary of State for Education and Employment and the Secretary of State for Wales appoint the Registrars who are responsible for maintaining separate registers of independent schools.

*** Proprietor, headteacher, other members of staff checked against List 99 and DH Consultancy Index before provisional registration granted. Criminal record checks requested by DFEE.

Section 87 of the Children Act requires independent boarding schools to safe-guard and promote the welfare of pupils and local authorities to inspect the welfare arrangements.

**** Local Authorities' Independent Registration and Inspection Unit.

^ These are: school accredited member of one of Independent Schools Joint Council (ISJC) associations and subject to inspection by ISJC with reports going to LA; has governing body or equivalent; most children go home at weekends or are visited regularly; LA, OFSTED, ISJC reports have identified no serious welfare concerns; the Registrar has not asked LA to visit.

^^ The Education Act 1996 provides for a Notice of Complaint to be invoked on one or more of these grounds: unsuitable or inadequate accommodations, inefficient and unsuitable teaching, proprietor or any other teacher or employee being 'not a proper person', failure to promote and safeguard children's welfare.

^^^ Under S87(4) of the Children Act local authorities have power to notify the Secretary of State for Education and Employment if they consider that a school is not safeguarding or promoting a child's welfare. LAC (95)1 advises that such notifications should be in separate reports.

+ Published by HM Chief Inspector of Schools in England as required under the Education (Schools) Act 1992.

++ Schools open to accommodate 4 or more children for more than 295 days in a year. Schools approved to admit children with statements of special educational need are exempt from the requirement to register as a children's home.

+++ The 1993 Regulations disapply the Arrangements for Placement, Reviews and Representation Regulations as well as several Regulations in the 1991 Children's Homes Regulations including Regulation 19 on notification of significant events to Secretary of State and Regulation 32 on visits by the local authority.

TABLE C: SPECIAL SCHOOLS – REGISTRATION, APPROVAL AND INSPECTION

Type	Registered by	Approval Process	Inspection by Education Agency (OFSTED)	Inspection by Welfare Agency	Cancellation of Registration	Status of Reports
Independent	See Table B above.	After being granted final registration, may gain approval* from SofS for Education for the placement of pupils with statements of special educational needs. Optional whether to apply for this. Terms of approval specify numbers, ages and gender of children and type of disability. Schools granted approval exempt from requirement to register as children's homes– see above.	HMI registration inspection as for independent schools. HMI advise on meeting Approval Regulations requirements and on proposals to vary terms of existing approval. Full inspections by OFSTED teams of registered inspectors every 4 years. HMI from time to time. Full inspections by HMI of schools not approved for SEN children catering wholly or mainly for such children on consent basis. Other HMI inspections depending on degree to which schools give cause for concern.	LA under S87 of the Children Act.	Same process as for independent schools listed in Table B.	Full inspection reports by HMI or registered inspectors are public documents. Other reports by HMI– eg registration inspections, approval inspections– are not public documents but are reflected in letters to the school. S87 reports not public documents. Sent to DFEE (SEN Division) and school.
Non–maintained	N/A	Approved by SofS**.	HMI advises whether schools meet requirements in Approval Regulations and on any proposal to vary terms of existing approval. OFSTED full inspection every 4 years.	Not subject to S87, but LA under duty to inspect under provisions in S62 of the Children Act***. S62 does not specify inspection frequency.	N/A. SofS may withdraw approval of special school.	Full inspection reports public documents. Any S62 reports would be public documents under provisions of LAC (92) 14 and LAC (94) 16.

Maintained^	N/A	Approved by SofS**	HMI advises whether schools meet requirements of Approval Regulations and on any proposal to vary terms of existing approval. OFSTED full inspection every 4 years.	Not subject to S87.	N/A. SofS may withdraw approval of special school.	Full inspection reports public documents.

* The Education (Special Educational Needs) (Approval of Independent Schools) Regulations 1994 govern the process and prescribe: 'every person who is a proprietor .... shall be a fit and proper person so to act.', residential care staff are suitable and sufficient in number, the proprietor of a boarding school to make provision' as may be necessary .... to safeguard and promote the welfare of the boarders at all times.', changes of proprietor and significant changes of staff to be notified to Secretary of State (SofS), written reports on child to the placing LEA at least once a year, the school, if requested by the LEA, to take part in any review of the statement, death of child to be notified to parents, LEA and SofS, placing LEA or SSD to have access to school at reasonable times, information to be supplied in prospectus including arrangements for pastoral care and for school discipline. SofS for Education has power to withdraw approval if it fails to comply with any of the requirements specified in the Regulations. No minimum period is specified by law if the proprietor is consulted and asks for time to put matters right. Otherwise the proprietor must be consulted summarily where this is necessary or expedient in the interests of the health, safety or welfare of the children.

** The Education (Special Schools) Regulations 1994 govern the process and prescribe: school to have governing body, whose composition and functions are to be approved by SofS, with duty to 'make such arrangements for safeguarding and promoting the welfare of the pupils as shall have been approved by SofS.' The Regulations also prescribe the information to be published by the governing body.

*** S62 provides LAs with a duty to satisfy itself that the welfare of any children, whom they have placed and who are being provided with accommodation by a voluntary organisation, is being safeguarded and promoted. The Children Act definition of voluntary organisation is ' A body (other than a public or local authority) whose activities are not carried on for profit.' The Education (Special Schools) Regulations provides that it is a condition of approval that a non-maintained special school shall not be conducted for profit.

^ LEA maintained residential special school and grant maintained residential special school.

APPENDIX E: RESPONSES TO THE REVIEW

The Review received written and oral responses from the organisations and individuals listed below. Those marked * met members of the Review as well as making a written submission. Those marked ** made oral responses only. In addition, a number of telephone responses to advertisements in local papers and radio were received.

A Voice for the Child in Care*

Advice, Advocacy & Representation Service for Children

Afzal - Dr Ghazala

Amies - Mrs Clare

Anderson - Professor Ewan*

Approach

Association of Chief Police Officers*

Association of County Councils*

Association of Directors of Social Services*

Association of London Government

Association of Metropolitan Authorities*

Association of Workers for Children with Emotional and Behavioural Difficulties

Audit Commission

Barking & Dagenham London Borough

Barking & Dagenham London Borough - Children & Families Services

Barnardos*

Barnett - Mr B

Beedell - Christopher B.Sc. C.Psychol.

Berridge - Mr David - Luton University

Bessels Leigh High School Trust

Birtenshaw Hall School

Blom-Cooper - Sir Louis QC*

Brand - Mr Don*

British Agencies for Adoption and Fostering (BAAF)

British Association of Social Workers*

Brown - Mr Ben

Brown - Mrs L.

Bryden-Brook - Mr Simon

Burnett Swayne

CSV - People for People

Caldecott College

Cambridgeshire County Council Social Services

Camden Social Services - Children & Families Division

Carebase

Caring for Children

Carroll - Mr Seamus

Central Council for Education and Training in Social Work (CCETSW)*

Chaundy - Mrs Jan

Cheshire County Council Social Services*

ChildLine*

ChildLine Cymru/Wales

Children in Wales*

Children's Rights Officers' Association

Clwyd Independent Panel**

Commission for Racial Equality

Community Practitioners' and Health Visitors Association

Conroy - Mr Matthew

Cooklin MB ChB MRC Psych - Dr Ruth. S.

Council for Disabled Children

Dartington Social Research Unit

Elliott - Ms Michele - Kidscape**

Farmer - Dr Elaine (Bristol University)

Fenton - Mr Andrew (Orkney Seven Action Group)

Friends of New Barns

Gabbitas Educational Services**

Gallagher - Mr Bernard (Manchester University)

Gale M.P. - Mr Roger

Glebe House - Friends Therapeutic Community Trust - & Michael

Glenthorne Centre

Gloucestershire County Council

G.M. Special Schools Heads Group

Grimwood - Mr Roy

Groome - Mr Richard

Hall - Mr Alan

Halstead - Miss Clare

Hames - Mr Michael**

Hamilton - Mrs Elizabeth

Hanvey - Dr Chris*

Heller - Ms Claire

Herring - Ms Tina

Hertfordshire County Council

Hounslow London Borough - Jo Blake, Liz Cooper, Sheila Lycholit

Incorporated Association of Preparatory Schools (IAPS)

Independent Panel of Investigations into Children's Services

Independent Representation for Children in Need (IRCHIN)

Independent Schools Information Service (ISIS)**

Independent Schools Joint Council (ISJC)*

Institute for the Study and Treatment of Delinquency

Jackson - Professor Sonia (Children in Wales)*

Jones - Mr Peter

Jones - Ms Adrianne **

Jordan - Mr Malcom - (Ashley Maynard Associates)**

Kahan - Dr Barbara O.B.E.*

Keeler - Mrs L.

Kent County Council

Kirklees Metropolitan Council

Kirklees Metropolitan Council Social Services Department

Kurtz - Dr Zarinna & Tumim - Lady Winifred

Lanes

Lancashire County Council

Latham - Mrs I.L.

Lee - Mr Paul**

Leeds Children's Right Service

Leicestershire County Council Social Services Department*

Lindsay - Dr Michael J.

Loader - Dr Peter MBBS MRCPsych

Local Government Management Board

Lowenstein - Dr L.F.

MacDonald - Karen

Manson - Mr David J.

Maudsley Family Research Studies

McMullen - Ms E. Jane

McParlin - Peter

Merton London Borough

MIND

Millington - Mrs Sheila

Morgan - Dr Roger**

Morris - Mr Edward

Mulvaney - Ms Joanne

NCH Action for Children

NCH Action for Children - Newcastle Children's Rights Service & Who Cares? - North East

NSPCC*

National Association for the Care and Resettlement of Offenders

National Association of Head Teachers (NAHT)

National Association of Head Teachers in Wales

National Association of Inspection and Registration Officers (NAIRO)

National Association of Probation Officers

National Association of Schoolmasters Union of Women Teachers

National Council of Voluntary Child Care Organisations*

National Criminal Intelligence Service**

National Foster Care Association*

National Institute for Social Work (NISW)*

National Union of Teachers

National Youth Agency

New Scotland Yard - Chief Inspector Jim Reynolds**

Nicholls - Mr J. on behalf of Association of Educational Guardians for the International Students*

Norwich - Professor Brahm**

Norwood Child Care

Office for Standards in Education (OFSTED)*

Office of Her Majesty's Chief Inspector of Schools in Wales

Orchard Lane Initiatives Ltd

O'Neill - Mr Freddie

O'Toole - Mr Kevin

Parents Action Group - Mrs J. Robinson

Park - Mr Robert

Pomeroy - Mr G.E.

Prison Reform Trust

Public Concern at Work

Quaker Heads' Conference

Ramsbotham - Sir David - HMI Prisons **

Redgrave - Mr Kenneth BA, MNRHP (NC), FRSH, MNBRCP

Robertson - Ms Jayne

Rome - Mr T.

Royal College of Nursing

Royal College of Psychiatrists - Child and Adolescent Section

Royal National Institute for the Blind (RNIB)

Saddington - Mr Alex**

Scope

Secondary Heads Association (SHA)

Service Children's Education (UK)**

Shaftesbury Homes & Arethusa

Sinclair - Professor Ian & Ian Gibbs - York University

Smith - Mr Graham - Chief Inspector of Probation**

Smith - Ms Gerrilyn

Smith - Professor Peter K.

Snook - Mr E.H.

Social Care Association (SCA)*

Society of Education Officers

Society of Local Authority Chief Executives (SOLACE)

Somerset County Council

South Devon Healthcare

Stevenson - Professor Olive**

Suffolk County Council Social Services

Thames/Anglia Heads of Inspection and Registration Group

Thayer - Ms Pamela

The Bridge

The Charterhouse Group

The Children's Society

The Headmasters' and Headmistresses' Conference

The Hesley Group*

The Howard League for Penal Reform

The Learning Agency

The Local Government Association**

The Lucy Faithfull Foundation

The National Association of Independent Resources for Children*

The National Heads of Inspection and Registration

The Nugent Care Society

The Nugent Care Society - CLUMBER LODGE

The Nugent Care Society - NAZARETH HOUSE CHILDREN'S VILLA

The Peper Harow Foundation

The Refugee Council

The Suzy Lamplugh Trust

Thomas Coram Foundation

Thompson - Mr G.A.

Thornton - Mrs L.W.

Thurnham M.P. - Mr Peter*

Union of Muslim Organisations of U.K. & Eire

Voice of Young People in Care Ltd (VOYPIC)

Voices From Care**

Voluntary Organisations Consultancy Service

Wales Advocacy Unit

Warner - Mr Norman*

Webster - Mr Richard

Weightman - Ms Christine

Welsh Local Government Association*

Westminster City

Whittle - Mrs Ann

Who Cares? Trust**

Williams - Ms Keeley

Woodhead - Mr David (ISIS)**

York City Council - Children's Services Division

York University - Dorothy Whitaker, Lesley Archer, Leslie Hicks

Young - Ms Sonia

APPENDIX F: PLACES AND ORGANISATIONS VISITED

The Review visited the places and organisations listed below. Organisations marked * arranged special presentations for the Review.

Children in Wales *

Former Leicestershire County Council *

London Borough of Kingston

Meadows School, Southborough, Kent

Mill Grove, Woodford, Essex

National Children's Bureau*

National Council for Voluntary Child Care Organisations*

NSPCC*

Social Care Association Annual Conference and AGM*

State Boarding Schools Information Service (AGM at St George's School, Harpenden, Hertfordshire)

The Dragon School, Oxford

The Lucy Faithfull Foundation*

Voices from Care*

Voluntary Organisations Consultancy Service

Welsh Local Government Association

West Midlands Child Care Consortium

Young Offenders Institution, Feltham (by invitation of the Howard League)